An Introduction to Narratology

'Fludernik's *Introduction to Narratology* will give undergraduate majors and graduate readers a formative overview of international narrative scholarship, as well as a practical manual for informed critical and interpretive practice.'

Bruce Clarke, *Texas Tech University, USA*

'Written by one of the world's leading narrative scholars ... *An Introduction to Narratology* is an excellent starting place for student readers coming to the field for the first time. It is also a first-rate reference work for more advanced students and for other readers who want to learn more about this excitingly active and diverse area of enquiry.'

David Herman, *Ohio State University, USA*

An Introduction to Narratology is an accessible, practical guide to narratological theory and terminology and its application to literature.

In this book, Monika Fludernik outlines:

- The key concepts of style, metaphor and metonymy, and the history of narrative forms
- Narratological approaches to interpretation and the linguistic aspects of texts, including new cognitive developments in the field
- How students can use narratological theory to work with texts, incorporating detailed practical examples
- A glossary of useful narrative terms and suggestions for further reading.

This textbook offers a comprehensive overview of the key aspects of narratology by a leading practitioner in the field. It demystifies the subject in a way that is accessible to beginners, but also reflects recent theoretical developments and narratology's increasing popularity as a critical tool.

Monika Fludernik is Professor of English at the University of Freiburg, Germany. She is the author of *The Fictions of Language and the Languages of Fiction* (Routledge, 1993) and *Towards a 'Natural' Narratology* (Routledge, 1996), which was the co-winner of the Perkins Prize of the Society for the Study of Narrative Literature.

An Introduction
to Narratology

Monika Fludernik

Translated from the German
by Patricia Häusler-Greenfield and Monika Fludernik

 Routledge
Taylor & Francis Group

LONDON AND NEW YORK

First published in German as *Einführung in die Erzähltheorie*
© 2006 by Wissenschaftliche Buchgesellschaft, Darmstadt

First published 2009
by Routledge
2 Park Square, Milton Park, Abingdon, OX14 4RN

Simultaneously published in the USA and Canada
by Routledge
270 Madison Ave, New York, NY 10016

Routledge is an imprint of the Taylor & Francis Group
Translation © Wissenschaftliche Buchgesellschaft, Darmstadt 2009

Typeset in Minion by
Keystroke, 28 High Street, Tettenhall, Wolverhampton
Printed and bound in Great Britain by
TJ International Ltd, Padstow, Cornwall

British Library Cataloguing in Publication Data
A catalogue record for this book is available from the British Library

Library of Congress Cataloging in Publication Data
Fludernik, Monika.
[Einführung in die Erzähltheorie. English]
An introduction to narratology / Monika Fludernik ; translated from the
German by Patricia Häusler-Greenfield and Monika Fludernik.
p. cm.
Includes bibliographical references and index.
1. Narration (Rhetoric) I. Title.
PN212.F5613 2009
809'.923—dc22
2008032785

ISBN10: 0–415–45029–2 (hbk)
ISBN10: 0–415–45030–6 (pbk)
ISBN10: 0–203–88288–1 (ebk)

ISBN13: 978–0–415–45029–4 (hbk)
ISBN13: 978–0–415–45030–0 (pbk)
ISBN13: 978–0–203–88288–7 (ebk)

Contents

List of figures

Preface

This volume was conceived as a textbook for students at the beginning of their academic career. It could form part of an introductory course to narrative studies or of an introductory module in literary studies. Although most of the examples are taken from literatures in English, the book attempts to cater to a wider audience of literature students in foreign language departments. It could also serve as a brief introduction for more advanced readers with no previous exposure to narratology who wish to catch up with developments in this field.

This introduction differs from the many other available textbooks on narrative and narrative theory in two strategic ways. First, I have tried to integrate narratological analysis with more general issues concerning reading of narrative and literary texts. These include the framing of books by the means of blurbs and cover texts, censorship, and questions of mimesis and realism as well as stylistic considerations and the use of metaphor in narrative. Second, the volume reflects my own particular line of narratological thinking and the tradition from which it developed. Thus it is the only available English language textbook on narrative studies with a heavy emphasis on German research in narratology. It also foregrounds linguistic and diachronic aspects of narrative studies.

In addition to these content-related departures from the familiar model of introductory accounts of narrative, the book also offers two chapters designed to meet the pedagogical needs of teaching staff: a chapter of textual interpretations that illustrates narratology in its practical application and one containing advice on how to avoid some of the more common terminological pitfalls that can be encountered when writing about narratives. The volume is rounded off with a glossary and an up-to-date bibliography.

This book is a translation of the second edition of *Einführung in die Erzähltheorie*. In the interests of the wider English-speaking readership, two chapters (9 and 12) have been replaced by new versions since the originals used German example texts. In the book as a whole, too, many of the German-language examples have been replaced by English illustrative material in order to facilitate matters for an international readership more attuned to literature in English. I have also found it necessary to rewrite passages in earlier chapters to clarify and explain more fully what I was trying to illustrate. Never has it become more obvious to me how different even quite simple German academic discourse is from that in English, how the order of presentation and the logic of combining arguments are handled in entirely untranslatable ways in the two languages. The text printed here is therefore a rewriting as well as a translation of the original German volume. It tries faithfully to do the same things as the original, but achieves this objective by sometimes introducing different sentences and different example passages from those employed in the source text.

My most extensive thanks go to Patricia Häusler-Greenfield, without whose enthusiasm, professional know-how and willingness to revise and rethink, and without whose patience with my perfectionist quibbling, this text would not have been completed in its present form. It has been a great joy to work with her on this book, and I have found our discussions entirely fascinating and inspiring, especially on how some things just cannot be expressed in a certain way or how a specific word will just eventually make all the difference to a sentence. I should also like to take this opportunity to thank Pat for being a superb teacher of writing in English while I was still in a junior position in Vienna. I have profited immensely from her instructions on how to combine verbs and nouns or nouns and adjectives in English and on how to listen to the cadence of syllables in a sentence to produce a euphonious discourse in my favourite non-native language. My own students, I am sure, are currently learning a great deal from the lessons I have absorbed from Pat.

Finally this brings me to the thanks due to other parties involved in this project. My gratitude extends first and foremost to Luise Lohmann, who has (wo)manfully struggled with typing and formatting the many versions of the chapters. I would also like to thank Carolin Berger-Krauße and Jeff Thoss for help with bibliographical items and proofreading. Special thanks go to Jan Alber for compiling the index.

This translation, like the original, is dedicated to my academic teachers in narratological thinking – Dorrit Cohn and Franz Karl Stanzel, with somewhat belated wishes for their eighty-fourth and eighty-fifth respective birthdays in August 2008. Without their example and inspiration my own narratological research would never have been possible.

1 Narrative and narrating

When we speak about narrative today, we inevitably associate it with the literary type of narrative, the novel or the short story. The word *narrative*, however, is related to the verb *narrate*. Narrative is all around us, not just in the novel or in historical writing. Narrative is associated above all with the act of narration and is to be found wherever someone tells us about something: a newsreader on the radio, a teacher at school, a school friend in the playground, a fellow passenger on a train, a newsagent, one's partner over the evening meal, a television reporter, a newspaper columnist or the narrator in the novel that we enjoy reading before going to bed. We are all narrators in our daily lives, in our conversations with others, and sometimes we are even professional narrators (should we happen to be, say, teachers, press officers or comedians). On occasion, we even take on the role of narrator: for example, when we read bedtime stories to small children. Narrating is therefore a widespread and often unconscious spoken language activity which can be seen to include a number of different text-types (such as journalism or teaching) in addition to what we often think of as the proto-typical kind of narrative, namely literary narrative as an art form.

Narrative is everywhere

But that is not all. As research is showing increasingly clearly, the human brain is constructed in such a way that it captures many complex relationships in the form of narrative structures (Polkinghorne 1988), metaphors or analogies. Just as we may describe a personal relationship metaphorically as a house that one partner has built painstakingly and lovingly and which the other casually allows to deteriorate until the plaster crumbles and the roof caves in, we may also conceive of each of our lives as a journey constituted by narration. Throughout our lives, things frequently happen without prior warning and bring about radical changes in the course of events, for example the first unexpected meeting with one's future partner. In reconstructing our own lives as stories, we like to emphasize how particular occurrences have brought about and influenced subsequent events. Life is described as a goal-directed chain of events which, despite numerous obstacles and thanks to certain opportunities, has led to the present state of affairs, and which may yet have further unpredictable turns and unexpected developments in store for us. It is therefore not surprising that psycho-analysis should have incorporated the telling of the patient's life story into the therapeutic process; indeed, many psychologists give the act of narration a central position in therapy (Linde 1993, Randall 1995).

The significance of narrative in human culture can be seen from the fact that written cultures seek their origins in myths which they then record for posterity. In an explana-tory process rather like that of individual autobiographical narratives, historians then begin to inscribe the achievements of their forefathers and the progress of their nation

Narrative and story

down to the present in the cultural memory in the form of histories or stories. Other areas of culture and society also create their own histories. There is historical linguistics, which 'narrates' the development of European languages from proto-Indo-European to present-day Dutch, French, Slovenian or Hindi. And, in the same way, there are music history, literary history and the history of physics. The nation state has its own story. So does current progress in genetic engineering, and the rise and fall of institutions (such as mercantilism or slavery) are also represented in narrative form. Narrative provides us with a fundamental epistemological structure that helps us to make sense of the confusing diversity and multiplicity of events and to produce explanatory patterns for them.

Narratives are based on cause-and-effect relationships that are applied to sequences of events. In historiography, a number of different narrative explanatory models have been applied. From a safe distance one might – to borrow a metaphor from biology – talk about the birth, maturity and demise of a nation. One can also analyse the series of contingencies that have resulted in a particular state of being. One example of this might be the question of why Minnesota has come to have such a strong ethnic German community. (This cannot be described as the inevitable result of a developmental process but is rather related to the chance events of expulsion and resettlement in the age of the Counter-Reformation.) But there are also non-narrative models of historical explanation, such as those which assume that history follows certain natural laws, or those which conceptualize current events as recurrences of crucial moments in a nation's history: 9/11 as a 'repetition' (also in the Freudian or Derridean sense) of Pearl Harbor.

Definition: What is narrative?

Having said this, we may well ask: what is **not** some kind of narrative, or rather, how should narrative be defined in order to distinguish it from non-narrative discourse?

So far we have made use of the term *narrative* in a way that reflects its popular usage, namely with a multiple meaning. In order to arrive at an explanation for the particular type of narrative involved in a story, we must now turn to the useful distinctions made in narrative theory (also known as narratology), which will clear up at least some of the confusion.

We said above that narrative is derived from 'narrate' and that narration is a very widespread activity. Narrative is therefore closely bound up with the speech act of narrating and hence also with the figure of a narrator. Thus one could define everything narrated by a narrator as narrative. But what is it, exactly, that a narrator narrates? Is it a particular novel? Or is it the story that is presented in this novel?

Narrative act – narrative discourse – story

At this point Gérard Genette's distinction between the three meanings of the French word *récit* ('narrative') provides a way out of our dilemma. Genette draws a distinction between *narration* (the narrative act of the narrator), *discours* or *récit* proper (narrative as text or utterance) and *histoire* (the story the narrator tells in his/her narrative). The first two levels of narrative can be classed together as the *narrative discourse* (Fr. *discours*; Ger. *Erzählerbericht*) by putting together the narrative act and its product, thus making a binary distinction between them and the third level, the story (Fr. *histoire*; Ger. *Geschichte*). The story is then that which the narrative discourse reports, represents or signifies.

Story as fable and plot

These distinctions enable us, for example, to account for the fact that the same story can be presented in various guises. The life story of Charlemagne may be told in a number of ways in different historical works, and the story of Snow White in Grimm's version is totally different from modern reworkings or parodies of the story's content. Whereas in the fairy tale the stepmother's cruelty, with its cannibalistic traits, is foregrounded, and eating in general plays an important role, in modern versions of the Snow White story the excessive cruelties of Grimm's fairy-tale world are often eliminated, and instead the potentially scandalous role of Snow White in the household of the seven (male) dwarfs gives cause for speculation.[1] Thus different narratives focus on quite different aspects of the story; or, more precisely, the stories that we reconstruct from different narrative texts often complement each other. By means of parody or by reflecting current issues and concerns, they fill the gaps that earlier versions of the 'same story' (fable) left in their presentation;[2] or they simply rewrite the story, for example from a feminist viewpoint. There is, therefore, a level of the story (the fable) that may be taken as the starting point for all Snow White narratives. Moreover, there are numerous textual or narrative manifestations of this fable in the different sequences of events and character constellations, that is to say, in the different plots that constitute the level of the fictional worlds in the many Snow White narratives. The existing texts about Snow White differ from each other quite markedly despite their common core, the fable.

In this respect fictional narrative, whether in fairy tale, novel or television film, differs radically from historical writing. The author of a novel or a film script develops a fictional world and produces both the story and the narrative discourse that goes with its product, the narrative text. Historians, by contrast, construct the most convincing and consistent account of events possible from their sources (which may also be narratives). What is most important here is that they are not allowed to contradict the statements made by their sources without good reason (such as the unreliability of the author of a source text or problems with dating). The historian is not free to invent his/her own story; the only room for speculation is in the areas of indeterminacy between the fixed points provided by historical sources. Despite these restrictions, historical discourses do not tell a single, unambiguous story since each historian has a particular view of things and tends to emphasize certain aspects of the age and the events being described while omitting others.

History and storytelling

History always has to do with perspective. No historian or novelist can ever reproduce *in toto* the (real or fictional) world, otherwise s/he would undergo the same fate as Tristram Shandy in Laurence Sterne's novel of the same name (1759–67). After several hundred pages of narrative, Tristram has still not managed to describe his birth, since he is so carried away by the minutiae of the prehistory of his conception. But narrative also involves selection. Every history, moreover, can be traced back to a particular perspective. It betrays the view of the author, his/her nationality and place of origin, the age in which s/he writes (or wrote), and it is tailored to a readership which has certain prejudices, historical convictions and expectations. History as historiography is never objective, however great its commitment to telling the truth. History teaching in schools, for example, has traditionally subscribed to the notion of the nation state, one result of which has been an analysis of the state's relations with other nations in terms of the friend/enemy binary oppositional metaphor. Another consequence of this is that the events of world history have been presented predominantly from 'our' (i.e. a European or Western) point of view. Events that were of consequence for the nation state tend to be consistently upgraded and included in the historiographer's text and plot, while events and developments of central importance abroad are often relegated to the periphery or else left out altogether. History teaching in the West has therefore reflected the enduring Eurocentrism of Western democracies, and in this context the empires of the Chinese, the Moghul dynasty in India or the history of Africa before its colonization by Europe have received scant attention.

Thus far, we have established that fictional narratives create fictional worlds, whereas historians collectively seek to represent one and the same real world in explanatory narrative and from a variety of different perspectives. As readers, we construct the story (characters, setting, events) from the narrative text of a novel, whereas in historical writing it is the historians who produce a story on the basis of their sources and set it down in verbal form. We may represent this as shown in Figure 1.1 below.

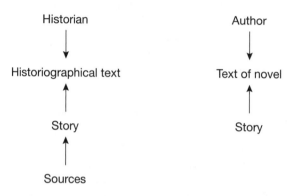

Figure 1.1 Story in history and the novel

To return to the fairy tale: if one identifies narrative with story (fable), then representations of this story in other media are also narratives. In the English-speaking world it is therefore customary to analyse not only the novel and the film as narrative genres but also drama, cartoons, ballet and pantomime.[3] In this sense, the ballet *Sleeping Beauty*, which presents an underlying story that also exists as a narrative in the form of a fairy tale, could be seen as an alternative manifestation of the same story (fable). The Russian Formalists, who were active in the 1920s and 1930s, coined the useful term *fabula* (E. *fable*) for this basic level of narrative. It can also be regarded as the source of a number of versions of the same story, in different media. In what follows I shall therefore make a distinction between the fable (*story*) and the more particular realization of the subject matter at the level of the *plot*, that is to say that level of the narrative which is reconstructed by the reader from the discourse as the narrative's 'story'. I will refer to this in future as the *plot level* or *fictional world*. (The Russian Formalists called it *syuzhet*, but this term is open to misunderstanding since the term *sujet* in other languages tends to refer to the thematic level of a narrative.)

The narrator
Let us return to the question of how narrative is to be defined. In German-speaking countries, definitions tend to be rather narrow and relate to the figure of the narrator. This is bound up with the etymologically more closely related German expressions *Erzähler* ('narrator') and *Erzählung* ('narration'). Thus, narrative is the story that the narrator tells. German research here continues the tradition of Goethe's tripartite distinction between epic, lyric and drama whereby the epic is the prototypical narrative category. The epic has a bard, a narrator who tells the story. According to this traditional view there are, therefore, literary genres with an underlying story – drama, for example – but these are not genuinely narrative since they normally do not have a narrator persona as teller of the story.[4] Narrative is therefore defined as 'story plus narrator', as is represented in Figure 1.2.

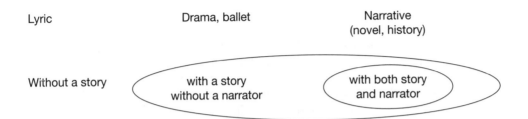

Figure 1.2 Narrative as defined by the presence of a narrator

In such a conception of narrative, narrative is merely a subset of the genres that include a story.

In the Anglo-Saxon world, on the other hand, as a result of Seymour Chatman's influential book *Story and Discourse* (1978), a broader definition of narrative has emerged, which also includes media other than purely verbal (oral or written) narrative discourses. Gerald Prince, in his standard work *A Dictionary of Narratology* (1987), still defines narrative thus:

> **Narrative:** The recounting [...] of one or more real or fictitious EVENTS communicated by one, two, or several (more or less overt) NARRATORS to one, two or several (more or less overt) NARRATEES.
>
> (Prince 2003: 58)

Chatman, on the other hand, defines *narrative* as a conjunction of discourse and story, but extends the definition of discourse to cover several media. Moreover, by analogy with the narrator in the traditional mould, he introduces the figure of a 'cinematic narrator' who is comparable to the narrator in the novel and fulfils a similar mediating function in the presentation of the story. Since the present introduction has been designed for the benefit of students pursuing introductory courses in a range of language and literature departments, I shall concentrate more on the traditional verbal narrative medium and consider film and drama only in certain chapters. Especially in the analysis of plot and action schemas, drama will figure prominently since the analysis of plot in the novel and the treatment of plot in drama are very largely in agreement.

The term *plot analysis* brings me to a further point, namely the significance of action sequences for the definition of narrative. Traditionally, a story is understood as a sequence of events that has a beginning, a middle and an end. It normally creates suspense as a result of complications in the middle part that are cleared up when these conflicts are resolved at the end of the work. The quotation from Prince cited above seeks to restrict narrative in a minimal version to 'one [...] or several' events. But this is only an extreme version of the thesis which holds that story and action exert a reciprocal influence on each other.

Story and action

Such a mutually interdependent relationship between story and action is, for the most part, the norm – in most narratives the story is concerned with chains of events. Events are, therefore, a characteristic feature of narrated worlds. Many narrative genres rely almost exclusively on the reader's interest in what happens next ('And what happened then?'). Yet the primary concern in narratives is not actually chains of events but the fictional worlds in which the characters in the story live, act, think and feel. New theoretical proposals in narratology, such as *possible-worlds theory* (see Chapter 10) and 'natural' narratology (Fludernik 1996) have therefore focused on the existence of fictional characters in a fictional world. From the point of view of cognitive theory, acting, thinking and feeling are constitutive to human existence in this world. Therefore, the existence of a human character in and of itself will produce a minimal level of narrativity for the play or fiction in which s/he occurs. Rather than basing narrativity on plot or on the presence of a teller figure, these theories take the presence of a character to be sufficient to produce narrativity.

The emphasis on the 'human' character is crucial. One criterion of what makes a narrative a narrative is the requirement of having a human or human-like (anthropomorphic) protagonist at the centre. Texts describing genes during cellular fission are only 'narrative' to the extent that they outline sequences of events. But it is agreed among narratologists that 'real' narratives are those that have human protagonists or anthropomorphic characters (the talking hare in the fable, the speaking car, and so on). Even if not all narratives place the thoughts of the characters at the centre of the story, the representation of the interior world of the protagonists is characteristic of a fictional narrative since it is only in fiction that it is possible to see into the minds of other people (Hamburger 1957/1993). However, in order to take account of the discovery that sequences of events in factual texts are also in some sense narrative, I introduce the term *narrative report* for sequences of events and note that narratives typically include chains of events in report form, and that these reporting sections are also employed in non-narrative genres such as a biological essay on cellular fission.

A final criterion for what does or does not constitute a narrative results from the temporal location of what happens in a narrative. This also relates to the centrality of the protagonists as 'real-world' figures from a cognitive point of view. The existence of every human being is bound to a specific time and place. What happened before this moment is past, though fixed in memory, and what comes after will be the future, which will turn into the present and, ultimately, the past. One important distinction, therefore, between the lyric and the narrative is that poems frequently do not situate their speaker in a particular time or space, so that the existential location of the ego in time and space which is typical of narrative is missing. This also means that such poems cannot be classified as narrative.

Definition

Summarizing the criteria outlined above, we can now define narrative as follows.

A narrative (Fr. *récit*; Ger. *Erzählung*) is a representation of a possible world in a linguistic and/or visual medium, at whose centre there are one or several protagonists of an anthropomorphic nature who are existentially anchored in a temporal and spatial sense and who (mostly) perform goal-directed actions (action and plot structure). It is the experience of these protagonists that narratives focus on, allowing readers to immerse themselves in a different world and in the life of the protagonists. In verbal narratives of a traditional cast, the narrator functions as the mediator in the verbal medium of the representation. Not all narratives have a foregrounded narrator figure, however. The narrator or narrative discourse shape the narrated world creatively and individualistically at the level of the text, and this happens particularly through the (re)arrangement of the temporal order in which events are presented and through the choice of perspective (point of view, focalization). Texts that are read as narratives (or 'experienced' in the case of drama or film) thereby instantiate their narrativity (Fr. *narrativité*; Ger. *Narrativität*).

The penultimate sentence of this definition refers to stylistic techniques in narratives which I will describe in detail in Chapter 4. For instance, narratives sometimes start out with a final state of affairs and then trace all the events leading up to it, as for example in *One Hundred Years of Solitude* (1967) by Gabriel García Márquez. Likewise, narratives may choose between a number of different perspectives, for example that of portraying the events from the point of view of the narrator or of one of the characters, or of allowing the reader an insight into the thoughts of one character but not of the others. In films these effects are often achieved by the use of close-ups. These possibilities will be discussed in Chapters 4 and 8. Thus between the plot and the discourse levels of a narrative, various kinds of restructuring take place, which are also conditioned by the different media of representation. Dramas, films and novels shape their surface discourse in different ways.

In this chapter, we have seen that there are fictional (invented) and non-fictional   Summary
narratives, and that there are verbal (novels and conversational narratives), visual (ballet) and verbal-visual (drama, film) narratives. Verbal narratives frequently have a narrator who produces the narrative discourse or narrative *text*. From the text the reader constructs the underlying world and *story* or action structure (also called the *plot*), which is a manifestation of the fable or network of motifs of the story. These relationships can be represented as in Figure 1.3.

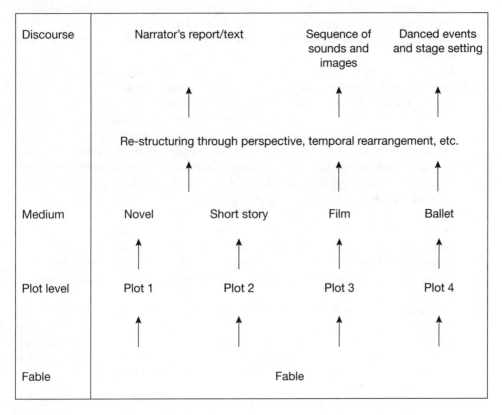

Figure 1.3 Fable, plot and discourse in different media

2   The Theory of Narrative

Definition

Narrative theory – or to use the internationally accepted term *narratology* (Fr. *narratologie*; Ger. *Erzähltheorie*[1]) – is the study of narrative as a genre. Its objective is to describe the constants, variables and combinations typical of narrative and to clarify how these characteristics of narrative texts connect within the framework of theoretical models (typologies).

Linguistics as model

The methods of narrative theory are inspired by modern linguistics, which demonstrates through a synchronic analysis of the language *system* (Saussure's *langue*) how language material develops meaningfully from the opposition and combination of basic elements (phonemes, morphemes, syntagms, etc.). In a similar fashion, narrative theory tries to trace how 'sentences turn into narrative' (to pun on the title of Grabes 1978), or, in other words, how the narrative emerges from the narrative text, the words on the page. In Chapter 1, we already discussed the difference between story and discourse (Fr. *histoire* vs. *discours*; Ger. *Geschichte* vs. *Erzähltext*) – a distinction that is modelled on the linguistic categories of *histoire* and *discours* established by the French linguist Émile Benveniste (1902–1976). It should be noted that, for many narratologists, the story level is a kind of *langue* or system, whereas the narrative discourse (i.e. the narrative text as we encounter it in the arrangement of sentences and paragraphs that we are reading) can be interpreted as *parole* (manifestation). At the same time, the temporal reordering we find in the discourse as compared to the order in which events in the story actually happened (see Chapter 4) can be discussed using linguistic models, especially syntactical paradigms. A change in the sequence of plot elements (for example, a narrative beginning *in medias res* with several flashbacks) can be compared to variations in word order, or to the transposition of constituent parts from deep to surface structure in generative grammar. In the 1960s and 1970s, for example, an entire school of text linguistics established *text grammars*. They tried to divide narrative texts into what they called *narremes* and analysed these in various combinations (see van Dijk 1972).

Considering how linguistics has served as a paradigm for narratology, it comes as no surprise that narratologists' models are primarily structuralist and dominated by binary oppositions (story vs. discourse, narrator vs. narratee [Fr. *narrateur* vs. *narrataire*; Ger. Erzähler vs. Adressat], homodiegetic vs. heterodiegetic[2]). However, many typologies also rely on triads,[3] and the German tradition known as morphology favours organic/biological metaphors.[4]

Staking out the field

As is the case with all fields of study, narratology first has to define its area of research. For this reason, every narrative theory establishes a definition of narrative at some point (cf. the discussion on the concept of narrativity in Chapter 1). On the whole, narrative theory is *text*-oriented; the contexts of production, publication, distribution and reception of narratives occupy an area on the periphery of narratology and relate more to the historical/situational research done in literary studies. Nevertheless, we shall briefly discuss the conditions of production and the physical appearance of narrative texts in Chapter 3.

As we saw in Chapter 1, narratives create (fictional) worlds[5] in which human beings exist and interact within life-worlds that are almost completely the same as the real world. As a consequence of this illusionism (see Chapter 6), all systematic narrative typologies include sections describing the figures of narrator and narratee, the representation of space, time, and acting *personae* ('actants'[6]) on the story level, as well as sections on different narrative levels (frame stories etc.) and the structure of the plot. The analysis of the relationship between story and discourse plays a major role in discourse-oriented narratology (in the models of Genette, Prince, Chatman, Stanzel, Lanser and Fludernik). The structure of the narrative discourse is foregrounded in this type of narratology. It deals, for instance, with narrative perspective (see Chapters 4 and 9), the representation of thought, or the discursive rearrangement of plot events. Other concerns in narrative theory include the distinction between fictional and non-fictional texts, and the influence of the medium of representation on narrative (novel/short story vs. film, drama, cartoons and the like, conversational narrative, cyber-fiction, and narrative in poetry, painting and music).[7]

Where should we locate narrative theory in the overall academic landscape? Narratology has traditionally been a sub-discipline of the study of literature and also has particularly close ties to poetics, the theory of genre, and to the semiotics, or semiology, of literature. Like genre theory, narrative theory deals with the distinctions between lyric, drama and epic, but it also focuses on typological, historical and thematic issues in relation to narrative subgenres such as the *Bildungsroman*, the Gothic novel, the novel of consciousness, the fable, the anecdote, the short story, etc. Such issues are naturally part of the basic repertoire in any kind of literary study. Narratology shares many characteristics with poetics because it analyses – although only as regards narrative – the characteristics of (narrative) literary texts and their aesthetic (narrative) functions. And finally, narratology resembles semiotics in so far as it analyses the constitution of (narrative) meaning in texts (films, conversational narratives, etc.).

Narratology in the context of literary and cultural studies

Despite its affinities with poetics and semiotics, narratology's relation to literature remains unclear. Possible applications of narratological insights extend far beyond literary narration and can even include therapeutic uses. However, it is precisely in the study of the highly complex genre of the novel that narrative theory has gained recognition and provided countless insights that are also relevant to literary analysis in general.

The relationship between narrative theory and interpretation is particularly controversial.[8] While narratology sees itself in principle as the *theory* that analyses the what and the how of narration, which it tries to systematize, many narratologists stress the fact that descriptive narratological categories also provide them with ideas that are decisive for their interpretive textual work, and most literary theorists would argue that the precision of narrational terminology is helpful in arriving at clearer interpretations of texts.

Narrative theory undoubtedly has its closest affinities with comparative studies and text linguistics since narratology's most prominent feature is its implicit universal validity. The models of Gérard Genette and F. K. Stanzel, to mention just two of the most important and widely applied typologies, feature text examples from more than one national literature. The claim to universality of narratological descriptive models may also be seen in narrative theory's connections to text linguistics, which also aims to explain how texts function per se. In study programmes entitled 'Literature and Linguistics' or 'Stylistics', which are very common in the United Kingdom, literary texts (verse, drama, prose) are analysed using methods from text linguistics, for example. Within this discipline, the insights into narrative texts produced by narratology are generally used to analyse narration as a text-type. A more detailed, practical illustration of the cooperation between the study of linguistics and literature will be provided in Chapter 5.

History of narrative research

The theoretical examination of narration goes back to Friedrich Spielhagen and Otto Ludwig's research on the novel (Spielhagen 1967 [1883], Ludwig 1891). However, linguists around the turn of the twentieth century were also gaining an understanding of narratological issues in the course of their study of the Romance languages (Charles Bally and others) and of English (Fritz Karpf). These theorists studied the French phenomenon of the *imparfait* (the backgrounded past tense) in Flaubert's novels and his representation of speech and thought in so-called free indirect discourse (more on this in Chapters 7 and 8).

Early classics

Important contributions to narrative research were made in the early twentieth century by Käte Friedemann (1910), Percy Lubbock (*The Craft of Fiction*, 1921), E. M. Forster (*Aspects of the Novel*, 1927) and Henry James (in the prefaces to his novels collected in *The Art of the Novel*, 1934). The first peak was reached by German narrative theory in the 1950s when some of the classics still studied today were published: Eberhard Lämmert's *Bauformen des Erzählens* ('Forms of Narrative', 1955), F. K. Stanzel's *Die typischen Erzählsituationen im Roman* (1955; translated as *Narrative Situations in the Novel*, 1971), and Käte Hamburger's *The Logic of Literature* (1957/1993). These typologies are still of relevance to German narratological research today. Norman Friedman's article on point of view (1955) was published around the same time in the United States. Slightly earlier, the book *Theory of Literature* by René Wellek and Austin Warren (1949) had begun to introduce formalist (and narratological) research to English-speaking countries, thereby spreading the insights of the Russian Formalists, such as Viktor Shklovsky, Boris Eichenbaum and Jurij Tynjanov, and of the Prague School. Russian 'narratology' (never so named), which was founded by the Formalists, became influential through the work of Roman Jakobson (who dealt more with poetry but gave essential, methodological impulses), V. N. Vološinov,[9] Mikhail M. Bakhtin, Boris Uspensky and later the text linguist and semiologist Jury Lotman. Another important figure of the Prague school of structuralism was the Czech literary theorist Jan Mukařovský, who had a decisive influence on what later became narratological structuralism. The most influential Russian narratologist is Mikhail Bakhtin, whose two books *The Dialogic Imagination* (1930s) and *Problems of Dostoevsky's Poetics* (1963) had a significant impact on the study of speech and thought representation and on the development of cultural studies.

French structuralism

The epoch regarded today as the classical phase of narratology developed as a strand within structuralism in France and includes the work of Claude Bremond, Algirdas Julien Greimas, Tzvetan Todorov, Roland Barthes and Gérard Genette. This research was significantly influenced by the studies of folk tales conducted by the Russian scholar Vladimir Propp (1895–1970). Propp's *Morphology of the Folktale* (1928), which had a direct influence on Bremond, opened up the possibility of a narrative grammar which would allow all narratives to be broken down into a limited number of basic forms and components. Propp's model, according to which the Russian folk tales he analysed consisted of thirty-one functions such as those of the hero, the (magic) helper and the antagonist, influenced, among other things, Bremond's and Greimas's model of actants. Furthermore, it also enabled the extension of structuralist methods in the direction of generative grammar (Noam Chomsky) with its transformations from grammatical deep structure to surface structure. Propp therefore paved the way for the text grammars to come, in which deep-structural narremes are transposed to the textual surface of sentences and paragraphs.

However, it was Gérard Genette, a specialist in rhetoric, who played the decisive role in the further development of narrative theory. The third volume of Genette's trilogy *Figures*, including *Discours du récit* (1972), focused almost entirely on the narrative discourse of the novel. He brought together the insights of many earlier researchers to create a new terminological framework that was constructed in accordance with strict, binary principles. Because of the delayed impact of structuralism in the United States, Genette's model did not become well known until just before the development of post-structuralism in English studies and literary theory. In North America his model found many followers, of whom the most important were Gerald Prince, Seymour Chatman, Dorrit Cohn and Susan Lanser. References to the work of these authors will occur throughout this book.

Narrative theory has also established itself in German-speaking countries, where it enjoys a high reputation and is an integral part of the curriculum for students of literature. Stanzel's narrative situations were and still are standard teaching material at universities, while his revised version of the model in *A Theory of Narrative* from 1979 (published in a revised version in 1982 and now in its eighth edition) has received international recognition since it was translated into English in 1984. Along with Stanzel and Lämmert, the German scholars Helmut Bonheim and Wilhelm Füger also made decisive contributions to narratology.

In the United States, narrative research has changed a good deal since the advent of post-structuralism and in many respects adopted ideas from the most diverse theoretical trends. As a result, psychoanalytical models have been integrated into narrative research (Brooks 1985, Chambers 1984), feminist approaches applied (Warhol 1989, Lanser 1992) and discourse-critical and generally ideological models favoured (Cohan and Shires 1988, Armstrong and Tennenhouse 1993, among others). A major narratological school developed around Wayne C. Booth, whose *The Rhetoric of Fiction* (1961) continued and perfected the tradition of Lubbock, Friedman and James. Booth and the so-called Chicago critics instituted narratology as linked to narrative rhetoric. Present-day representatives of the school (James Phelan, Peter Rabinowitz) continue to focus on the rhetorical aspects of narrative (Phelan 2007). Phelan is also editor of the official journal of the American-based Society for the Study of Narrative Literature (SSNL), *Narrative*, and Ohio State University in Columbus, Ohio, Phelan's current base, houses Project Narrative, a narratological research centre (see projectnarrative.osu.edu).

Besides psychoanalytic, feminist, ideological, rhetorical and ethical approaches, there is extensive research that focuses on formal and logical models (Gerald Prince, Thomas Pavel, Marie-Laure Ryan, David Herman). The conferences held by the Society for the Study of Narrative Literature are evidence of the impressively broad scope of North American narrative research and of its integration of diverse theoretical models, from post-colonialism to queer theory.

Recent developments

Among the most notable narratologists of the present are researchers from Jerusalem and Tel Aviv (where the narratological journal *Poetics Today* is published), such as Meir Sternberg, Shlomith Rimmon-Kenan and Tamar Yacobi. Younger German narratologists include Wolf Schmid, Manfred Jahn, Ansgar Nünning, Monika Fludernik and Werner Wolf. A strong narratological tradition also flourishes in France, Scandinavia, and Spain, as well as in Belgium, the Netherlands and many of the former Eastern Bloc countries.[10]

Journals

Some of the most important journals of narratology are *Poetics Today*, edited in Tel Aviv; *Style* (DeKalb, IL), *Narrative* (Columbus, OH), *Journal of Narrative Theory* (*JNT*, formerly called *Journal of Narrative Technique*; Ypsilanti, MI) and *Narrative Inquiry* (Worcester, MA), all published in the United States; as well as *Poetica* and *Germanisch-Romanische Monatsschrift*, published in Germany.[11]

Narrative research today

In the last few years, narrative research has extended its scope beyond the theoretical question 'What is narrative?' and integrated the leading theoretical debates (from feminism to post-structuralism) that originated in the United States. Although in the past two decades narratology has often been declared dead, at the moment there appears to exist a veritable boom, as reflected in the number of recent monographs on narratological subjects and the popularity of the annual conference of the Society for the Study of Narrative Literature (SSNL). Ohio State University Press is publishing an extremely successful series on the theory and interpretation of narrative. Several introductory and reference works have appeared in the past few years: Lothe (2000), Cobley (2001), Abbott (2002), Keen (2003), Herman/Vervaeck (2005), the *Routledge Encyclopedia of Narrative Theory* (Herman *et al.* 2005), the *Companion of Narrative Theory* (Phelan/Rabinowitz 2005) from Blackwell, and a *Cambridge Companion to Narrative* (Herman 2007). In Germany, the ongoing interest in narrative theory is sustained by a series of handbooks devoted almost exclusively to narratology (*WVT–Handbücher zum literaturwissenschaftlichen Studium*) as well as a new series entitled *Narratologia* published by de Gruyter, most of whose volumes are in English. In addition to this surge in publications, the so-called 'narrative turn' in the social sciences has had a crucial effect on generating an interest in narrative and theoretical models of narration (Hyvärinen 2006). To sum up, at the beginning of the twenty-first century, far from being on its last legs, narratology is not only alive and well but flourishing.

3   Text and Authorship

In this chapter we shall be looking at phenomena that are usually excluded from Narrative and context traditional theories of narrative: publishing, the staging of plays and the production, publication, distribution and reception of narrative texts in the real world. The marginalization of these areas in classical narratology is clearly justified: when doing a close reading of a text a literary critic must of necessity ignore such sociological aspects. Close reading, after all, tries first and foremost to tease out what exactly the text 'means' and what it is that comes across to the reader in stylistic and narrative terms. Yet over the past two or three decades there has been a tendency to investigate literature from a sociological perspective and, more specifically, to look at its consumers and users: in other words, to pay more attention to contextual features.

In particular, the rise of New Historicism as practised by American scholars has led to an increased focus on text-context relations, with ideological issues and aspects of reception theory playing a central role. Stephen Greenblatt, the most prominent American New Historicist, is concerned with how literary and non-literary discourses – in the Foucauldian sense of the term – exercise power, participate in power relations or undermine them. Other scholars devote more attention to censorship, the publishing media and institutions, and the reader her/himself (cf. Smith 1993, among others).

Among literary specialists there is currently a renewed interest in the author. Roland The author Barthes's contention that the author is dead did not prove particularly useful to British Cultural Studies and the New Historicism. These approaches foreground the idea of the author as a conduit for ideologically charged discourses rather than as an individual responsible for her/his text. At the present time, narratologists are also more immediately concerned with the figure of the author. Of particular interest are texts produced by members of ethnic minorities or more generally groups suffering from discrimination: post-colonial texts, literature of migration, women's writing. Narratologists are also focusing on texts which undermine the author – narrator distinction. This category includes, among others, older narratives in which the narrator insists on being one and the same person as the author. A good example of such a text is Aphra Behn's classic narrative *Oroonoko* (1688), a romance with a peripheral first-person narrator who presents herself as the author. It is, for instance, quite true that Behn took to London the feathered Surinam Indian headdress she refers to in her role of first-person narrator in the novel; the headdress was even used as a prop in Dryden's play *The Indian Queen* (1663/64). Moreover, there is a whole series of postmodern novels in which the genres of autobiography and first-person novel coalesce so that it becomes difficult for the reader to decide if the narrator is merely a fictional persona or actually the author in person. Henry Miller's *Tropic of Cancer* (1934) can be cited as an example of this kind of ambivalence: Miller himself regarded the text as autobiographical whereas readers have held it to be fictional (cf. Cohn 1999: 35).

Last but not least, there are even signs of a 'return of the author' in narratological studies as demonstrated, for instance, by the work of Fotis Jannidis (1999). In fact, the figure of the author is already well established in narratological discourse in the guise of the implied author (Booth 1961), although the extent to which the implied author has the status of a person is disputed. When the implied author embodies and puts into practice the 'intentions' of the text, s/he is conceived of as a real person (only people can have intentions); when described as the text-as-a-whole, or the implied meaning of the text (cf. Chapter 4 and Heinen 2002), the implied author becomes a rather nebulous construct devoid of any anthropomorphic features. This is why Genette and Cohn firmly reject the idea of the implied author and abide by the dyad of narrator/author (Genette 1988: 135–54; Cohn 1999: 132–49; Cohn 2000).

Gender of the author

A particularly contentious aspect of authorship is the gender of the author: male or female. This question has always been sociologically relevant, but was largely ignored, since authority was by definition male and hence authorship implicitly suggested a male writer. Using a male nom de plume, a pen name, particularly in the nineteenth century, was an important strategy employed by women to get their works published and make them known to a wider audience. In English literature one can point to the example of Mary Ann Evans, better known as George Eliot. Works by women were often dismissed as trivial, even when – or perhaps because – large numbers of such works were on the market. (Male authors had to compete with a veritable flood of 'scribbling women'.[1])

Écriture féminine?

Text-oriented literary studies has also concerned itself with the gender of the author. Here the focus has been on linguistic differences between feminine and masculine discourse, most notably in the ideas of feminist literary theorists such as Luce Irigaray. Irigaray argues for the existence of what she calls *écriture féminine*, a feminine way of writing. Notwithstanding this, the linguistic experiments of many postmodern women writers (like Monique Wittig) do not differ fundamentally from the experiments of male authors, which also push language to its very limits. Male and female postmodernist writers use the same kinds of strategy for different ends, however: Samuel Beckett, for instance, when playing with the dissolution of syntax, pursues existential questions of the human condition, whereas Wittig is more concerned with language as body-centred, with constituting gender as being in language. What is more, we should note that readers are only too willing to assume that women writers whose first names are not instantly identifiable as female are male. Yet both male and female writers regularly produce first-person narrators of the opposite sex, without any perceptible difference in style. Conversely, there are languages and styles in which particularly 'masculine' or 'feminine' elements predominate in accordance with gender (Japanese can here be adduced as a striking example), with the result that a narrative can, in a sense, perform 'femininity' or 'masculinity'. As Robyn Warhol (1989) notes, many Victorian women writers make use of such performative femininity. The gender of the author, then, is not directly obvious from a text, and a marked femininity of the narrative discourse need not indicate a female writer.

Be that as it may, we shall not pursue these complex and controversial matters any further in the present chapter. Instead, we shall look at some basic aspects of context that could be relevant for interpretive purposes.

The author

The author of a text is not necessarily the person who composed that text. As Harold Love explains in his book on textual criticism, there are different kinds of authorship: for example precursory authorship, executive authorship, declarative authorship and revisionary authorship (2002: 40–50). A precursory author is the author of a source that has a decisive influence on a text (for example, Holinshed's *Chronicles*, which were the starting point for Shakespeare's history plays). The executive author is responsible for the creation of the text, in other words s/he writes down the words on the page or composes text on the keyboard. (A scribe or typist, however, only copies already composed text and is not identical with the executive author.) The declarative author is the person who features as author on the title page, even if s/he has had nothing whatsoever to do with producing the text (in contrast to the executive author who could conceivably be a kind of 'ghost writer'). The revisionary author is responsible for amendments to the text and is often the publisher or editor of a work, or a relative/descendant of the author. As we can see, there is no unique, simple definition of authorship, especially when one takes into account the emergence of authorship as a legal concept. In his book on Shakespeare (2003), Lukas Erne reminds us that the notion of authorship for plays only came into being in the Elizabethan period. Prior to this, it was the players and/or company that were held to be responsible for the pieces they performed.

The eighteenth century was a watershed in publishing, one of the reasons being that copyright, which had been vested in the publishers, was returned to authors. Before this, a publisher had been able to pay an author a pittance and then, should the published work be a success, reap all the rewards for himself. The modified system did not particularly benefit the authors, though, as pirated editions, especially in North America, ate into their income until well into the nineteenth century.[2]

Literature has always been subject to censorship. During the Middle Ages censorship was practised by the Church and directed against blasphemy and heresy. One of the results of the emergence of the nation state in the sixteenth century was political censorship. For instance, in England, a pamphlet attacking Elizabeth I's projected marriage to a Catholic fell victim to the censor (and its author was punished by having his hand cut off).[3] Stage plays with politically sensitive themes were also affected (cf. Clare 1990 and Dutton 1997). For instance, the Scots at the court of James I protested against Chapman's, Jonson's and Marston's drama *Eastward Ho!* (1605) because of a passage deemed insulting to the King and his countrymen, and as a result of this the authors were arrested. Political censorship was again extremely prevalent in the late eighteenth century in the wake of the French Revolution. Thus the radical writer William Godwin was obliged to disseminate his social criticism in the form of a novel, *Caleb Williams* (1794). His radical philosophical tract *Political Justice* (1793) was only spared censorship because the book was so expensive that the masses feared by the government could not afford to buy it.

Ever since the nineteenth century censorship has mainly addressed issues of sexual morality. Both Flaubert's *Madame Bovary* (1857) and Oscar Wilde's play *Salomé* (1896) were prohibited because of their outspoken portrayal of allegedly immoral behaviour. In the twentieth century, the description of child abuse in John McGahern's novel *The Dark* (1965), the stoning of a baby on stage in Edward Bond's play *Saved* (1965) and the unpatriotic stance on the Northern Ireland conflict expressed in Howard Brenton's

Authorial functions

Censorship

The Romans in Britain (1980) all aroused fierce controversy. Although censorship was abolished in most European countries in the course of the twentieth century, the Catholic Church still has its Prohibitory Index (Index Librorum Prohibitorum). Religious censorship continues to flourish, as witness the fatwah pronounced against Salman Rushdie because of his novel *The Satanic Verses* (1988), or the calls for prohibition articulated by Catholic believers against the Austrian action painter Hermann Nitsch and his representations of Christ on the cross.

For narratologists, the fact that literary narratives frequently escaped political and religious censorship because of their fictional nature is certainly significant. Instead of writing an inflammatory speech criticizing the politics of the day, a tried and tested ploy is to write a play featuring similar circumstances – set in classical times. In *The Island* (1973) Athol Fugard mirrors this strategy, targeting the African struggle for independence and criticism of the inhuman apartheid regime in South Africa. In a play-within-a-play we see two Robben Island prisoners perform *Antigone*. Admittedly, even a classical drama can cause consternation among particularly nervous rulers. This could explain why some of Shakespeare's plays were forbidden in totalitarian states in spite of the fact that they had got past the censors in Queen Elizabeth's time. The treatment of political themes in allegorical drama is of particular interest for the narrative theorist. Plots are frequently utopian. In the fictional world, the freedom fighters triumph; the dictator is punished. The fact that the stories portray the thoughts and feelings of the victims signally contributes to the political impact of such works. Narrative is particularly well suited to conveying arguments by implication.

Publishing

Simply writing a book does not guarantee its being read. When, as was the case in the Elizabethan period, many authors circulated text in manuscript form, they could be fairly certain of reaching their readership. From the eighteenth century onwards, however, it was the printer/publisher who called the tune. Authors either dedicated their work to a patron who then paid for publication, or the publisher worked at his own risk and was, in consequence, mainly interested in printing texts that would sell well. Laurence Sterne, for instance, had problems finding a publisher for his *Tristram Shandy* (1759–67), which went on to become a cult novel.

At first sight, such issues seem to have little to do with the text itself. Yet the mechanics of publishing and distribution do exert a considerable influence over the type of narrative produced.

To begin with, what the text is like will depend on the preferences of its audience. Significant change can only be brought about by those who are willing to risk doing something new. The adaptation of classical texts and the continuity of literary traditions handed down from antiquity were of central importance until the mid eighteenth century, whereas nowadays success through innovation is the most important criterion in determining literary merit. Literary historians are not the only scholars interested in such historical developments; narratologists also concern themselves with new trends in narrative, such as the introduction of chapter headings, or with the often playful modifications of the epistolary novel during the eighteenth century, and of course the newest strategies of experimental novels.

In Britain, another central influence on narrative writing was the existence of circulating libraries or lending libraries and the practices these adopted. As they charged a fee per volume, the libraries preferred novels with three volumes, thus creating the predominant genre of the 'three-decker novel'. The fee not only affected the length of novels, but also their structure. Similarly, nineteenth-century serial publication in parts at fortnightly intervals meant that these narratives reached a suspense point at the end of each of their instalments.[4]

Since the twentieth century and at the present time, marketing strategies have also had a considerable impact on the nature of narratives, as they also did, for that matter, in the eighteenth century. Barchas (2003: 3–5) points out that in *The Tatler* Jonathan Swift's poem 'Description of a Morning Shower' was printed just above a colourful assortment of advertisements. Thus the many objects washed up by the Fleet river in the poem, including a dead cat, are reflected in the panoply of goods advertised on the page.

Distribution and promotion

Advertising and marketing are important for attributing a narrative text to a particular genre. This is evident from the fact that the book trade categorizes novels as 'crime' or 'bestsellers', among others. Leading British bookshops have sections for 'fiction' (novels and short stories), 'crime', 'history' and 'autobiography', but also, interestingly, for 'English literature' (where you will find the Penguin Classics, for example, while new writing and popular novels are shelved under 'fiction'). The short descriptions (or blurbs) on the back cover of texts or on the inside flap of hardback books also play their part in the marketing game. With a brief summary of the theme of a novel and, often, details of the setting and characters, they inform and help potential readers decide whether to buy the book or not. Currently many British and American blurbs feature numerous quotations from reviews, which are also intended to fuel a desire to purchase the book. Verdicts from customers on websites such as http://www.amazon.co.uk as well as comments on readers' sites like http://books. guardian.co.uk/bookclub can also influence our first impression of a particular narrative text.

Such contextual features of narratives are of narratological interest as they lead to a preliminary categorization of the text and thus influence its reception. They also furnish information about the interests and preferences of those who act on such information, enabling authors to find out what the public would like to read. Of course, a multiplicity of readerships is being addressed: in some markets a very clear distinction is drawn between literary and popular fiction, as can be seen from the comments on the jackets of newly published works of serious literary prose or those found in the Penguin Classics series. Elizabeth Gaskell's novel *North and South* (1855), for example, is presented with, on the back cover, a comment from a literary historical perspective in bold print followed by a brief account of the themes and main characters:

The blurb

> **Although only lately rated among Elizabeth Gaskell's best work *North and South* is a novel that is remarkable, and triumphantly successful, on many levels.**
>
> As the title suggests, it is primarily a study of the contrast between the values of rural southern England and the industrialized north; but through the medium of its central characters, John Thornton and Margaret Hale, it also becomes a profound comment on the need for reconciliation among the English classes, on the importance of suffering, and above all on the value of placing the dictates of personal conscience above social respectability. And in Margaret Hale, whose intensity, spiritual isolation and passion electrify the book, Mrs Gaskell created one of the finest heroines of Victorian literature.
>
> (Gaskell 1986: back cover)

The text draws attention to the fact that this is one of the novelist's most important texts, now regarded as her best novel, and urges the cultivated reader to tackle this work should s/he not yet know it. The oppositional pairs town/country and industrial/rural are mentioned in explanation of the title and locate the work within the tradition of the Victorian social and industrial novel. Margaret Hale, the female protagonist, is described in glowing terms ('electrify', 'finest heroines'), which makes a browser look forward to reading the book.

In the English-speaking world, new fiction is often marketed extensively and aggressively, with widespread use of hype and hints at sexual explicitness. Here is a relatively harmless example, part of the text from the back cover of Hanif Kureishi's *The Black Album*:

> Shahid, perilously fond of sex, drugs, rock 'n' roll, attends a lusterless community college in London. He wants to please the conservative Muslims in the flat next door but is enthralled by the gorgeous Deedee Osgood, an X-popping, rave-hopping, radical college professor with a penchant for sex in taxis. Set in 1989, the year the Berlin Wall fell and the fatwah was imposed against Salman Rushdie, *The Black Album* is a naughty, provocative, exhilarating novel by a phenomenally talented young writer who richly captures the ebullience – and confusion – of living.
>
> (Kureishi 1995: back cover)

The adjectives 'naughty, provocative, exhilarating' and the noun 'ebullience' are calculated to appeal to the more unconventional reader. By contrast, the Gaskell blurb seeks to lure the reader with an emphasis on moral seriousness and clearly addresses a well-read audience. The text for the Kureishi novel instead focuses on entertainment, hybridity and chaos. These very different marketing strategies could be seen as linking in with the narrative technique of the respective novels. Gaskell's text aims to create harmony out of initial social discord, whereas a chaotic assortment of themes is reflected in the structure of Kureishi's narrative. The blurbs offer a foretaste of the reading experience to come.

Cover design
One last point needs to be addressed before we turn to questions of reception. The layout and illustration of a book's cover and the design of its title page strongly influence consumer behaviour when the reader is able to choose from a number of editions from a range of newly published books. These graphic features also arouse or confirm certain assumptions about the content of the work (crime novel, thriller, romance, blockbuster, literary fiction). For decades the novels of William Faulkner, for instance, were published with sexually explicit covers. One can imagine that readers seduced by the prospect of sensational immorality may well have been put off by the complexity of Faulkner's language, got bored and set the book aside with a yawn, without ever having reached the 'saucy bits'. In the meantime, Faulkner, now considered one of the masters of modernist American literature, is accorded covers more appropriate to his status as a classic writer.

Empirical literary studies
Literary scholars have also begun to look into text reception. This work involves carrying out empirical tests. Early research into reader response was speculative: proponents such as Wolfgang Iser and Hans-Robert Jauss based their ideas concerning the reactions of potential readers on an analysis of their own responses or referred to the comments of established literary scholars about published books or productions of plays. This kind of investigation should not be dismissed out of hand. The trained eye of an experienced reader is able to predict many reactions on the part of literature

fans with a certain degree of accuracy. But the subjective responses of literature specialists may render them blind to other possible types of reading. Empirical literary studies, with its flagship institution IGEL (*Internationale Gesellschaft für empirische Literaturforschung*, founded in 1987), has always argued that reader response findings should be cross-checked and validated. There have been various attempts to put this into practice. In Germany, empirical literary studies are mainly carried out by Siegfried J. Schmidt (Siegen) and his associates. A respected practitioner in the Netherlands is Gerard Steen. Werner Faulstich/Hans-Werner Ludwig's *Erzählperspektive Empirisch* (1985) and Bortolussi/Dixon's *Psychonarratology* (2003) are the two outstanding examples of the results of this kind of work, which is also relevant for narratology.

Most empirical studies use students with little or no experience in literary studies as guinea pigs, for obvious reasons: they are still 'unspoilt'. The results obtained in this way are frequently open to criticism from a literary angle, since the informants generally have little experience of reading and do not find it easy to understand the texts. Testing complex narratological categories is even more challenging and difficult. Bortolussi/Dixon change sentences in texts, for example, in order to obtain different responses to the original and to the amended text, and then test theories such as the text's potential to generate sympathy based on the extent of the foregrounding of characters' consciousness. However, many texts are more complex than the experimenters would have them be, and interference from other quarters may also occur. It may sound logical that the more insight one obtains into a quarrel between a man and a woman, the more readers will take the part of the person whose point of view they are familiar with because they learn about that person's thoughts. However, the impact of the situation itself – the woman feels exploited, the man feels trapped – should not be underestimated. Each individual reader will have her/his opinion on this issue. Another point not taken into account is that female readers might sympathize with the woman's position, and male readers with the man's, no matter how much insight is given by the author into the consciousness of the protagonists. The realization that reader response can be extremely gender-specific is very valuable, but only results in yet more methodological problems for empirical researchers.

The findings of cognitive linguistics and literary studies over the last twenty years are less concrete, but potentially more reliable. Back in the 1980s, Israeli scholars identified so-called primacy and recency effects in the reading process (Hrushovski 1982; cf. Stockwell 2002). Information occurring early in a narrative activates a framework into which further information can be fitted. As a result of the primacy effect, a considerable amount of material which is inconsistent with this frame has to accumulate before the reader is willing to break out of her/his conceptualizations of the situation. The idea of the recency effect, on the other hand, is useful for explaining the impact of recently mentioned material on the reader. In order to disambiguate personal pronoun references (anaphors) one normally refers back to the immediately preceding person or thing – these are considered to be salient – and not to possible antecedents further back in the text. Such matters may become relevant for narratology in a discussion of the use of pronouns *he* or *she* at the beginning of a paragraph, for instance, although other factors (narrative situation, existence of competing protagonists) can also play a role. | Cognitive approaches

A purely text-based approach to narrative writing sidesteps interesting issues to do with its production, circulation and reception. In this chapter we have discussed some of the contextual features that may influence narrative texts. These aspects can only be | Summary discussed as contexts; in contrast to text analysis, there is no terminology for and systematic description of these available as yet. Notwithstanding this, context should be taken into account when interpreting texts, particularly if the aim is an ideological or gender-specific reading.

4   The Structure of Narrative

We can distinguish two layers in every narrative: the level of the world represented in the story and the level at which this representation takes place. In the novel, the latter level is that of the narrative discourse (level of narrative mediation). In the case of first-person and authorial narratives, this is the narrator's discourse. (As examples of first-person narratives one can mention Günther Grass's *The Tin Drum* and *David Copperfield* by Charles Dickens; novels like Henry Fielding's *Tom Jones*, Balzac's *Old Goriot* or Goethe's *Elective Affinities* are authorial narratives.) The narrator may either figure in the plot (first-person narrative: the narrator reports what s/he has experienced her/himself) or, alternatively, stand aloof from the world of the characters and describe the fictional world from his/her perspective as authorial narrator. In narratives with a prominent narrator figure, the narrative discourse simulates the situation of a story-teller telling the story to his/her listeners. Sometimes, however, this layer of the narrative structure may not be immediately obvious, and so the reader has the impression that there is no narrator at all. First and foremost, this holds true for modern psychological novels in which the account of what happens is filtered through the consciousness of one of the characters in the story. F. K. Stanzel categorizes such texts as prototypes of what he calls the *figural narrative situation* (see Chapter 9). *(margin: Level of representation and level of the represented)*

In the English-speaking world the terms *overt* and *covert* (Chatman) are often used to refer to an easily identifiable as opposed to a concealed narrator. An *overt narrator* is one that can be clearly seen to be telling the story – though not necessarily a first-person narrator – and to be articulating her/his own views and making her/his presence felt stylistically as well as on the metanarrative level. Stanzel refers here to a *personal(ized) narrator*; in English the term *dramatized narrator* is also used (Booth 1961). A particularly sophisticated form of overt narrator, according to Stanzel, is the embodied 'I'. The narrator is drawn in considerable detail, even down to providing a description of his/her physical appearance. Such a narrator takes an active part in the story, sits at his/her desk, contemplates the apple trees in blossom and has a spouse or child, a personal history and a gender which are clearly indicated. In Fielding's novel *Joseph Andrews* the narrator tells of Lady Booby, who is rent by conflicting passions. Her vacillation is compared to the dilemma of a jury trying to weigh up the relative merits of the arguments put forward in court. *(margin: The narrator)*

> So have I seen, in the Hall of Westminster; where Serjeant Bramble hath been retained on the right side, and Serjeant Puzzle on the left; the balance of opinion (so equal were their fees) alternately incline to either scale. [. . .] 'till at last all becomes one scene of confusion in the tortured minds of the hearers [. . .] Or as it

happens in the conscience, where honour and honesty pull one way, and a bribe and necessity another. – If it was only our present business to make similies, we could produce many more to this purpose: but a similie (as well as a word) to the wise. We shall therefore see a little after our hero, for whom the reader is doubtless in some pain.

(*Joseph Andrews* I, ix; Fielding 1986: 62–3)

Here the narrator notes that he has been physically present at such legal proceedings (he is an embodied narrator). Later in the passage, he mainly features as a storyteller who draws parallels, thus becoming active on the metanarrative level. He closes the paragraph by returning to the story, or rather to the main protagonist, Joseph Andrews. In some postmodern short stories, for instance, the plot is so attenuated that the main focus of attention is on the desperate narrator sitting at his/her desk, incapable of squeezing out any words whatsoever.

A *covert narrator*, on the other hand, is linguistically inconspicuous; s/he does not present him/herself (one could almost say: itself) as the articulator of the story or does so almost imperceptibly:

On a cold and starry Christmas-eve less than a generation ago, a man was passing along a lane in the darkness of a plantation that whispered thus distinctively to his intelligence. All the evidences of his nature were those afforded by the spirit of his footsteps, which succeeded each other lightly and quickly, and by the liveliness of his voice as he sang in a rural cadence.

(*Under the Greenwood Tree* I, i; Hardy 1998: 7)

On the north-eastern shores of England there is a town called Monkshaven, containing at the present day about fifteen thousand inhabitants. There were, however, but half the number at the end of the last century, and it was at that period that the events narrated in the following pages occurred.

(*Sylvia's Lovers* i; Gaskell 1982: 1)

Other media   At the level of representation, film is shaped by a combination of visual and acoustic elements. Narratologists and film studies specialists differ in their terminology here. Chatman contends that there is such a thing as a 'cinematic narrator'; Jahn (2003) refers to a 'FCD/filmic composition device'; Bordwell and Branigan, on the other hand, reject the idea that there is a narrator as such in the medium of film at all. Similarly, the level of representation is different in ballet and in cartoons, for example, depending on the medium. Drama, too, poses serious problems for a definition of the discourse level and a narratorial persona. Although there are many plays that have a kind of narrator on stage (as in Thornton Wilder's *Our Town*), and though some late nineteenth-century plays have stage directions that smack of authorial narrative (Shaw is notorious for this), in general the 'narrative discourse' of drama is taken to be that of the performance, where there exists no communicating narrator persona. One may therefore be tempted to introduce a 'dramatic composition device' by analogy with film.[1] In painting and music (cf. Wolf 2002) it is particularly difficult to perceive events in chronological order (painting) or to correlate elements in the represented world (persons, objects, actions) with the level of representation (music). Recurring motifs or characters are, for example, encoded in sound sequences in the music theatre of Richard Wagner. But even in the case of programme music such as the *Symphonie fantastique* by Berlioz there remains a sizeable body of music which it is not easy to relate to a fictional world.

The *narratee* (Fr. *narrataire*; Ger. *Leserfigur*) is the intrafictional addressee of the narrator's discourse. S/he may also be a fictional character: the narrator tells the story to a friend, for instance, in other words to someone who belongs, just as the narrator does, to the fictional world even though this person is not active on the plot level and exists only 'offstage'. The narratee is rather nebulous in most novels, although s/he is usually implicitly or explicitly identified as male or female. Laurence Sterne's celebrated addresses to 'Dear Madam' or George Eliot's evocation of a male reader ('you must be an exceptionally wise man, who . . . never . . . threw yourself in a martial attitude' *Mill on the Floss* (Eliot 1980: II, iv, 154) are typical examples of this gendering process. The reader is frequently admonished to become active, 'I leave you to imagine the agreeable feelings with which Philip went to Mr Deane the next day' (Eliot 1980: 546). S/he can even take shape as a character in the true sense of the word. In Italo Calvino's *If on a Winter's Night a Traveler* (1979) the narratee is told to close the door so that he can read in peace. We subsequently learn of the narratee's trip to the bookshop, where he bought the novel he is reading now (see p. 31 below). The narratee

An *implied reader*, on the other hand, is located at the opposite end of this scale of concreteness. He or she is a projection from the text and is perceived by the reader as acting out the role of an ideal reader figure, although the real reader may not actually assume this role. In ironic texts, the implied reader position is understood to be filled with somebody capable of enjoying the ironical remarks by the narrator, and the real reader will ideally take on that role. The implied reader

As well as drawing a distinction between the level of representation and the level of the represented, we may also distinguish between other basic structural features of narrative. For instance, no matter what the medium is, all narratives are structured externally as well as internally. External and internal narrative structures

External paratextual structuring elements include, for example, the title page of a book, or the comments about it on the back cover, or short excerpts from reviews on the first pages, or notes about the author and her/his other works, or information from the publishers about titles by other writers in the same series. Also to be included are tables of contents, forewords, introductions, editorial comments, bibliographies and the like. In his *Paratexts* (first published in 1987 as *Seuils*) Gérard Genette distinguishes between several kinds of paratext: what he calls the 'peritext' of the editor, the author's name, the title of the book, the dedication, the epigraph, various types of forewords and introductions, titles and headings within the text, notes and the 'epitext' at the end of a work. We have already discussed some such paratexts in Chapter 3. In the case of the screening of films in the cinema, trailers and credits can be included in this category. In the theatre, the programme may be considered one such paratext, and perhaps even the curtain. Paratexts

The visual presentation of the text of a novel also counts as an external narrative structure in so far as it is not mimetically motivated. We are talking here about typographical elements such as the choice and size of font, marginal notes or illustrations accompanying the text. Here the borderlines between the part played by the author and by the editor are difficult to draw precisely. In contrast, differences in print type (use of italics or bold print, capital letters) which serve to render volume or pitch (in dialogue), interior monologue (as opposed to words from the narrator which are not italicized, for instance), or fantasies (as opposed to real events and objects in the fictional world) have to be considered part of the internal structure. In theatre and film, similar effects can be achieved through the means of lighting, sound, colour, perspective, close-up or fade-out shots. For instance, memories can be filmed in black and white or sepia, present-day action in colour. In the theatre, the dimming of light may be used to signal memory episodes.

The main point here is to distinguish between publishing or marketing-related paratexts and those that are relevant to the narrative. For example, the title of a novel, play or film is clearly important for the narrative as it is usually determined by the author as opposed to the publisher and taken to signal something crucial about the story. Yet the title is still not part of the narrative proper but one of its metanarrative elements. In film it is quite clear that the title is part of the narrative discourse; like the credits, which roughly correspond to the list of dramatis personae in a drama, it is often superimposed on the opening sequence of the film. The same holds true for the important structuring elements (chapter divisions and chapter headings). Some lengthy works consist of several parts or books, with a fair number of chapters in each, for example, Fielding's *Tom Jones* or Victor Hugo's *Les Misérables*.

Chapter divisions

The practice of dividing texts into chapters only goes back as far as the early modern period, although we find it somewhat earlier in German literature than in English. Analogous to the division into acts in drama, such a division was often introduced into works of fiction that were originally without chapters. Novels without chapters can be found as late as the mid-eighteenth century and are becoming more common again in contemporary fiction. Even if chapter divisions are present, their function is sometimes reader- rather than content-related. Their purpose is not necessarily to reflect important stages in the plot but to chunk the text into bite-sized pieces for the reader.

Notwithstanding these remarks it is, however, clear that as units of text chapters frequently fulfil three functions:

- They mark a change of scene or a shift of focus to other characters. A new chapter makes it easier for the reader to adjust to a different strand of the plot, often a flashback, a tale within a tale or the citation of documents of some kind (an exchange of letters, diary entries etc.; cf. Nischik 1981, Fludernik 2003a).
- Chapter headings as metanarrative elements enable the narrator to play games on a metafictional level. These tricks may leave their mark on the text in an intentionally arbitrary division of the narrative into chapters or in metanarrative comments on the chapter breaks.
- They permit the narrator to expound at length on generic, aesthetic and metanarrative matters. This is particularly noticeable in Henry Fielding's *Tom Jones* (1749), where each book of the novel is prefaced with a chapter from the narrator, expounding his (or Fielding's) narrative poetics.

Examples

Tom Jones contains examples of particularly striking and amusing divisions into chapters and chapter headings:

The remainder of this scene consisted entirely of raptures, excuses, and compliments, very pleasant to have heard from the parties, but rather dull when related at second hand. *Here, therefore, we shall put an end to this dialogue, and hasten to the fatal hour* when everything was prepared for the destruction of poor Sophia.

But this being the most tragical matter in our whole history, *we shall treat it in a chapter by itself.*

(Fielding 1996: XV, iv, 697–8; my emphasis)

These are the closing sentences after a conversation between Lady Bellaston and Lord Fellamar, in which they plan Sophia's rape. This assault on her chastity will be forestalled in the following chapter by the unexpected arrival of her father, Squire Western. The final section of Chapter 4 heralds a change of time and place, and a metanarrative comment on the portrayal of the events in question is appended in a separate chapter.

Fielding's chapter headings also show the narrator teasing or misleading the reader. They may even state the opposite to the contents of the chapter, and this strategy can be exploited for comic effect. For instance, Chapter 4 quoted above is headed, 'By which will appear how dangerous an advocate a lady is when she supplies her eloquence to an ill purpose' (p. 696). Alongside such moralizing chapter headings there are others that focus on the reader's reactions: 'Containing some matters which may affect, and others which may surprise, the reader' (XV, v, 698). Others shroud forthcoming developments in mystery and build up suspense: 'Short and sweet' (XV, viii, 714) or have to do with purely structural matters: 'In which the history is obliged to look back' (XVI, vi, 755). They can be witty and amusing: 'A most dreadful chapter indeed; and which few readers ought to venture upon in an evening, especially when alone' (VII, xiv, 336). This practice is not particular to Fielding but can also be noted in German and French chapter headings (Wieckenberg 1969, Schnitzler 1983).

Nevertheless, chapter divisions in novels are not used in a totally consistent way. The majority of chapter breaks are pragmatically motivated: they divide long stretches of narrative into more easily digestible morsels. Some authors, especially nineteenth-century ones, are particularly adept at chapter management. As a result of the serial publication of their works in periodicals, writers such as Charles Dickens were obliged always to end their instalments on a note of suspense, develop each and every strand of the plot in each episode and structure each instalment quite unmistakably as a sequence of three to four chapters.

Structuring elements resembling chapters are also to be found within films, and not only in early productions which actually signalled a change of scene by means of written messages to the audience ('Ten years later' or 'Meanwhile, back at the ranch'). To the best of my knowledge, this aspect has been somewhat neglected in film studies. In the meantime, a similar kind of structuring is quite clearly noticeable in films made for television because these have to take commercial breaks into account, the element of suspense clearly playing an important part in deciding where and when the breaks are to occur. With DVDs, moreover, films are divided into scene sequences and in some cases these are given individual titles. In theatre performances, visual markers (curtain, music, shifting of props) indicate scene and act changes. (But not always: in plays with multi-scene acts, the interval or intervals will tend to superimpose their structure on the five acts.)

Text–internal narrative structures

Narrative levels

To begin with, a distinction has to be made between various levels of narrative. Thus, in accordance with the well-known communicative model of narrative (A. Nünning 1989, Coste 1989, Sell 2000), there is a level at which the narrator (that is to say a narrator who is constituted in the text) communicates with a narratee. This level of narration or narrative communication can be either implicit or explicit. For instance, in Lilian Faschinger's *Magdalena the Sinner* (*Magdalena Sünderin*, 1995), the narrator addresses her interlocutor directly: 'And now you will listen to me, Reverend Father' (1996: 1). The narrator addresses her remarks to a fictional character, who exists intra-textually as a fully-fledged character at the plot level, someone who listens and who also acts. The communicative situation in the narrative discourse is that of the confessional. Other novels feature narrators who seek to impress, mislead or win over their inter-locutors. Such intra-fictional narratees are not as common as are relatively vague and unspecified extradiegetic narratees with whom the real reader can readily identify or from whom s/he would perhaps like to distance her/himself. When the narrator apostrophizes her narratee as 'dear reader' in women's writing of the Victorian period, this implies a high degree of intimacy with the real reader. Laurence Sterne's 'Dear Madam' comments, on the other hand, often level a charge of naivety or stupidity at the narratee and are actually a metafictional ploy which uses irony to distance the reader from this fictional reader role.

Implied author and implied reader

Some narratologists postulate a second set of communicative relations around the narrator/narratee relationship, namely those between what Booth terms the 'implied author' and the 'implied reader' (Iser). The *implied author* is in actual fact not a character but a construct of the reader or interpreter, who tries to determine the 'meaning' of the work in question. Sentences such as 'In *Little Dorrit* Dickens seeks to demonstrate the power of social constraints' construct an intention on the part of the 'author' based on the reading of the novel and on one's speculations as to what it might mean. In this case 'Dickens' in the sentence cited is not the historical person Charles Dickens (the real author) but the product of ideas about the work's purpose developed by the reader. Similarly, the *implied reader* (Fr. *lecteur implicite*; Ger. *impliziter Leser*) and the real reader are not one and the same; the implied reader is constructed by the critic who predicates a particular reader response on the work. Thus it can be said that many of Dickens's novels embody a very bourgeois world view, in spite of containing a good deal of social criticism. In point of fact, these texts tend to uphold the Victorian work ethic and condone the Victorian mystification of sexuality. The implied reader will be a contemporary agreeing with those views, a role into which the actual reader may or may not slip.

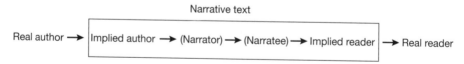

Figure 4.1 The narrative-communicative situation (see Chatman 1978: 151)

Functions of the narrator

What exactly are the various functions of the narrator in a narrative text? Hitherto our focus has been on the communicative function. Narrators, however, fulfil a number of other functions and we shall go on to look at these briefly.

The remarks which follow are based on Nünning (1989, 1997b), who provides the most exhaustive account of narratorial functions. To begin with, a narrator has a narrative function: it is s/he, technically speaking, who presents the fictional world. Narrator may remain covert in this function and need not feature overtly as narrator. Secondly, the narrator comments or expounds: s/he explains why events occur, ascribes them to political or social circumstances and conditions, indicates what it is that motivates the characters and so on. This particular function requires an overt narrator, for the most part one who refers to her/himself by a first-person pronoun. It is important that such comments and explanations refer to the story world. Their main purpose is to arouse the reader's sympathy or antipathy for certain characters (Ger. *Sympathielenkung*) and to develop a normative framework for the story world and the reader's reception of it. Thirdly, the narrator often functions as a kind of philosopher or moralist who articulates universally valid propositions, especially in the case of sentences in the so-called gnomic present (for example, 'Man is an animal that has degenerated as a result of learning to speak' or 'Boys will be boys'). In such cases, an overt narrator's remarks pertain to the real world and not just to the fictional world of the characters, even if they are declaredly intended to apply to the latter. The narrator's gnomic statements serve to point out the general rules which help to explain events on the story level. Moreover, they create a system of norms intended to make it easier for the reader to interpret the text. Fourthly, the narrator has discursive functions which have to do with the communicative situation of narration (directly addressing the narratee, making metanarrative comments about the process of telling the story). Naturally, all these functions often become blurred in the sentences which constitute the text, for instance when the narrator's description of a person contains evaluative adjectives, that is to say when functions 1 and 4 above are combined.

In specific circumstances a narrator will lose credibility because s/he violates valid social norms in word or deed. Such an *unreliable narrator* (Fr. *narrateur non-fiable*; Ger. *unzuverlässiger Erzähler*) may give a distorted picture of (fictional) reality as a result of being obsessed by certain ideas (so, for example, one could view the embedded narrator of Tolstoy's *Kreutzer Sonata* as obsessive, with mad ideas about marriage). Alternatively the narrator may reveal her/himself to be an immoral or dishonest person (Jason Compson in William Faulkner's *The Sound and the Fury*, 1956). S/he may also turn out to be a naive and unsuspecting party to the events portrayed, lacking any grasp of the background to the story – in contrast with the reader, who arrives at an understanding of the situation by dint of reading between the lines. The narrator in Maria Edgeworth's novel *Castle Rackrent* (1800), the servant Thady, is a striking example of such a naive unreliable narrator. In German literature one could point to Serenus Zeitblom, the unreliable first-person narrator of Thomas Mann's *Doctor Faustus* (1947), since he has only a very vague notion of what happens to Adrian Leverkühn, the hero.

The 'discoverer' of this type of narrator, Wayne C. Booth, in his theory links the unreliable narrator to the figure of the implied author (Booth 1961). A reader only realizes that a first-person narrator is unreliable because s/he assumes that the implied author holds views in direct conflict with those held by the first-person narrator. Unreliable narrative discourse creates the impression that the implied author is communicating with the reader behind the first-person narrator's back. The narrator is deliberately presented as a figure whom the reader discovers to be lacking in credibility. An unreliable first-person narrator functions, therefore, as a sign of the fictionality of the text – real first-person narrators may unmask themselves, but they

The unreliable narrator

are not made to look ridiculous on purpose and by means of textual manipulations. In a revision of Booth's theory, Ansgar Nünning, for his part, has proposed an analysis of the unreliable narrator (1998) which is firmly rooted in a reader-response framework. He also points out the importance of signals and clues in the text: first-person narrators like those in many short stories by Edgar Allan Poe render themselves suspicious by repeatedly claiming to tell the truth, the whole truth and nothing but the truth.

Fallibility

Whether we can also describe authorial narrators or reflector figures as unreliable is disputed among narrative theorists. In this connection, Seymour Chatman has introduced the notion of *fallibility* with reference to reflector characters: Bloom in Joyce's *Ulysses* is not unreliable, but he is fallible as a result of his limited view of events: he is not able to comprehend the world of the novel in the breadth and depth available to the omniscient narrator.

Characters as narrators

Beneath the level of communication between narrator and narratee, another, intradiegetic level of communication exists, that of the communication between characters. This communication may include the telling of stories; hence some characters become narrators. They tell these stories to other characters, who thus become narratees. Such embedded narrative acts are located on the story level (to use Genette's terminology: they are *intradiegetic*); the story that is told in these acts of narration is situated at a lower level, one that Bal calls *hypodiegetic*. (Genette's term for this is *metadiegetic*, a rather unfortunate choice since the prefix 'meta', as in meta-linguistic etc., regularly denotes a comment on something, in other words it signals a superordinate level of discourse.)

Frame narratives

As well as internal narratives, there are also frame narratives. Frames (shown by the square brackets in Figure 4.2) may be found either at the beginning, or at the end, or both at the beginning and end of a narrative. Nelles (1997) calls the first type *introductory framing* (cf. A in the diagram) and the second *terminal framing* (cf. B). In addition, frame narratives can also be interpolated at some point in the text (*interpolated frame*, cf. D). McHale (1987: 117) characterizes Type A as 'missing end frame' and Wolf labels Type B as 'missing opening frame' (Wolf 2006: 185–7).

Examples

Henry James's novella *The Turn of the Screw* has only an introductory frame, in which a group of friends swap ghost stories until we arrive at the narrative proper, the story of the governess and the ghosts (Type A). Joseph Conrad's novel *Heart of Darkness* begins with a scene in which Marlow, the first-person narrator, and his friends are sitting in a boat on the river Thames. Then comes Marlow's story, and at the end of the book we find ourselves once more in the company of his listeners in the boat. This is a good example of Type C. Examples of interpolated frames (Type D) would

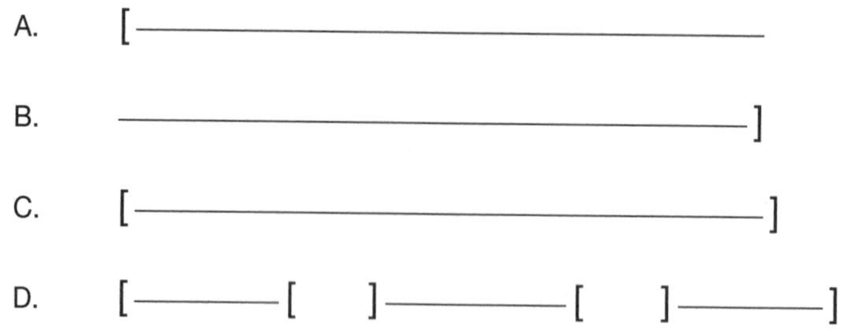

A.   [————————————————————————

B.   ————————————————————————]

C.   [————————————————————————]

D.   [————[   ]————[   ]————]

Figure 4.2 Four types of frame narrative

be Theodor Storm's novella *The Dykemaster* (*Der Schimmelreiter,* 1888), in the course of which the school-master breaks off his narrative many times, or Tolstoy's novella *The Kreutzer Sonata* (1889). (In fact, there are some minimal interpolations even in *Heart of Darkness.*) Terminal framing (Type B) is the rarest and most striking type. Examples of Type B are often texts in which the internal narrative is not told as such but takes the form of a vision from which the reader is rudely ejected at the end of the text. An example would be Thomas Pynchon's *Gravity's Rainbow,* where (at least, according to one reading of this text) the whole novel turns out to be a film which Slothrop has just been watching.

When characters themselves tell stories, the narrative level to which they belong   Multiple framing
also constitutes a frame. Thus frames and the stories contained in them are recurring elements that may nest inside each other as in Figure 4.3 below, like the proverbial Chinese boxes, or Russian dolls.

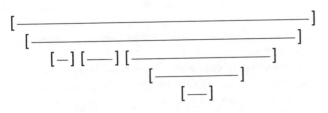

Figure 4.3 Multiple framing

The best-known texts with a frame structure are the tales from the *Arabian Nights* (cf. Ryan 1986). Recent work on frame narratives has stressed that framing may occur on the vertical as well as on the horizontal narrative level. In other words, the framed story can, as in the case of the *Arabian Nights* tales, be a story told by one character, and in this story another tale is told, and so on (vertical axis). The framed narrative is part and parcel of the intradiegetic level. Frame narratives may also be found next to each other, without any explicit reference to verticality. An example of such horizontal framing is the editorial preface. Furthermore, Nelles (1997) makes a distinction between epistemic and ontological framing, that is to say between framed stories which are the product of a character's imagination and those which did, in fact, happen.

Narrative and plot

Although discourse narratologists have mainly focused on the discourse level of narra-   Plot
tive, the level of the story itself is equally important. Here let it be noted that I am not so much concerned with the events themselves as with the plot, in other words with a logically structured story that spells out motivations. Such a plot precedes medial-ization, whether this be in the form of verbal narrative, film or drama (cf. Chapter 1).

At the story level it is usually axiomatic that one has a combination of *setting* and *actants.* Paradoxically, this renders the building blocks of traditional stories merely existential and therefore static. In narratives, characters and settings generally feature in descriptive passages – a time frame only emerges as the result of sequences of actions on the part of the characters. In this connection, Chatman distinguishes between *events* and *existents* at the story level. However, if one takes characters to embody human characteristics, then one can regard their actions as part of their existential grounding, and describe the setting as dynamic, a kind of environment which includes events and developments that impact on the protagonists from outside. The best concise account of plot studies is that provided by Jan-Philipp Busse in Wenzel (2004).

Plot strands

The work of Propp and Bremond dealt only with the structure of linear sequences of actions. This was undoubtedly the case because what is most important for us in fairy tales are the deeds of the hero as he tries to fulfil the tasks imposed on him. Subsequent researchers have turned their attention to the ways in which the various strands of a plot converge or diverge. Indeed, texts of a certain length often feature various settings within a space and a number of actants, all of whom will be brought together by a time shift or change of scene: a move from country estate to townhouse, or from the army in the field to the bosom of the family. Such spatial and temporal coordination between characters is not unproblematic: for example, how do you ensure that the various protagonists and their stories will connect within the same time frame? A popular solution is to have two or more characters meet, whereupon the newly introduced characters review what has so far happened in their lives, thus bringing the stories of all parties up to date. In classical drama, in order to bring plot strands together and update them, much recourse is had to messengers; sometimes letters (serving as interpolated stories) are used for the same purpose.

Alternative worlds

Recent research has drawn attention to virtual sequences of actions and to strands of action that are logically irreconcilable (Ryan 1991). Readers empathize with characters and become emotionally involved with possible developments desired by the protagonists: for example, they hope the hero will get to meet his beloved at the ball, whereas actually such a happy meeting is delayed or prevented by unexpected events. Postmodern narratives have also popularized the technique of *uchrony* (Rodiek 1997) or the genre of the *parahistorical novel* (alternative historical novel; see Helbig 1988). Such texts portray events which diverge from the course of history as we know it. For example, in Philip K. Dick's *The Man in the High Castle* (1962), the Allies lose the Second World War. In science fiction, the existence of parallel worlds or universes makes structuring the plot a difficult task. Bremond alludes to the convoluted plots so typical of the ontological playfulness of this genre. He postulates a choice of two courses of action at each stage of the narrative. For instance, the hero reaches the castle and (a) enters or (b) rides on. In interactive cybertext narratives the reader is even in a position to decide whether the story continues with (a) or (b). In stories with alternative plot strands both courses of action are 'real', and the consequences of these actions come to exist alongside each other. Hilary Dannenberg provides an in-depth discussion of such experiments, which she calls 'ontological plotting' (2004a, 2004b, 2008).

Let us now move on from the plot level to the communicative level, and thus to the narrator.

The narrator: person

First-person and third-person narrative

In thinking about the relationship of narrators to the figures they tell about – the term for this relationship in narratology is *person* – we are exploring another set of basic aspects of the structure of narrative. Take our day-to-day spoken interaction, for instance: here we find many accounts of things that happened to us. Kurt tells us about his adventures in India, for instance, and how he narrowly escaped death in an accident involving a taxi. This kind of first-person narrative focuses on exciting events. Furthermore, these events are authenticated by Kurt's account of them. He is not only present in the here and now but was present when they occurred, and very much in the thick of things. Since a first-person narrator is one of the characters in the plot, Genette describes first-person narrative as *homo*diegetic (narrator = character). In the case of Kurt, because he is the main protagonist and is giving an account of an adventure he was personally involved in, he would be classed by Genette as an *auto*diegetic narrator.

Although first-person narrative predominates in conversational narrative, there are also stories in which we relate events that happened to others, who have normally told us about it. The urban legend of the huge spider lurking in the bunch of bananas at the supermarket and then running amok in someone's kitchen would be a typical example of this. In this case, the narrator and the protagonist are different individuals, which is why Genette refers to these as *heterodiegetic* narratives (narrator ≠ protagonist). In contrast to what happens in spoken interaction, in literature the world of the third-person narrator is completely separate from that of the characters in the story. For example, the narrator of a fairy tale, with his special 'teller of tales' tone, never takes on the same solid contours as a friend telling us about his parents' experiences in New York. This friend – let us call him Peter – is standing next to us as he tells his story, and we can see him gesticulating wildly as he speaks. In literature, however, the level at which the story is mediated to the reader is usually perceived as being of secondary importance in relation to the plot. The narrator is frequently nothing more than a disembodied voice.[2]

The distinction we have just made between first- and third-person narration (or homodiegesis/heterodiegesis) includes further possible variants. In fact, the range of possible relationships that narrators, narratees and characters can enter into is potentially rather wide. *We*-narrative is fairly common in spoken interaction: couples, soldiers, sportspeople, students, scouts – they all experience exciting events together and then give their accounts of these in the first person plural. But we can also tell and write about *other* people in the plural (*they*-narrative), although the use of such narratives is much rarer. In narratological studies *we*-narrative has mainly been analysed by Uri Margolin and Brian Richardson (for instance, Margolin 2000, Richardson 2006).

We-narratives

Second-person narratives, which tell the story of a narratee, are a particularly interesting case. In fiction in English and in the Romance languages one finds a fair number of works tailored along these lines. Italo Calvino's *If on a Winter's Night a Traveller* (1979) begins by addressing the reader and then continues with a description of how this reader went to a bookstore and purchased the book being read.

You-texts

> You are about to begin reading Italo Calvino's new novel, *If on a winter's night a traveler* [*sic*]. Relax. Concentrate. Dispel every other thought. Let the world around you fade. Best to close the door; the TV is always on in the next room. Tell the others right away, 'No, I don't want to watch TV!' Raise your voice – they won't hear you otherwise – 'I'm reading! I don't want to be disturbed!' Maybe they haven't heard you, with all that racket; speak louder, yell: 'I'm beginning to read Italo Calvino's new novel!' Or if you prefer, don't say anything; just hope they'll leave you alone.
>
> (Calvino 1982: 9)

In Calvino's text the reader perceives her/himself as being urged to carry out the actions described. Only later, when extensive use is made of the past tense, and more and more personal details about the *you*-protagonist are revealed, does it become clear that 'you' must definitely be a fictional character.

Many *you*-texts are written from the subjective perspective of the character referred to by 'you', but without a narrator figure or a narratee (addressee) emerging from the text. This is true of Ilse Aichinger's story 'Spiegelgeschichte' (1949; 'Story in a Mirror'), in which a woman relives her life backwards, and her death at the end of the story coincides with her memories of being born. In postmodern writing various experiments with personal pronouns have explored other options: we come across texts with invented pronouns or with an impersonal pronoun like *it* or *one* (Fr. *on*; Ger. *es, man*; see Fludernik 1996: 222–236).

Generally speaking, all the pronouns mentioned so far refer to protagonists in the narrative. The narrator, if referred to by a pronoun, is always 'I', even when we are looking at a third-person novel or a *you*-text. The narrator speaks (hence 'I'); the persons s/he speaks of are 'I', 'he', 'she', 'we', 'you', etc. We can only speak of first-person narrative when the narrator is also a character. Genette neatly sidesteps this terminological tangle with his terms homo- and heterodiegesis. However, the complex differences between heterodiegetic *he, they* or *you*-narratives, or between homodiegetic *I* and *we*-narratives, cannot be encompassed in one simple binary opposition.

Time

Let us move on now from the level of communication to the level of the story world. Here the structuring of the narrative in time is another very important element. On the one hand, the sequence of the events which feature in the story has to be compared with the order in which these events are depicted at the level of representation, in the narrative discourse. On the other hand, discrepancies between story time and discourse time must also be taken into account.

Discourse time and story time

Story time is very often discussed under the heading of *tempo* or *pace*. Basically, what is at issue here is how reading or viewing time compares with the actual duration of the events described. The pace of a narrative derives from the relation between discourse time and story time (Günther Müller 1948). It is rare for story time and discourse time to be isochronic. In most cases *anisochrony* – to use Genette's term – may be observed. According to Genette, Chatman and others, there are five different and distinct possible patterns.

a) In *summary*, discourse time, as opposed to story time, is speeded up. For example, at the beginning and end of novels the protagonist's early years or her/his life after the denouement (for instance, after marriage) are often summarized in single chapters. Thus, in the following invented example, the hero's childhood is presented in four densely packed pages, whereas subsequent phases of his life (for example, his first term at university) are covered in five pages.

Section of text	Chapter 1	Chapter 2	Chapter 3
Pages	3, 4, 5, 6	7, 8, 9, 10, 11	12, 13, 14
Period of time covered	20 years	3 months	1 day

Figure 4.4a Example of narrative tempo: summary

b) The narrative is speeded up slightly (see 'Chapter 2' in Figure 4.4a). Lämmert calls this *accelerated narration* (Ger. *geraffte Erzählung*; 1955: 84).

c) In *isochrony* the discourse time is identical with story time. This form can only occur when the words of characters are rendered verbatim or a blow-by-blow account of a series of rapid actions is given, as might be the case with the description of a fist fight, for instance. Even, 'He climbed the stairs and knocked at the door' is not, strictly speaking, isochronic: ascending the stairs certainly takes longer in real time than knocking at the door, though both occupy the same amount of textual space and time in the narrative discourse. Film, of course, is much more mimetic in this respect: in this medium actions are generally portrayed as lasting as long as they do in the real world. But here too, as everywhere, selection is at work: in films car journeys, for example, or doctor's consultations, sleeping, and other such activities are radically speeded up, or omitted, as they are in the novel.   Isochrony

d) In narrative discourse descriptive passages or the portrayal of mental processes slow down the pace of the action. The cinematic equivalent of this would be *slow motion* photography. Chatman refers to this device as *stretch*, Bal as *slow-down* and Lämmert as *time-extending* narration (Ger. *zeitdehnendes Erzählen*). The most striking examples of this type can be found in death scenes in which the whole of the protagonist's life unfolds before her/his eyes. The relatively brief moment when death occurs is filled out with many pages of description (see Figure 4.4b: 'Chapter 8').   Stretch

Section of text	Chapter 7	Chapter 8	Chapter 9
Pages	35–40	41–55	56–59
Period of time covered	2 days	1 hour	7 days

Figure 4.4b Example of narrative tempo: stretch

e) Last but not least, it may be that passages of text, for instance descriptions of landscape, of states of mind, or of socio-historical background, do not correlate at all with any action in the world of the story. Genette calls this category 'pause' (cf. Figure 4.4c: 'Chapter 35').

Section of text	Chapter 33	Chapter 34	Chapter 35
Pages	320–340	341–55	356–60
Period of time covered	3 months	1 day	0

Figure 4.4c Example of narrative tempo: pause

f) The opposite holds true when something that occurs in the fictional world is not mentioned at all on the level of narrative discourse. Such narrative *ellipsis* is mainly used to create suspense. In point of fact, ellipsis is just the most extreme form of speeding up, which is also highly selective. A good deal of information which would overburden the narrative with details is simply filtered out. As the eponymous hero of Sterne's novel *Tristram Shandy* explains, if you were to describe the events of your life in minute detail, just as they occurred, you would be dead long before reaching the end of your autobiography: Ellipsis

> I am this month one whole year older than I was this time twelve-months; and having got, as you perceive, almost into the middle of my fourth volume – and no

farther than my first day's life – 'tis demonstrative that I have three hundred and sixty-four days more life to write [...] the more I write, the more I shall have to write.

(IV, xiii; 1987: 286)

We should remember, though, that this model, which is based on the ideas of Genette and Chatman, focuses exclusively on events that make it possible to quantify story time. Postmodern texts in which the time covered in the fictional world is not specified are not susceptible to the kind of structuring in which duration is measured. There are some texts which withhold information about the sequence of events and actions in time; here we can speak of *achrony* as discussed below. There are also texts in which the actual duration of events cannot be ascertained at all. Moreover, recent research by Kathryn Hume (2005, 2006) has extended the notion of speed to cover different types of speed at the levels of story, discourse and narration.

	Narrative time (nt)			*Story time* (st)
Ellipsis	Narration stops	$(nt=)\ 0 < n\ (=st)$		action continues
Speed-up	Narration	$nt < st$ (not so long as)		action
Scene	Narration	$nt \approx st$ (concurrent)		action
Slow-down	Narration	$nt > st$ (longer than)		action
Pause	narration continues	$(nt=)\ n > 0\ (=st)$		action stops

Figure 4.5 Five types of relationship of discourse time to story time (modelled after Martínez/ Scheffel 1999: 44)

Chronology: analepsis

Let us turn to the relationship of events in the fictional world and in the narrative discourse. Most stories are structured chronologically. However, some novels, epic poems and films may begin with a flashback providing a swift summary of the events leading up to the story, or they may plunge their addressees into the thick of the action – a highly effective attention-getter. Drawing on the work of Genette, narratologists have paid particular attention to *anachrony*, in other words to deviations from chronological order. The most common of these is the *flashback*, also called *analepsis*, in which prior happenings are recounted, often as part of something the hero/heroine remembers; sometimes the purpose is to explain unexpected events which have just been related. In the traditional novel, analepsis is often signalled by a tense shift to the pluperfect (past perfect). In film, past events and the memories of the protagonists can be marked by dissolves, or sometimes by a switch to black-and-white photography. Michael Ondaatje's *The English Patient* (1992) makes extensive use of analepsis; in the film version of the novel, as in the text, the events leading up to Almásy's serious burn injuries are only revealed slowly, in a series of flashbacks.

Prolepsis, achrony

The reverse case, foreshadowing or *prolepsis*, is rather rare nowadays, although it does occur somewhat more frequently in the novels of the nineteenth century: 'Her

[Grushenka's] old merchant friend was seriously ill by this time, "failing", as they used to say in the town, and in fact *he died within a week of Mitya's trial*' (*The Brothers Karamazov*, XI, i; Dostoevsky 1998: 707; my emphasis). What is known as *achrony* is typical of postmodern experimental texts. With such texts, it is difficult to ascertain whether one event follows the other in chronological order; sometimes it is even impossible to determine if events are presented in any kind of chronological order at all. For example, the celebrated millipede in Alain Robbe-Grillet's novel *Jealousy* (1957) cannot be fitted into the action at any one particular moment in a series of plot events. It is also not clear whether the man squashes the creature once or on several occasions. Under the heading of 'frequency', Genette also makes a distinction depending on whether something is recounted once only (singulative), whether one and the same event is depicted several times (repetitive) or whether more than one similar event is told once only for the sake of abbreviation (iterative). The millipede which keeps re-surfacing in Robbe-Grillet's text could, therefore, be a repetitive element; it stands for the hero's obsession with the insect, which he cannot get out of his mind.

Presentational modes

Telling versus showing

In considering important aspects of narrative structure, we also have to look at how the action is rendered. The choice here is between two basic techniques. One of these uses a narrator to tell the story explicitly, whereas the other seems not to require a narrator as mediator at all. These techniques are not only relevant to the overt/covert narrator dichotomy pointed out at the beginning of this chapter, but also, and especially, apply to *mediated* vs. *immediate* narrative (Stanzel) and the distinction between *reporting* and *scenic* presentation (Ger: *berichtende* vs. *szenische Darstellung*, Otto Ludwig). The terms *telling* and *showing* (which go back to Percy Lubbock) can be applied to film and drama, too. In novels and oral story-telling we generally find narrators whose job it is to put the story across to the addressees. But on the stage and in cinematic narrative such narrator figures are few and far between, with the notable exception of plays like Thornton Wilder's *Our Town* (1938) or Bertolt Brecht's *Mother Courage* (1939). In film versions of literary texts one often finds framing narrator figures: they feature in *voice-overs* or in a sequence inserted at the beginning of a film showing the first-person narrator writing the text. In some films, the level of narration is transposed into the film as in the celebrated screen version of John Fowles's *The French Lieutenant's Woman* (1970), where the self-reflexive narrator figures as the producer of the film.

In Stanzel's theory of narrative, the distinction between *showing* and *telling* is a central concern, as expressed in the *teller mode* vs. *reflector mode* dichotomy. In scenic presentation, for instance in drama, it seems as if the action were taking place before our very eyes, without any mediation. The reflector mode thus correlates with an *illusion of immediacy*. Traditionally, however, stories are told, and a person tells them to us, so that we actually see before us a *teller* who mediates the story to the reader or audience. In the novel, a narrator persona often provides a similar illusion of communication and direct address.

Focalization, perspective, point of view

Reflector mode

Showing, apparently unmediated presentation of events and people, can only occur in conversational exchanges which a novel quotes verbatim or in the context of drama or film. However, the novel also offers the additional option of seeing things from the point of view of a particular character. In such cases this character serves as a focalizer or lens; the story is put across to the reader through the filter of the focalizer's thoughts and perceptions. Such a character in a novel has a camera in her/his mind, so to speak. In his theory of the novel Stanzel calls these characters 'reflector figures' since they 'reflect' the story to the reader rather than telling it to them as a narrator persona would. The term *reflector* derives from Henry James, who called some of his focalizers, like Strether in *The Ambassadors*, 'reflectors'.

Figural narrative situation

I have chosen a short story by Somerset Maugham as an example of a figural narrative situation – a narrative in which one (or more) reflector figures play a major part in representing events. The tale begins as follows:

> He came back into the kitchen. The man was still on the floor, lying where he had hit him, and his face was bloody. He was moaning. The woman had backed against the wall and was staring with terrified eyes at Willi, his friend, and when he came in she gave a gasp and broke into loud sobbing. Willi was sitting at the table, his revolver in his hand, with a half empty glass of wine beside him. Hans went up to the table, filled his glass and emptied it at a gulp.
>
> ('The Unconquered'; Maugham 2000: 343–4)

The story is filtered through the perceptions and memories of Hans, but we only learn who 'he' is towards the end of the paragraph. This opening contains elements that are typical of what is termed an *etic opening* (a term coined by Roland Harweg). There is no antecedent for the personal pronoun 'he'; the pluperfect is used instead of the present perfect tense ('had backed'), thus situating us at a point in time at the end of a sequence of unknown events, which are of course known to the protagonists. Likewise, the objects and setting are taken for granted and therefore referred to by the definite article: 'the kitchen', 'the man', 'the floor', 'the wall', 'the table'. We seem to move into the perspective of Hans and see the world from his vantage point. No attempt is made to introduce the reader to the protagonists' situation. We have to piece the connections together, slowly, and work out who Hans and Willi are, what has happened to the man and woman.

Perspective

At this point we should note that narratives may be told from the perspective of a narrator, from that of a character and, last but not least, from a neutral, impersonal perspective (also known as 'camera-eye'[3]). A distinction can be made, then, between embodied and impersonal points of view, and between external and internal ones. 'Embodied' here would mean that the reflector figure is fleshed out as a character so that one can assume that s/he has a subjective position on various matters. Consequently, we can identify four different possible perspectives in novels.

A new model

In this model the terms 'external' and 'internal' are defined as positions from which a perspective is gained (external relating to the extradiegetic level and internal to the diegetic). 'Embodied' means that the perspective comes from an anthropomorphic figure whose brain interprets what s/he sees and who is able to make statements about

Vantage point	Embodied	Describes psychological states of others	Impersonal
External (extradiegetic level)	So-called omniscient narrator	Yes	Impersonal, 'omniscient' (covert narrative)
Internal (diegetic level)	First-person narrator	No	Neutral perspective
	Reflector figure	No	0

Figure 4.6 Forms of focalization

her/himself. 'Impersonal' means the opposite: the focalizer gives away nothing about her/himself. A first-person narrator is an embodied narrator but is located on both the external *and* the internal level. In the reflector mode there is no such thing as an internal impersonal (neutral) perspective since a reflector figure as defined here perceives the world through her/his own mind. This model focuses exclusively on visual perspective and access to consciousness, it does not take ideological perspective into account (Uspensky 1973; cf. Chapter IX) nor does it consider stylistic idiosyncrasies attributed to various characters. To my mind, these last should be treated under the heading of 'tone' or 'voice'.

The terminology proposed here differs from that of Genette and Stanzel (cf. Chapter 9). The most commonly accepted models of focalization are very confusing, I believe, so the model presented here diverges somewhat from established practice. By way of clarification, I shall briefly explain the customary terminology, albeit without covering the model recently presented by Nieragden (2002), which starts out from and refines the work of Mieke Bal.

In the English-speaking world it is traditional to speak of *point of view*, which corresponds to *narrative perspective* (Ger. *Erzählperspektive*). Traditionally, the aim is to make a distinction between narratives in which the story is filtered through the consciousness of a character (reflector figure) and those in which there is a view from 'outside' (defined in different ways). Stanzel's dichotomy between *internal* and *external perspective*, in combination with the notion of *narrator* vs. *reflector mode*, is an attempt to reconcile this distinction within the scope of one model. In the domain of *mode* (oppositional pair: narrator vs. reflector) the emphasis is on who or what mediates the story (the narrator's language or the mind of the reflector figure). As far as *perspective* is concerned, an outside (and unrestricted) view of the fictional world (= external perspective) stands in contrast to a view from within, which is limited to the knowledge and the perceptions of the reflector figure (= internal perspective).

In opposition to models which seek to cover and combine consciousness, language, position (intra-/extradiegetic) and point of view, Genette and after him Mieke Bal

Point of view and perspective

Focalization

radically restructured the concept of point of view and introduced the narratological term *focalization*. A basic premise of their model is a distinction between *perspective* or *mode* ('Who sees?') and *voice* ('Who speaks?').

Genette distinguishes between *zero focalization* (Fr. *focalisation zéro*; Ger. *Nullfokalisierung*) on the one hand, and, on the other, a pair of terms defining restricted points of view, *internal* and *external focalization* (Fr. *focalisation interne/externe*; Ger. *limitierte Sicht*). Zero focalization corresponds to Stanzel's authorial narrative situation, in which the authorial narrator is above the world of the action, looks down on it and is able to see into the characters' minds as well as shifting between the various locations where the story takes place. This perspective is unrestricted or unlimited in contrast to the limitations of internal and external focalization. In the case of internal perspective, the view is restricted to that of a single character; in that of external perspective to a view of the world from outside, allowing no insight into the inner workings of people's minds. The Genettean model is, however, inconsistent, since the reflector character is presented by means of internal focalization but s/he sees *other* characters under the restrictions of external focalization. By drawing a distinction between the *focalizing instance* and the *focalized*, and between visible and invisible focalized objects, Mieke Bal managed to improve on the terminology. In a figural narrative such as James Joyce's *A Portrait of the Artist as a Young Man* (1916), Stephen Dedalus, the reflector figure, is the focalizer or the focalizing instance. For him, his own self is an invisible focalized object (he can see and discuss his own thoughts and feelings). By contrast, in the world, such as the people around him, Stephen can only contemplate visible focalized objects. (Invisible objects, other people's minds, cannot be focalized.) In an authorial narrative like Fielding's *Tom Jones*, the focalizing instance is actually the narrator, who sees visible and invisible focalized objects in the fictional world. (Bal calls Fielding's narrator a *narrator-focalizer*.) In a first-person narrative (Dickens's *David Copperfield*, for instance) the narrator is the focalizing instance, but he is just as limited in his perspective as the reflector figure Stephen Dedalus: his own self excepted, he can only perceive visible focalized objects. So Bal explains limited perspective as a restriction of perspective to an external view of invisible focalized objects. (Seeing oneself is always possible. Thus the authorial narrator has access to her/his own thoughts, although this perspective only applies on the level of the narrative discourse.)

By contrast, in my model restricted perspective is not considered (see Figure 4.6). Instead, access to the minds of others is postulated as a useful category. My diagram distinguishes between embodied and impersonal (disembodied) narratorial media. The ability to see into other people's minds is possible only from an external vantage point. Only on the extradiegetic level is it possible to look into characters' minds, irrespective of whether the narrator is an overt, personalized or dramatized narrator or a covert one. On the other hand, first-person narrators and reflector figures can only 'see' their own past or present thoughts. (I am here excluding prophetic and supernaturally gifted narrators as well as recent experiments with omniscience in first-person narrative, cf. Heinze 2008.)

Perspective structure

Drawing on Manfred Pfister's work on dramatic theory, Ansgar Nünning reintegrates the term *perspective* into narratology, concentrating on the structure of related perspectives in literary works. Pfister had used the concept of perspective structure to discover the meaning or the underlying intention of dramatic texts (which do not usually feature narrators) by comparing and collating various perspectives (that of the audience, of the dramatis personae). The ideological positions of the individual characters may all tend in the same direction (*closed* perspective), so that a consensual answer to the questions arising in the play is implied. A good example of a closed perspective is *King Lear*. When the characters merely serve as mouthpieces for the author, though, Pfister calls this perspective *aperspectival*. For instance, the medieval morality play provides one single, God-given moral perspective. Yet the various world views represented on stage may take us into quite different ideological directions: here the perspective is *open*. Modern plays by Ibsen, Brecht and Anouilh are good examples of open perspective structure.

In Nünning's adoption of Pfister's model, the characters' and the narrator's perspectives have to be set in relation to the meaning of the text overall. In traditional narrative the *viewpoint* (or *point of view*) of the narrator is often a privileged, closed perspective. The perspective structure remains open if the text provides no clear and obvious guidelines for the readers to decide between the narrator's views and those of the characters. Nineteenth-century novels such as those of George Eliot are typical examples of a closed perspective structure. Open perspective structure, on the other hand, is characteristic of modern texts such as the novels of Virginia Woolf: here the separate 'truths' of the individual characters cannot be reduced to a common denominator.

These comments on traditional as well as on more recent theories and models conclude our survey of the most important narrative categories. In the following chapter we shall turn our attention to the surface structure of texts.

5   The Surface of Narrative

In this chapter we shall be looking at the language of narrative; in particular we shall be investigating how words and sentences turn into stories. This last phrase echoes the title of Herbert Grabes' classic essay 'Wie aus Sätzen Personen werden' ('How Sentences Turn into People', Grabes 1978). My prime concern in this chapter will not be how a narrative is constructed but rather the process by which, at the discourse level, elements susceptible to linguistic analysis serve to generate specific reader responses or even create the fictional world itself.

How sentences turn into fictional worlds

Let us start out from the assumption that the language of narrative creates possible worlds: sentences use words to create characters, incidents, settings in time as well as in space, and put these various elements into some kind of order. This would not be possible without the help of the reader's imagination: the reader supplies missing information using concrete pictures and ideas of her/his own, although some aspects of the fictional world will always remain vague or unclear. Various points that must be made explicit in drama or film are often left open in novels: the characters' clothes, for example, the arrangement of furniture, the protagonist's hair colour etc. It is easy to demonstrate this openness of verbal narrative if we take the opening of a novel like the following:

> Lieutenant-Commander Peter Holmes of the Royal Australian Navy woke soon after dawn. He lay drowsily for a while, lulled by the warm comfort of Mary sleeping beside him, watching the first light of the Australian sun upon the cretonne curtains of their room. He knew from the sun's rays that it was about five o'clock: very soon the light would wake his baby daughter Jennifer in her cot; and then they would have to get up and start doing things. No need to start before that happened; he could lie a little longer.
>
> (*On the Beach*, i; Shute 1966: 7)

We learn who Peter Holmes is, that he has a daughter and that he is in Australia, but we do not know how tall he is, what colour are his eyes or hair, how old he is, and so on. Satirical texts are particularly given to such indeterminacy, whereas more deliberately realistic works try to convey much more specific information. Compare the following two extracts from Eliot and Hardy:

> When old Mr Gilfil died, thirty years ago, there was a general sorrow in Shepperton; and if black cloth had not been hung round the pulpit and reading-desk, by order of his nephew and principal legatee, the parishioners would certainly have

subscribed the necessary sum out of their own pockets, rather than allow such a tribute of respect to be wanting. All the farmers' wives brought out their black bombasines; and Mrs Jennings, at the Wharf, by appearing the first Sunday after Mr Gilfil's death in her salmon-coloured ribbons and green shawl, excited the severest remark. To be sure, Mrs Jennings was a newcomer, and town-bred, so that she could hardly be expected to have very clear notions of what was proper; but, as Mrs Higgins observed in an undertone to Mrs Parrot when they were coming out of church, 'Her husband, who'd been born i'the parish, might ha' told her better.' An unreadiness to put on black on all available occasions, or too great an alacrity in putting it off, argued, in Mrs Higgins's opinion, a dangerous levity of character, and an unnatural insensibility to the essential fitness of things.

('Mr Gilfil's Love Story', i; Eliot 1985: 119)

The man was of fine figure, swarthy, and stern in aspect; and he showed in profile a facial angle so slightly inclined as to be almost perpendicular. He wore a short jacket of brown corduroy, newer than the remainder of his suit, which was a fustian waistcoat with white horn buttons, breeches of the same, tanned leggings, and a straw hat overlaid with black glazed canvas. At his back he carried by a looped strap a rush basket, from which protruded at one end the crutch of a hay-knife, a wimble for hay-bonds being also visible in the aperture. His measured, springless walk was the walk of the skilled countryman as distinct from the desultory shamble of the general labourer; while in the turn and plant of each foot there was, further, a dogged and cynical indifference personal to himself, showing its presence even in the regularly interchanging fustian folds, now in the left leg, now in the right, as he paced along.

(*The Mayor of Casterbridge*, i; Hardy 1986: 69)

Eliot's satirical portrait of narrow-minded small-town gossip does not leave any space for extensive description of the characters; all we learn is that there was a transgression of propriety of dress, but this leaves the looks of the women involved open for the reader's (or a film director's) creative imagination. Hardy, by contrast, is so specific in his description that our liberty of imaginative engagement becomes severely curtailed.

A verbal text, then, will often (but not always) let the imagination run free, within certain limits fixed by the concrete details that the text provides. The names of characters – particularly in first-person novels of the twentieth century – are often not revealed until late in the text, for instance in the course of a phone call rendered in direct speech. Other information is also dished out in small helpings as the text proceeds. The reading process is shaped by assumptions deriving from the words the reader has read. Such expectations are partly confirmed and fulfilled, but they must also sometimes be modified, and fleshed out in more detail. The picture of the possible story world is thus rounded out and becomes a point of orientation, taking on quasi-referential characteristics. This point (i.e. realism in fiction) will be discussed in more detail in Chapter 6.

In the following, we shall restrict ourselves to a consideration of the linguistic means used to project the fictional world of the text.

Space/time

Deixis

A picture of the fictional space in which a narrative takes place can be evoked by direct deixis both in the interaction between characters in a novel and in the direct speech of interlocutors in conversational exchange. Examples of deixis are phrases like *here in Berlin* or *on the other side of the world*. Just as the first-person singular pronoun refers to the speaker, so *here* signifies that the speaker finds her/himself in Berlin, and *at the other side of the world* implies that she/he is probably somewhere in Europe. A novel normally presupposes that the speaker (narrator) and addressee (narratee) are situated within the same framework of reference: in the examples above they share a European, German, Berlin-based perspective on things. Directly deictic, concrete, spatial references that do not correspond to the reader's real-world position serve to intensify the fictionality of a text. So, if the narrator confronts us with sentences like 'It's cold here on Mars. I like to think back to our days together on Uranus', we tend to expect a science fiction tale, complete with aliens, and we are no longer surprised by any other strange features of the setting.

Setting

Most realistic narrative texts create the impression of being authentic by embedding fictional agents in imagined settings, although they make frequent reference to real places. Novels set in London, Vienna or Moscow are legion, and countless descriptions of landscape exploit our prior knowledge of the scenery in question: it only takes a few hints (skiing holiday in the Tyrol, chalet, mountain peak, gentian and edelweiss) and we fill in the details automatically. Nevertheless, this does not make a novel's setting any the less fictional – literary London in the novels of Dickens is not the real London. Specific allusions to real places in prepositional phrases ('in a little hamlet at the foot of the Matterhorn') disguise this fictionality, however, and prompt the reader to flesh out the setting in her/his head. As in several other instances (the representation of speech in novels, for instance; see Chapter 7), reality is conjured up by using clichés to prompt readers to apply schemata already familiar to them.

Apart from deictics and prepositional phrases of place, descriptions are the other main means of characterizing settings, of putting flesh on the bare bones of places, as it were. Descriptions also have a crucial part to play in presenting the dramatis personae of a story. Each description contains essential and evaluative elements. It puts an object or a subject in the limelight and specifies objective characteristics (height, hair colour) as well as using culturally or socially marked modifiers (*nonchalant behaviour, lush grass*) or, for people, even providing an evaluative description (*cunning expression; hideous laughter; a delightfully coquettish gesture*). Sternberg (1974), Bal (1982) and Mosher (1991) and Wolf/Bernhart (2007) have all made notable contributions to the literature on exposition and description.

The opening passage of many traditional tales consists of a formula which could be expressed in grammatical terms as shown below,

[PP – time] [PP – place] Verb [Adjective] [NP]

where PP stands for prepositional phrase and NP for nominal phrase: *In the middle of the last century there was a rich man in Tuscany who . . .* or *At the beginning of our decade there was a poor family in Salisbury who. . . .* The following is a more elaborate realization of the same formula:

It was the opening of the season of eighteen hundred and thirty-two, at the Baths of WILDBAD.

The evening shadows were beginning to gather over the quite little German town; and the diligence was expected every minute. Before the door of the principal inn, waiting the arrival of the first visitors of the year, were assembled the three notable personages of Wildbad, accompanied by their wives – the mayor, representing the inhabitants; the doctor, representing the waters; the landlord, representing his own establishment. Beyond this select circle, grouped snugly about the trim little square in front of the inn, appeared the townspeople in general, mixed here and there with the countrypeople in their quaint German costume placidly expectant of the diligence – the men in short black jackets, tight black breeches, and the three-cornered beaver hats; the women with their long light hair hanging in one thickly-plaited tail behind them, and the waists of their short woollen gowns inserted modestly in the region of their shoulder blades.

(Collins 1995: 9)

In this opening passage from Wilkie Collins's novel *Armadale* (1866), a particular moment in time and a particular place are mentioned. The time is narrowed down to the evening and the place is specified as the entrance to an inn. The focus turns to the three most eminent people in the town, and to the townspeople gathered there, who are then described in more detail. In this first section of the novel (of which only the beginning is cited here), the time, the place and the protagonists of the story are presented. Subsequently we learn that the month is May and that we are somewhere in the Black Forest.

That is not all, however: the passage quoted contains a further hint, one of a purely linguistic nature. The use of the progressive tense ('were beginning') in the description of the early evening signals that all this is background information and that soon something will happen to disturb the peaceful scene, namely the arrival of the stage-coach, and with it the main protagonist. Thus, the time frame is narrowed down from the year to the month indicated (May), and from thence to a particular moment on a specific evening. This is where the narrative proper can be said to commence.   `Specifying time`

Unlike information relating to place, points in time or periods are realized linguistically by prepositional phrases and deictic words (*now, nowadays*). As texts unfold, references to time function more simply than references to place. Sequence in time is signalled by a range of adverbs of time and adverbial phrases (*after, then, later, the next morning*). References to intervening periods of time are often located at the beginning of chapters (*six years later, the next day*), together with information about changes of scene. Two features are specific to time referencing: simultaneity and anachrony.   `Sequentiality of events`

Simultaneity plays a significant role in locating a narrative in time. It often serves to bring together various strands of action: *While the Seifferts were still at table, Captain Koss took the train to Prague.* Here again, conjunctions and adverbial phrases of time have a crucial part to play. In English and in French the choice of tense is also important (the progressive tense, *l'imparfait*). Furthermore, it is possible to incorporate events that are already over by a particular stage in the narrative: 'meanwhile' or 'in the meantime' (Fr. *pendant ce temps*; Ger. *inzwischen*) plus the pluperfect tense bring together chains of events with the circumstances resulting from them. While sequentiality and thus strict adherence to chronological order are the norm, so that simultaneity stands out as an exception, this situation is reversed in respect of place and space: spaces are   `Simultaneity` static; what needs to be stressed is change of scene. Many narratives switch to and fro between two (or more) locations. Key points in the plot are reached when characters travel from one location to another, or converge in one place; in so doing they bring the separate plot strands together.

Anachrony   Anachrony, as we saw in Chapter 4, refers to breaks in the chronology of a story. The narrative discourse then turns back to events which happened previously (analepsis) or jumps forward to discuss what will happen later (prolepsis). Such leaps in time are frequently marked by the choice of particular tenses. Analepsis is signalled by the pluperfect (*She* **had** *first* **met** *Jean at a party* . . .; *Il y a plusieurs années qu'il* **avait rencontré** *M. Berthold à Genève* . . .; *Vor Jahren* **hatte** *er einmal in einem Wirtshaus übernachtet*), which marks anteriority when used in conjunction with the traditional narrative past tense (Fr. *passé simple*; Ger. *Präteritum*,). In traditional past-tense narrative, prolepses are rendered in the conditional: *Twenty years later he* **would** *recall these words with terror; Plusieurs années plus tard, Bournel* **se souviendrait de** *cette affaire miraculeuse; Noch lange* **würde** *er sich dieser Worte besinnen*.

The remarks in the preceding paragraph belong more properly to the section below on the use of tenses in narrative, but tense features extensively in almost every area of the surface of narrative. Having dealt with how place and time are realized in the narrative discourse, I shall now focus on the verbal means employed to create the characters in a novel and look at the role of language in structuring and contouring the plot.

Fictional characters: how characters are introduced

Emic openings   So, let us return to Herbert Grabes' perceptive question (1978), 'How do sentences create people?' Uri Margolin has worked extensively on the presentation of character in narrative texts (1990, 1995, 1996). He discusses all conceivable constellations and combinations. Looked at from the textual point of view and from that of the reader, it seems important that characters (like objects and places) are introduced by means of reference. The customary way to do this is to give the text what Harweg terms an *emic opening*, that is to say to introduce characters by an indefinite article and a modifying phrase (indef. ART + (adj.) NP), for example *Once upon a time* **a** *rich farmer lived in a small town*. This indefinite reference is followed up by the use of the definite article and/or a proper name: ***The** farmer's name was* **George** *and he had three daughters,* **the** *youngest and most beautiful of whom was called* **Arabella**. The network of references ('daughters', 'the youngest of whom' etc.) helps the reader find her/his way through the text. In traditional authorial narrative, in other words in texts where a third-person narrator relates a story which has nothing to do with her/him, this shift from indefinite to definite articles and names occurs very frequently. It is also common in retrospective first-person narrative.

Descriptive reference   As well as the practice of referring to characters by name, other options are available, of course. Such strategies are particularly common in nineteenth-century texts. In such cases the aforementioned George would be referred to as *the farmer* or *the father*. In many Victorian novels pars pro toto locutions are used extensively to identify characters: *the man with the silken shirt, the boy in the red hat*, etc. As can be seen, synecdoche and metonymy (e.g. father – daughter) play a major role in introducing the actors in a narrative since they offer access to the social, spatial and visual contexts of the story and to information about the characters. Entire plot sequences are sometimes built on metonymical relations (e.g.: cause – effect) just as they are on conversational adjacency pairs. This is also demonstrated by the standard action pairs of provocation and challenge, attack and revenge, or jealousy and murder. Chapter 7 includes further comments on metonymy and metaphor.

Modern narratives, particularly those which show a fondness for internal focal-   Etic openings
ization, i.e. those which use reflector figures and offer an account of what happens through the eyes of these reflectors, treat persons and objects from the fictional world as given, known and therefore in no need of being introduced. In *etic openings* typical of reflector-mode narratives, it is therefore common to encounter naming with no accompanying explanation, the use of pronouns without antecedents ('referentless pronouns' or 'nonsequential sequence signals', Backus 1965) as well as noun phrases with definite articles ('familiarizing articles', Bronzwaer 1970) before any people or objects have been properly introduced by indefinite ones.

> *She* was sitting on *the* veranda.
> (Somerset Maugham, 'The Force of Circumstance';
> Maugham 1992: 42; my emphasis)

> *Il* tenait une lettre à la main, il leva les yeux me regarda puis de nouveau la lettre puis de nouveau moi, derrière lui je pouvais voir aller et venir passer les taches rouge acajou ocre des chevaux qu'on menait à l'abreuvoir, la boue était si profonde qu'on enfonçait dedans jusqu'aux chevilles mais je me rappelle que pendant la nuit il avait brusquement gelé et *Wack* entra dans la chambre en portant le café disant Les chiens ont mangé la boue, je n'avais jamais entendu l'expression . . .
> (*La route des Flandres*; Simon 1960: 9; my emphasis)

> (*He* was holding a letter in his hand, he raised his eyes looked at me then the letter then me again, behind him I could see the horses being taken to the horse trough to drink, spots of chestnut red, mahogany, ochre, the mud was so deep that you sank into it up to your ankles but I remember that during the night there had been a sudden frost and *Wack* came into the room saying The dogs have eaten mud, I had never heard the expression before [. . .]
> (translation Patricia Häusler-Greenfield)

Although the second text here is a first-person narrative, it also focalizes from the perspective of the experiencing self, that is to say the character in the novel located on the plot level. This person knows who 'he' and 'Wack' are and therefore offers no further explanation. The most striking examples of etic patterns of reference can be found in interior monologue, for instance in Molly Bloom's soliloquy in *Ulysses*. In this representation of her mind, she refers to various different men as 'he' and 'him', making life extremely difficult for the reader, who has to work out from the context to whom she might be referring. Molly knows, of course, but since she has no interlocutor, there is no need for her to follow the rules of conversation (Grice's conversational maxims; cf. Grice 1975) out of consideration for her audience. After all, she is her own audience – she is talking to herself.

Moving on from the aspects of reference mentioned above, it is now time for us to   Descriptive
address the question of how characters are fleshed out by the use of descriptive   modifiers

adjectives, and more generally, by modifying phrases. We have already seen this process at work in the extract from Collins's *Armadale*. The figures in a story may be indirectly characterized by their actions, and adverbs make a significant contribution to this process as they concretize actions and words, and evaluate them, too. It is not so much what a character does and says that is important, but how s/he behaves or speaks: *in a leisurely way, agitatedly, preachily, shrilly, looking at the floor in embarrassment* etc. The adjectives and adverbs used in the course of a text often contribute more extensively to characterization than a detailed, one-off description of a person's appearance or disposition such as those we regularly find at or near novel openings:

> Emma Woodhouse, handsome, clever, and rich, with a comfortable home and happy disposition, seemed to unite some of the best blessings of existence; and had lived nearly twenty-one years in the world with very little to distress or vex her.
>
> (*Emma*, i; Austen 1971: 3)

Story and contouring

How do the events of a story acquire contours in the telling? Classical narratology used to stress the sequencing of what happens (*and then . . . and then . . .*) and the logical patterns of the plot (explaining motivation: *The king died and then the queen died of grief*, Forster 1927). However, this approach is inadequate when applied to longer stretches of text, as it does not account for overarching macrostructures. Here the idea of plot strands (in complex plots) and of their ravelling and unravelling, as well as the creation of suspense prove more relevant.

The structure of plot strands

In narrative, as in drama, the various strands of the plot often serve to reflect aspects of the main plot in the subplot. For instance, two couples are contrasted as they try to solve similar problems but in different ways. So, in many cases, the hero or heroine is compared with two other characters who take opposing courses of action, leaving it to the main protagonist to find the golden mean. For example, in Jane Austen's *Pride and Prejudice*, the attitude towards marriage of the heroine, Elizabeth, is contrasted with the emotional excesses of her sister Jane and the behaviour of her friend Charlotte, who, because of her straitened circumstances, cannot afford to marry for love. The way in which points of contact between various strands of action are managed is much more discourse-specific. As already mentioned, marking simultaneity by using *while* or *in the meantime* is one way of doing this. Another strategy consists in having major and minor characters encounter each other using the coincidence model, as Dannenberg (2004a, 2008) terms it. Subplots are only meaningful if they overlap with the main plot and the characters actually encounter each other. As an alternative to such a predictable coincidence, whereby two sets of characters, both of whom we have been following in separate chapters or sections of the novel, meet, we also find instances of characters or groups encountering unknown people. The story of these new characters is often unravelled, uncovering a subplot of which the reader was previously unaware.

Suspense

Suspense is created when concrete events are anticipated (prolepsis), and we are curious as to how they came about. As an example one can cite the beginning of Gabriel García Márquez's *One Hundred Years of Solitude* (1967), where we learn about the execution of the protagonist before we hear about his life leading up to this ending. Likewise, in crime novels, the body which will lead to the reconstruction of the murder is discovered at the beginning of the tale. Suspense is generated by withholding important information, for instance by introducing a mystery which is only solved at a later stage (see also Fill 2003). Ann Radcliffe's Gothic novel *The Mysteries of Udolpho* (1794) contains a large number of such moments, for example the explanation of the murder of St Aubert's sister, whose letters and miniature portrait St Aubert orders his daughter Emily to burn before his death. In *The Mysteries of Udolpho* these mysteries keep surfacing. Emily remembers her father pressing his lips to the miniature (which misleads the reader into suspecting a love affair with the unknown beauty). There are frequent passages alluding to Emily's horrified reaction to the object she glimpses behind the black veil. It is only much later that the reader is told, almost in passing, that the reason for Emily's fainting fit was not a corpse but a skeleton modelled in wax.

The use of repeated references and hints is not the only means of creating suspense. Metonymical devices also encourage readers to speculate. In an essay written in 1986, 'Embedded Narratives and Tellability', Ryan shows that plot is not merely driven by what characters actually do but also by their plans, wishes and possible alternative plot developments. In other words, suspense is generated by our empathetic immersion in the situation of the various characters. Will Emily manage to escape, for example, or will Montoni prevent her from doing so? At other points descriptions – in a kind of metonymical process – prompt readers to devise their own terrifying scenarios. An example would be the incident when Emily explores the tower in which her aunt is imprisoned and discovers the torture seat. This relic turns out to be dysfunctional but provokes Emily, and the reader, to anticipate cruelty of the worst kind on the part of Montoni. It also echoes the real tortures administered in the dungeons of the Inquisition, which the novel mentions but does not enlarge upon.

Metonymy

Oral storytelling and the episodic model

Conversational narratives, as well as many medieval and early modern texts, have a completely different narrative structure to that which we are accustomed to from novels. Spoken narratives are brief, for the most part, and so the structures we are accustomed to finding in novels (several different settings and strands of action, and an overarching build-up of suspense) do not occur. Echoing the views of William Labov, Joshua Waletzky and their followers, one could maintain that colloquial spoken narrative is an integral part of conversation, in other words it depends on some kind of interaction between speaker and interlocutor. The classic essay here is Labov/Waletzky (1967).[1] Narrative turns are frequently signalled by metanarrative utterances of the type: *That reminds me of when I was at school. Once something really weird happened. I must tell you about it* . . . In the example, the beginning of the story proper is signalled by a thumbnail sketch ('something really weird'), indicating what the story is really about, pre-empting what will be related in detail and creating suspense. (Labov calls this announcement of the subject the *abstract*.) In many conversational narratives in English, suspense is also created by pre-empting the story's climax. Livia Polanyi (1978) discusses instances in which the narrative starts off with a key utterance from the protagonist and only then fills in the necessary background details. Then comes a word-for-word repetition of the build-up to the climactic moment after which a fresh account of the climax is given in considerable detail. Such a strategy enlivens the narrative. We all know how frustrating the tellers of anecdotes can be if they go into tiresome and

Interaction

unnecessary detail before finally getting round to the point of their stories. By using the trick described above, an oral storyteller can retain the interest and attention of the listener who can, after all, demonstrate her/his impatience by yawning, not paying attention, or even by getting up and leaving.

In natural narrative we can distinguish two basic levels: the level of communication between speaker and listener(s) and the level of the story itself (Fludernik 1996: Chapter 2). The framing of the narrative, which belongs to the communicative level, consists of a characterization of the story at the beginning (*abstract*) followed by an explanatory introduction containing the necessary background information (*orientation*) and at the other end a coda and an overall assessment of the story. More precisely, these frame elements are the switch points that enable one to move from the communicative situation to the story proper and back again. However, the communicative level is also active during storytelling whenever the narrator addresses explanatory remarks (*delayed orientation*) or comments to his audience ('The house stands as you know, at the edge of the forest'; 'Of course, that's quite typical of Karl. He was never backward at making rude jokes.'). The listeners, too, are not passive – they nod, interject appreciative phrases (*Aha, right, I see*) and involve themselves by making comments (*Scandalous! Typical! That's terrible!*).

Episodic structure

Episodic structure is typical of the story level. Each episode ideally has three stages: the opening; the climax, including the incident schema; and the resolution. In its prototypical form a narrative episode correlates with a cognitive schema which involves changing location, encountering an unexpected event and reacting to this.

> Well, I go into this shoe shop and look around and who should I see trying on boots but my wife. And she claims she's too short of the readies to put a hot dinner on the table. So, I go straight up to her and ask her what she thinks she's doing.

Conversational exchanges frequently occur instead of incidence→reaction type sequences (for instance, unexpected or threatening remarks leading to witty or clever responses on the part of the storyteller). In natural narrative the point of the story cannot primarily be found in what happens – a report could do that job just as well. It is the entertainment value, the exceptional nature of the events narrated, and the story's moral (which Labov calls *point*) that make the tale worth telling (its *tellability*, to use Labov's term). The 'point' of recounting a heated exchange between a female traffic warden and a motorist would be that, in the end, the motorist is able to flannel himself out of a fine and comes across as a canny character. So, in the story he projects 'positive face', a self-image of shrewdness. In the 'shopping for boots' example quoted above, the storyteller comes across as a frustrated husband who thinks he has caught his spendthrift wife red-handed. In this case, his aim is not to save face or preserve status. He is trying to arouse sympathy or, perhaps, by giving a very extreme example, to put one over his mates during a session of swapping misogynist anecdotes.

Narrative episodes occur in succession, and the beginning and ending of a tale are clearly marked by the use of *abstracts* or *codas*. The three switch-points we have already discussed can easily be identified from various linguistic markers in the text. Three kinds of markers are used: tense (shift into historic present, and in English the use of the progressive form, in French *l'imparfait*); word order (adverbial phrases of time/ place are shifted to the beginning of sentences; the same holds true, at least in English, for prepositional phrases); and discourse markers. The latter are adverbials which have no lexical meaning as such but which fulfil a discourse function within a stretch of connected and coherent text. Within the three kinds of markers, the use of discourse markers is the most striking.

This linguistic category was popularized by Deborah Schiffrin (1987). It is usually taken to include adverbial phrases at the heads of sentences where, rather than fulfilling a clear semantic function, they help to structure spoken discourse, to modulate the interaction between storyteller and audience, or to signal a change of topic. In English, typical discourse markers would be *well, so, but, anyway*; in French *alors, puis, mais, enfin, quoi, hein, oui* (Gülich 1990); in German *da, doch, ja, nun, so, also* (cf. Weydt 1983). For example, in the sentence *Well, and what are you up to today?*, 'Well' does not mean 'good' but signals a change of topic. Such discourse markers are commonly found in all types of spoken interaction. As far as conversational storytelling is concerned, however, some may have a specifically narrative function. They can signal the three basic points in the structure of an episode; they can mark a transition from the communicative to the narrative level and vice versa; and they can moderate the interaction between storyteller and audience.

This does not mean that particular discourse markers only occur in specific contexts, as might be assumed. Most discourse markers (in English *so, anyway, but, and, well*) are used in various ways: the same marker can signal a shift in the level of narrative or the beginning of an episode; the same function (for instance, gathering up the threads of the narrative after an interpolated comment) may be carried out by a variety of markers (*so, anyway*).[2]

To a large extent, as the examples from conversational narrative have shown, we owe our ability to interpret stories appropriately to aspects of narrative discourse which can be described linguistically. In the final section of this chapter we shall consider how particular linguistic features can be exploited in experimental narratives.

Discourse markers

The creative use of pronouns in texts

Chapter 4 has already covered the narrative category of 'person' and has introduced *you*-narrative (singular and plural) and *we*-narrative, as well as *they*-narrative. In the context of experimental postmodern literature, a number of writers have played with the pronouns in the text, with a view to subverting traditional language patterns or to defending a particular ideological position. In English academic discourse, the automatic use of masculine pronouns after nouns which can refer to both males and females has been superseded by the use of both masculine *and* feminine anaphorics, for example *the teacher . . . s/he* or *he or she*. (In German, forms like *LehrerInnen* and *frau* instead of *man* are widespread.) Various female authors have also come out in protest against the grammatical bias in favour of the male sex and have tried to find alternative forms of expression. Second-person narrative, which, in the case of English is not marked for gender, is sometimes used to conceal the gender of a main protagonist, who is referred to only as *you* throughout. First-person narrative may also leave the question of the gender of the first-person narrator open, thus deliberately confounding readers

Concealing gender

as it undermines their cultural assumptions and prejudices. In English and in German this is relatively simple: one simply has to be careful not to describe any situation which would unambiguously indicate the gender of the protagonist. In languages such as French, on the other hand, in which adjectives agree with the number and gender of the nouns they modify, this is a much more challenging task as all such adjectives, and other constructions requiring agreement (*Coco est intelligente, je suis venue, il l'a vue*), have to be avoided in order to keep the reader in the dark as to the real gender of the hero – or heroine.

Invented pronouns

Another attractive, though little-used, option is to invent new personal pronouns. This is what June Arnold did in her novel *The cook and the carpenter* (1973). All the characters are referred to either by the names of their respective trades or, in the case of anaphoric references, these are replaced with *na*. (For instance, instead of *She looked at her hand* it says *Na looked at nan hand*). Madge Piercy's *Woman on the Edge of Time* (1976) uses the personal pronoun *per*.

You-narrative

In English and Spanish, second-person narratives are fairly common, whereas in German literature there are relatively few texts of this type. Concealing or not specifying the gender of a second-person protagonist is very common in second-person narratives in English. A good example is the gay novel *Nocturnes for the King of Naples* by Edmund White (1978), where the indeterminacy of the gender of *you* delays the reader's realization that the lovers whose affair is being described are a same-sex couple.

More frequently, second-person narrative concentrates on providing in-depth focalization through the eyes of the *you*-protagonist.

> Here is the lobby of the famous hotel you visit often for your amusement and have memorized: large, sturdy sofas and chairs of black leather and a dull checked fabric, beginning to show wear, arranged in uniform rows at the start of each day, leading out from two walls, with an aisle of perhaps twelve feet in the center, separating them. Dark, highly polished mahogany. Plants the height of men, which appear to be artificial but are, in fact, living in ornate gold-trimmed vases. Near the arched doorway there is usually activity, but back farther in the lobby everything is quiet. People walk lazily up and down the carpeted aisle, glancing at those who are seated, most of them older gentlemen, groggy with disuse. Music is being piped in, the same furry, glazed texture as the carpet; the music seems to be coming from a great distance and no one is listening to it. A few men are speaking softly to one another, but most are silent and solitary. Velvet drapes have been drawn over the windows that face the ocean, in order to eliminate the sunset.
>
> (Joyce Carol Oates, 'In a Public Place'; Oates 1975: 66–7)

By using the pronoun *you*, which ambivalently hovers between reference to the narratee/reader and the second-person protagonist, the effect of internal focalization is enhanced and takes on an almost hypnotic quality.

One

Beside the address pronoun, the impersonal 'one' (Fr. *on*, Ger. *man*) is a popular choice in experimental narratives, the main aim usually being to stimulate the reader's empathy for the protagonist. Celebrated examples of this technique are Monique Wittig's novel *L'Opoponax* (1964) and, in German, Gerhard Meier's *Der schnurgerade Kanal* ('The Straight Canal', 1977) and E.Y. Meyer's *In Trubschachen* (1973). In English, only brief passages in the opening pages of Christopher Isherwood's *A Single Man* (1964) and John Fowles's *Mantissa* (1982) have come to my attention. Meyer's novel is also interesting in that it frequently uses the conditional form, which leads us to a consideration of how authors play with tenses in their narratives.

Experiments with tense in narrative

As a general rule, narrative can only take place when the events related are already over. The traditional choice of tense is therefore the past tense. Nevertheless, examples can be found of concurrent narrating (sports reports, for example, in which the present tense occurs). The use of the so-called *historic present* is widespread in conversational storytelling: the narrative discourse is mainly in the past tense (or present perfect), with some stretches in the present, particularly when the tale reaches a climax. Overall, however, the most common narrative tense is the preterite.

The epic preterite

However, these remarks about the use of tenses no longer hold true for literary narratives of the late twentieth century. As Käte Hamburger explains in *The Logic of Literature* (1957), the past tense form used in German narratives is not a 'genuine' past tense. It simply serves to mark out a text as fictional. On the basis of F. K. Stanzel's work and subsequent studies of the use of tenses, we must conclude that the deictic function of such past tenses is, if not cancelled out entirely, then at least extremely limited. In other words, the past tense which normally fixes a 'here and now' pertaining to the speaker in relation to an event situated in the past loses this function of referring to past time pure and simple and adopts the function of signalling fictionality.

Analogous to the narrative turn in conversational narrative (where the narrators are allocated longer turns in the interaction), narrative discourse likewise profits from a framing that sets the story apart from author-reader interaction. The idea that the so-called epic preterite marks a text as fictional arises particularly in the context of figural narrative, in other words, whenever the story is filtered through the consciousness of a character in a novel. But, of course, such a narrative is not actually possible in real life so that the fictionality of such narratives does not necessarily derive from the use of the epic past tense. In fact, the reverse is probably true: the preterite gives the impression of being fictional because it occurs in a text that is obviously fictional.

In contrast, we should note that in first-person narrative and authorial narratives there is, in fact, a relationship of anteriority between the retrospective first-person narrator or the heterodiegetic narrator on the one hand and the level of the story on the other. Nevertheless, this traditional relationship can no longer be taken for granted in the twenty-first century as, alongside narrative in the English simple past tense, the French *passé simple* and the German *Mitvergangenheit* (preterite), alternative tense options have established themselves. In the course of the twentieth century, the *passé composé* in French (as in the example of Albert Camus's *L'Étranger*), and above all the narrative present, have come to rival the traditional preterite. The narrative present has become increasingly common since the 1880s, at the latest since the beginning of the twentieth century (Petersen 1992). The use of the present tense as the main narrative tense could be rooted in a desire to emphasize the immediacy of the narrative: it is particularly popular in figural narrative situations. Indeed, using the present tense has become so widespread that it hardly seems necessary to treat it as a special narrative device. Here is an extract from the novel *The Other Side of Silence* by André Brink:

Narration in the present tense

> Frau Knesebeck motions to a corner of the desk where Hanna can put down her latest offering.

But Hanna remains standing.

'What are you waiting for?' After a moment, Frau Knesebeck forces one of her thin-lipped smiles that look like wincing. 'Oh, I see.' She pulls open the drawer and removes the previous stack of papers, pushes them across the desk towards Hanna. 'Yes. Well.' She presses her fingertips together.

(Brink 2002: 89)

Out of context, the present tense here seems to invoke a series of almost cinematic images. But when a whole novel is written in this way, as is the case here, one notices this cinematic quality less and less. The effect simply wears off.

On the other hand, the use of the conditional, the future or even the subjunctive as the basic narrative verb form remains the preserve of a handful of postmodern texts. Examples are E.Y. Meyer's *In Trubschachen* (the *one*-novel mentioned above) for the conditional, the beginning of Michael Frayn's *A Very Private Life* (1968) for the future tense, and Ernst Jandl's play *Aus der Fremde* (1980), in which the dialogue is kept in the subjunctive mode. (This is a borderline case, however, since dramatic dialogue is not narrative.) To the best of my knowledge, no one to date has chosen the ponderous and therefore boring pluperfect tense as their main narrative tense for a novel or short story.

Summary

As becomes apparent in this chapter, it is certainly worthwhile incorporating the linguistic surface structure of texts into narratological analysis. After all, language is the medium of narrative texts, and an investigation of how this medium works and how the broad spectrum of options it offers is exploited in narrative will provide us with valuable insights.

6   Realism, Illusionism and Metafiction

Narrative realism

In Ian Watt's influential study *The Rise of the Novel* (1957), *realism* is presented as an Realism essential defining feature of novels. Watt does not refer here to the nineteenth-century literary movement known as *Realism*, characterized by Sir Paul Harvey (editor of *The Oxford Companion to English Literature*, 1932) as concentrating on 'truth to the observed facts of life (especially when they are gloomy)'. This literary movement goes back to a manifesto of 1857 by Champfleury (Jules Husson 1821–89), 'Le Réalisme'. As we are all aware, it was a forerunner of naturalism (Zola, Gissing, Hauptmann) and originated in the desire of writers to distance themselves from romantic idealism, melodrama and a starry-eyed lack of concern for contemporary economic and social issues. The works of Stendhal, Balzac and Flaubert provide early examples of realism, but it is primarily the Goncourt brothers in France, Theodor Storm and Wilhelm Raabe in Germany, and the English novelists George Eliot, Anthony Trollope, Elizabeth Gaskell, George Moore and Arnold Bennett who are classed as literary realists.

In Watt's work, by contrast, the term *realism* is used in connection with matters of Ian Watt style and narrative technique to refer to characteristic features of the novel when it emerged as a genre in the early eighteenth century (between Defoe and Fielding). These characteristics set the novel apart from the romances of the seventeenth century and the tales of court intrigue modelled on French texts (Eliza Haywood). Watt notes that novels are no longer set at court but in the world of the middle or even the lower classes. They no longer take place in Catholic countries overseas (Italy, Spain, France) but in Britain, and here particularly in London. This reflects a shift to a more profound concern with real life. Financial, economic and social matters assume more importance. The action no longer takes place abroad at a splendid royal court and no longer involves idealized heroes and heroines driven solely by moral, political or emotional concerns (in other words the classic heroic conflict between love and duty). Instead, the story is adapted to a middle- (or lower-middle) class readership, reflecting their struggle to survive and the despicable motives (greed, jealousy, cunning, hypocrisy) that may underlie their actions. It describes how the emerging middle classes behave and what they hope for or fear. Watt points out the meticulous evocation of the fictional world in these works: it is depicted down to the very last detail. Novels, according to Watt, create a vivid world which, to a large extent, replicates that of their real-life readers, in contrast to the vague and frequently geographically and historically erroneous information provided in romances. The London of Defoe's *Moll Flanders* or Fielding's *Amelia* is created by strategic references in the pages of these books to actual thoroughfares, buildings and shops. The names of the settings refer to real-life locations but, in the context of the narrative, they are just as fictional as the characters themselves. Increasingly, we find descriptions of objects similar to those with which readers are familiar; they tend to be goods that can be purchased, such as articles of clothing, furniture or conveyances.

This is not to suggest that novels, Victorian novels included, can provide a complete picture of such 'reality'. In point of fact, the illusion that a novel portrays the 'real London' and the 'real world' is a product of the reading process. By drawing on her/his own resources, the reader fills in the gaps and rounds out the picture provided in the text. When Moll Flanders enters a haberdasher's shop, and the narrator expounds knowledgeably on different qualities of lace, because of this the reader visualizes the bales of cloth – which are not elaborated on in the text – and imagines a typical haberdasher's establishment on the basis of her/his own personal experience. Likewise, the mention of a red shawl, a hat or gloves, evokes pars pro toto the image of a fashionably turned-out protagonist. To be sure, this only holds true for readers living at the time when the novel was written.

In other words, a detailed description of places, objects and clothing as well as of people (at least from Richardson on) conjures up a totality, a real world, thus creating the illusion that the novel is depicting reality. The same holds true for the psychology of the protagonists. Moll Flanders presents herself as an extremely complex character: she aspires to become a lady, she resorts to bigamy, theft and prostitution in order to solve her financial problems, yet she is nevertheless plagued by moral scruples. Because of this complexity she comes across vividly as a character and the reader perceives her as being both multifaceted and convincing. Although she is an imaginary person as opposed to a creature of flesh and blood, she comes across as far more authentic than the heroines of heroic tragedy or romance.

Roland Barthes

Barthes and Watt compared

With his notion of literary realism, which he believes is constitutive of the novel, Ian Watt anticipates Roland Barthes's ideas about the *effet de réel*, put forward in connection with Flaubert's novella *Un Cœur Simple* ('A Simple Heart', 1877; Barthes 1968). However, we should note that Barthes was concerned specifically with the role of unnecessarily detailed description in nineteenth-century French novels. According to him, it is precisely the superfluity of apparently pointless detail which authenticates the text as realistic: the details would not be there if they were not an integral part of true-to-life description. Thus Barthes's *effet de réel* is not applicable to all kinds of description; it only applies to apparently superfluous details which serve to evoke an impression of reality at a higher level of interpretation. Watt's notion of realism depends much more extensively on the mentioning of functional details (such as the chair one sits on at table, the spoon the cook uses to stir the pot or the dressing table at which the heroine sits to comb her hair). However, such functional details only create a possible world when metonymic processes of expansion are triggered during the act of reading. Watt's details activate *frames*, as they are called by linguists, schemata in which one part of the frame evokes the whole thing, for example: window – house; hedge – garden; tablecloth – lunch, etc. Barthes considers the extension of this dynamic at a point in the reading process when the fictional world has already been created: he focuses on the yellow mark on the tablecloth, which is what causes the cloth to be perceived as a quasi-real tablecloth and lends the scene an almost photographic quality. Details, as Barthes clearly demonstrates, enhance the illusion that a scene is 'real' and convince the reader that the world portrayed is very largely identical to the real world. In the nineteenth-century novel, the reader is encouraged to flesh out typical attitudes, motives or psychological states starting out from what s/he knows. The use of certain syntactic patterns, for example, evoking as they do familiar conceptual frameworks in the reader, would be typical of the techniques employed here.

> Miss Brooke had *that kind of beauty* which seems to be thrown into relief by poor dress. Her hand and wrist were so finely formed that she could wear sleeves not less bare of style than those in which the Blessed Virgin appeared to Italian painters; and her profile as well as her stature and bearing seemed to gain the more dignity from her plain garments, which by the side of provincial fashion gave her the impressiveness of a fine quotation from the Bible, – or from one of our elder poets, – in a paragraph of to-day's newspaper. She was usually spoken of as being remarkably clever, but with the addition that her sister Celia had more common-sense.
>
> (George Eliot, *Middlemarch*; Eliot 1986: 29; my emphasis.)

Formulas of typification

Formulaic expressions such as 'that kind of beauty' authenticate the story since they give the impression of a continuum between the real and the fictional world. In addition, a realistic novel will also seek to establish connections between the habitual moral positions and political views of its readership, and the actions and opinions of the characters in the story.

Realism in the novel is largely based on illusion: the trick is to make the world of the novel seem like part of the real world and not, as is generally claimed, to depict the real world. Instead of imitating reality, realistic novels refer to aspects of reality which are already familiar to readers; these are then perceived as part of a conceptual frame and ultimately integrated into the world the readers know. This explanation, however, only holds for texts about real events and actual locations in the reader's time. Watt's notion of realism may fit in neatly with the work of Flaubert and Defoe, George Eliot and Balzac, but if we turn to the Gothic novel, the historical novel dealing with distant eras (Flaubert's *Salammbô*, for instance) or indeed post-colonial fiction, we will become aware of certain limitations. In the above-mentioned cases there is only limited scope for the recognition of details since strange or unusual settings are deliberately chosen. A good deal of the charm of such texts is to be found in the exotic and escapist scenarios they offer the reader.

The illusion of reality

In texts of the type mentioned above, the impression of authenticity is often created in the way Barthes describes, by the use of unfamiliar details, local artefacts which seem fantastic to a Western reader, exotic vegetation (flora and fauna), or sections of text in the strange vernacular of the protagonists (cf. Chapter 7). Although this foregrounding of the Other serves to authenticate the foreign or fantastic – in other words, although it rewrites fictionality as historical or cultural difference – it does not convince us merely on account of the strange setting but also because of the universal nature of the human psyche and its transculturally valid qualities. The kind of literary illusionism which underlies Watt's realism and which is typical (but perhaps not constitutive) of the novel, is rooted in our perception that the minds of characters in novels, and in

Authenticity and psychological realism

stories in general, are similar to ours and are governed by comparable sets of circumstances. Even animals and robots in science fiction stories are psychologically accessible to us if we interpret them as functioning in the same way as we do. What has been termed psychological realism is just an extreme form of the general illusionism which can be found in narrative. Exactly how prototypical and cognitively convincing such narrative is perceived as being will depend on the experiential quality of the story world depicted.

Aesthetic illusion

Ian Watt's concept of realism has much in common with the notion of *aesthetic illusion* (Wolf 1993).[1] Narrative texts create the illusion that the fictional world is directly accessible while a text is being read, that it really does exist, and in the precise form in which it is described. Wolf characterizes aesthetic illusion as 'an illusion of experiencing reality' (31) and as the 'pleasurable experiencing of the illusion of quasi-authenticity conjured up by a work of art, coupled with an underlying awareness that it is not real but simply an illusion' (xi). Admittedly, aesthetic illusion is an element of all representational art, also painting and sculpture. The illusionism of realistic narrative concentrates on the evocation of a quasi-'real' fictional world, which includes all the figures populating it. This illusion is always evoked in literary texts, but it can also be punctured by the use of metafictional strategies (see below).

The authenticity of the narrative voice

Author versus narrator

One of the most significant achievements of narratology is the fact that nowadays we distinguish between author and narrator. Until the late nineteenth century, the author was held to be identical with the authorial narrator, although this patently cannot be said to apply to Dickens's late novels, *Bleak House* (1852–53), for example, where the narrator uses an extremely strange style, thus evoking a rather peculiar narrator figure. Authorial narrators in English novels of the nineteenth century, those by Scott, for example, or the early Dickens, Trollope, Thackeray or George Eliot, sound like tellers of fairy tales, chroniclers of local events, expert historians, satirists or moralists. This leads one to visualize the respective authors behind those narrative voices as figures who admonish, look down on others with disdain or have knowing smiles playing about their lips. We seem to be face to face with Meredith the master of irony, Gissing the social ethicist and George Eliot the wise moralist.

Madame Bovary: author ≠ narrator

Illogically, perhaps, it was the *Madame Bovary* trial of 1857, which followed the publication of Flaubert's novel a year earlier, that drew the separate identities of author and narrator to the attention of the literary elite (cf. LaCapra 1982). Illogical because, in reality, the discrepancy between the views of the author and the moral views of the world of the story was in dispute and, secondly, because the views that were considered morally reprehensible were held by a character in a novel and not by its author or narrator – a parallel here with Molly Bloom in James Joyce's *Ulysses*. What were regarded as Emma's blasphemies and her sexual misdemeanours stirred up controversy but, as the counsel for the defence claimed, they did not reflect the views of the author, Flaubert. He had made her actions the butt of his irony and ultimately punished Emma for them by having her die. From the narratological point of view, both prosecution and defence were guilty of confused thinking: their yardstick was inappropriate to the circumstances. *Madame Bovary* is for the most part a figural narrative; there is extensive use of reported thought and free indirect discourse, especially in the sections where Emma's reprehensible views are described. The narrator is only implicitly present as an ironic foil to Emma; for many readers who do not recognize the irony he disappears altogether. A typical example of this situation is the following passage, used by Hans-Robert Jauss to demonstrate that the italicized words are free indirect thought and not a comment on the part of the narrator:

> En s'apercevant dans la glace, elle s'étonna de son visage. *Jamais elle n'avait eu les yeux si grands, si noirs, ni d'une telle profondeur.* Quelque chose de subtil épandu sur sa personne la transfigurait.
>
> Elle se répétait: J'ai un amant! un amant! se délectant a cette idée comme à celle d'une autre puberté qui lui serait survenue. *Elle allait donc enfin posséder ces plaisirs de l'amour, cette fièvre de bonheur dont elle avait désespéré. Elle entrait dans quelque chose de merveilleux, où tout serait passion, extase, délire* . . .
>
> (*Madame Bovary*, quoted in LaCapra 1982: 57)

> But when she saw herself in the mirror she wondered at her face. *Never had her eyes been so large, so black, nor so deep.* Something subtle about her being transfigured her.
>
> She repeated: 'I have a lover! A lover!', delighting at the idea as if a second puberty had come to her. So at last she was to know those joys of love, that fever of happiness of which she had despaired! She was entering upon a marvelous world where all would be passion, ecstasy, delirium.
>
> (*Madame Bovary*, quoted in LaCapra 57–8)

The censors naturally targeted Flaubert's rather lukewarm criticism of Emma's behaviour. In their view, such moral turpitude should have been unambiguously pilloried by the narrator, leaving the reader in no doubt as to the rights and the wrongs of the matter. Although Flaubert ridicules Emma, making her the butt of his irony, he does not actually morally condemn her. No explicit moral judgement of the actions and opinions of the characters can be found in the novel. Flaubert offers a resolutely non-didactic and non-moralizing scenario, not in his role as author, as the censors wrongly assumed, but in the world view presented in the novel (attributable to the implied author or to the text as a whole).

In fact, then, the reproaches of the prosecution were actually justified: had he wished to condemn Emma, Flaubert would have had to devise a plot in which her husband caught her in flagrante and drove her out of the house in disgrace so that she ended up in the gutter as a prostitute rather than committing suicide out of desperation. But he is trying to counter this traditional pattern. Flaubert's ironic approach consists in having Emma fall victim to the illusions promoted by romantic love stories. She tries to compensate for the boredom and banality of her bourgeois existence by escaping into the world of reading and, subsequently, by entering into adulterous relationships. Imagination is the means she employs to break out of her humdrum existence, but she fails to take into account the realities of her situation and her place in society. Ultimately, Flaubert's book is a critique of a permissive society, but a critique that is much more subtle, compassionate and differentiated than that of any self-appointed moral authority. The fact that the narrator distances himself, actually all but disappears, enables us as readers to gain deep and intimate insights into Emma's feelings. Thus we realize how hopeless her situation is. This hopelessness is the product of social circumstances (her status as a woman, her lack of intelligence and education) and her emotions (her dream of happiness in love, which is doomed to be shattered).

So Flaubert's novel is not really the kind of book that lends itself to demonstrating the difference between real author and fictional narrator. This difference could have been brought out much more effectively in a novel where a notoriously conservative author has a narrator incite characters and readers to anarchy or terrorism. Nevertheless, Flaubert's show trial had the effect of undermining the notion of an author's responsibility for her/his characters and led people to question the idea that what a narrator says is necessarily what an author believes.

Traditional narrative theory treats the idea that author and narrator are not identical as axiomatic, even, or rather especially clearly, in the case of first-person narrative, which is merely pseudo-autobiography, after all. Fictional first-person narrators already existed in late medieval times. There are two sources for fictional first-person narratives: frame stories and medieval dream narratives. In accounts of dreams, which are actually a kind of frame story, too, the first-person narrator of the frame dreams that s/he experiences fantastic events. The story world is marked as fictional by the fact that it is part of a dream, whereas an autobiographical frame would authenticate it as true. A 'normal' frame story features protagonists who, for their part, also tell stories. The frame renders these narrators responsible for their stories – the views they express are not attributed to the author. Thus medieval frame stories anticipate the picaresque novel from Nashe to Defoe. In this genre, the non-identity of author and narrator is taken as given. At the same time, such framing functions as an authentification strategy, particularly when the frame is provided by an editor and fictional commentators. Furthermore, the frame soon acquired the functions of providing an ironic gloss and a fresh perspective on the narrative. In the case of earlier British literature, the 'preface' to Fielding's *Shamela* (1741) and the story-within-a-story structure of the Gothic novel (particularly striking in the case of Maturin's *Melmoth the Wanderer*, 1820) are good instances of this technique. In the literary and artistic heyday of the form, Bram Stoker's *Dracula* (1897) or the frame stories of Joseph Conrad and Henry James can serve as examples.

Basically, then, in the modern period, the distinction between author and narrator can only be regarded as innovative in third-person narrative. Narratologically speaking, this last development was a product of modernism. So, within narrative theory as a whole, the author/narrator distinction cannot be regarded as constitutive. It is a more recent development which has, in the meantime, come to predominate. In other words, in the same way as we find a continuum reaching from narrating to experiencing selves in first-person narrative, in the case of third-person narrative we should also assume the existence of a scale. This scale ranges from one end, where the historical existence of the narrator as a peripheral first-person narrator is made quite explicit (as in Aphra Behn's *Oroonoko*, for instance), to the other, the pole of complete non-identity, which is a regular feature of texts from the modern period. In between there could be placed a multitude of texts in which implied identity and non-identity are negotiable. This brings us to the subject of fictionality and how this is manifested in metanarrative and in metafictional passages in a particular story.

Margin notes:
Narrative frames as strategies of authentification

Summary: narrator versus author

Fictionality

Margin note: Hayden White

The issue of fictionality in narrative is complex and highly controversial. We may start out from the assumption, as we saw in Chapter 1, that novels, literary films, dramas, oral storytelling, history and autobiography may all be counted as examples of narrative texts. In this connection, Hayden White (1978) emphasizes the constructed nature of written history, an insight which is frequently (and wrongly) interpreted as referring to the fictional nature of historical writing. White contends that the naive view that historical events or facts 'exist' and only need to be 'written down' by historians goes back to an old-fashioned concept of mimesis, which is – incidentally – a literary notion. Second, he maintains that the so-called historical 'facts' and 'events' are only constructed by historiographical discourse and then have meaning attributed to them in a plot which is created by the historian. Finally, he claims that this process involves literary-rhetorical schemata which represent the course of history as tragedy, comedy, satire or farce. Since the same topics – the French Revolution, for instance – may be presented as tragedy, comedy or farce, the fictionalizing elements of historical writing are clearly located in the discourse of historiography. This can be analysed narratologically just as a novel can, and shows obvious fictional characteristics. The fictionality of narrative discourse, its teleological structure, its literary and rhetorical features all have no bearing on the truth of the content which is narrated. Every history takes what historians agree upon after the sources have been studied, and interprets this on the basis of speculation or by having recourse to fresh sources or new methods. In contrast to the novel, historical narrative can be proved false if new sources are found. So, the fictionality of history, according to Hayden White, has to do with the similarity between historical writing, especially that of the nineteenth century, and the discourse of the novel. It also derives from the fact that all plots are constructed, including historical plots in history texts.

In *The Fictions of Language and the Languages of Fiction* (1993a) Monika Fludernik shows that conversational narrative contains many fictional elements, and in *Towards a 'Natural' Narratology* (1996) she characterizes it as the prototypical form of narrative. She transfers the discourse of the academic historian from the genre of narrative to that of argument. Her concern here is to avoid limiting narrative to the reporting of sequences of actions – reports can also be found in argumentative texts, instructions and descriptions. The essence of narrative, in her view, is the communication of anthropocentric experience – the experientiality which is inherent in human experience – and this means drawing on fixed patterns of behaviour as well as conveying thoughts and feelings, and depicting perceptions and reflections. Hence, narrative is not merely a sequence of events; rather such sequences are an integral part of human experience and this is why they feature prominently in stories. Action is, however, not absolutely necessary in order to construct a narrative, as the plays of Beckett or the modern psychological novel show.

[margin note: Fictionality and conversational narrative]

The notion of fictionality is retained within this framework. In so far as narrative depicts psychological states, it is fictional since such states cannot be rendered except by using the techniques of fiction (cf. Chapter 7). Psychology is fundamental to narrativity: experientiality and consciousness are conditional upon each other. From this perspective, it is clear that academic history is not narrative but argumentative since it puts together arguments using existing sources and does not depict human experience. (The emphasis here is on *academic*: much historical writing is quite novelistic in structure and tone.) Oral storytelling, regarded as prototypical in Fludernik's model, is based on experientiality, since it is not events as such that are foregrounded but rather that which is surprising, exciting or terrible about them (*tellability*). The point is to come to terms with and interpret the experience. Fludernik does not recognize the

[margin note: Fictionality and narrativity]

existence of two types of narrative, fictional and non-fictional. Narrative is fictional per se, not because it is 'made up' or deals with fantastic occurrences, but because it is based on the representation of psychological states and mental perceptions.

The fictive

Alternative studies on fictionality are concerned with the notion of the fictive. Starting out from this concept, fictionality is seen as being fundamental to human action and behaviour. In play, we make up scenarios and characters, conjuring up virtual play-worlds from childhood on, a process strongly resembling storytelling (Currie 1990, Lamarque/Olsen 1994). The fictive is even more familiar from mathematics and in virtual scenarios: 'imaginary' numbers, 'assuming that, then . . .'. Although such virtual scenarios are central to play, where the imagination is allowed to roam free, until now there has been little research into their significance for literary narrative.

Signalling fictionality

Traditional studies of fictionality and non-fictionality in narrative discourse have tended to start out by postulating various narrative categories which, it is claimed, only exist in novels and not in real-life stories. The widely held view that metaphors can only exist, or at least are mainly found, in poetry has been discredited, for we find metaphors in advertisements and even in scientific papers. Similarly, the linguistic and narrative elements that are supposed to signal fictionality have also been recognized, in the meantime, as having a much wider distribution. There are no aspects of narrative which could be described as typically literary (Löschnigg 1999). For example, free indirect discourse occurs outside the novel, in conversational narrative and even in newspaper articles. Not to put too fine a point on it, any decision as to whether a text reports real events or imagined ones needs to be taken by the reader or listener, and this decision will depend on the context. Explicit comments on the part of the narrator and paratextual elements play a large part in this decision-making process. If a book is subtitled 'A Novel', or found at bookstores or in catalogues under the heading 'History', it will be read accordingly. Works which playfully send out contradictory signals, such as Wolfgang Hildesheimer's novel *Marbot* (1981), may well mislead and confuse the reader. Hildesheimer's novel purports to be a biography and did indeed confuse some reviewers when it was published. In fact, the book is a novel in the form of a pseudo-biography. What is crucial here is what the reader actually knows: the *form* in itself does not explain whether actual places and people are being described.

Three levels: story as *fictio*, *fictum* and *suppositio*

In short, I can only restate the fact that, with novels, reaching a decision on matters of fictionality versus non-fictionality (or literariness, for that matter) involves addressing the three following questions: whether the story is a construct (*fictio*), whether the events depicted are made up (*fictum*) and whether an object or a situation is virtual (*suppositio*). The first two of these are traditionally put together under the heading of 'fictionality' whereas the third, labelled 'fictivity', is mainly encountered in philosophy and mathematics and hardly features in literary theory at all. One can also note that when the concept of fictionality is used, it generally refers to *fictum*, and that truth in the historical or practical sense of the word can only be generated in context by comparison with other information. The fact that objects, people and places actually exist cannot be adduced from the text alone but must be supported by evidence from the context and other sources of information.

Metafiction and metanarration

At this point it might be helpful to clarify two concepts that are often used in connection with postmodern texts and are frequently regarded as signs of anti-realism:

metanarration and *metafiction*. We should note, to begin with, that these terms are often treated as identical in meaning, particularly in the English-speaking world. Metanarrative narratorial comments are widely seen as evidence of fictionality and so they are often considered to be instances of metafictionality. Such an equivalence cannot be taken for granted, however. On the contrary, metanarrative comments can considerably strengthen the illusionistic effect of a realistic narrative, as Ansgar Nünning has pointed out (Nünning 2004).

Metanarrative narratorial comments are to be found in texts dating from long before the twentieth century; indeed, they already existed in the Middle Ages. In conversational narrative, the so-called *abstract* can be counted as a metanarrative comment on the part of the storyteller, for example: 'Have I already told you about the time when the parrot came and perched on my head?' Metanarrative statements fulfil a wide variety of functions, most of them hardly noticeable as the phrases are so short, like the verb 'told' in the example above. Many purported metanarrative sections of narrative are actually metadiscursive (Fludernik 2003b, Engler 2004). They help readers to orientate themselves on the discourse level ('as we saw above' and 'as we shall see in the next chapter') and to shift their attention from one location or group of people to another more easily ('We shall therefore see a little after our hero', *Joseph Andrews*; Fielding 1986: 63).

In traditional narrative theory, metanarrative statements on the part of the narrator have been interpreted as being especially intrusive and as puncturing the illusion of reality. They draw attention to the figure of the narrator and to her/his role in mediating events, thus disrupting the apparently unmediated portrayal of the fictional world. These attitudes emerged with literary modernism, which in its turn developed as a reaction to the Victorian novel. However, such tendencies were much less pronounced in German than in English literature, a fact which is clearly evidenced by the emphasis placed on the narrator in the work of, say, Thomas Mann. The example of narrator-less, figural novels such as those of James Joyce and Virginia Woolf should not be exploited in order to condemn narratorial comment out of hand. As Ansgar Nünning so lucidly explains, the mediation level of narration even serves the purpose of creating a mimesis of the narrative process (Nünning 2001). The level of mediation is in itself so realistic that the reader feels s/he is in direct communion with the narrator. This results in a build-up of trust between reader and narrator, a feeling of closeness and reliability, which – in contrast to the stereotypical view of an intrusive narrator – helps to put across a convincing picture of the fictional world. Metanarrative comments enhance the credibility of the narrator: her/his difficulties in teasing out the truth of what happened or the search for the right words to use are taken by the reader as proof of authenticity. The narrator is not omniscient but makes an honest attempt to furnish a satisfactory account of what happened.

Metanarrative and mediacy

In addition to the above-mentioned type of comment which contributes to the *illusion* of authenticity, there are also metanarrative narratorial remarks intended to question the validity of the story or of the way in which it is presented. Such comments also give the impression that the narrative discourse is a constructed account (*fictio*) or that the story is only made up (*fictum*). Thus, at the end of Chapter 15 of *Joseph Andrews*, the narrator castigates human vanity and then addresses the narratee directly.

Metafictional metanarrativity

> I know thou wilt think, that whilst I abuse thee, I court thee; and that thy love hath inspired me to write this sarcastical panegyric on thee: but thou art deceived, I

value thee not of a farthing; nor will it give me any pain, if thou should'st prevail on the reader to censure this digression as errant nonsense: for know to thy confusion, that I have introduced thee for no other purpose than to lengthen out a short chapter; and so I return to my history.

(Henry Fielding, *Joseph Andrews*; Fielding 1986: 83–4)

We have here an example of a hostile tirade directed at the audience, long before Peter Handke's play *Publikumsbeschimpfung* (1966; *Offending the Audience*). Moreover, the narrator makes it perfectly clear that large parts of the preceding chapter were inserted as padding. As a result of this, the fictionality of the narrative discourse is clearly foregrounded. In Book III, Chapter 6, similar direct remarks from the narrator about his deliberate refusal to compare Joseph Andrews with a lion also emphasize the fictionality of the narrative discourse (228–9) and thus have a metafictional impact. We also find metanarrative comments with a metafictional thrust in the chapter headings, for instance in Chapter 10 of Book III, 'A Discourse between Poet and Player; of no other Use in this History, but to divert the Reader' (246).

Shattering illusions

In Fielding, the story itself is still seen as true, in spite of all the humorous comments about the presentation of events in the narrative discourse. However, in the work of the postmoderns and their literary antecedents, one also frequently comes across remarks characterizing the story as fictional. When the narrator in Diderot's *Jacques le fataliste* (1773–75) declares that it is up to him how the plot develops, he is emphasizing the fact that the story is made up.

You see, reader, how considerate I am. With a flick of the whip on the horses drawing the coach draped in black I could bring together Jack, his master, the tax officers, the mounted guard, and the rest of the procession, at the very next inn, interrupting the story of Jack's captain and provoking you as much as I pleased. But for that I would have to lie and I do not like lies unless they are useful and necessary. The fact is that Jack and his master never saw the black-draped coach again and, while still upset over his horse's antics, Jack continued . . .

(Diderot 1984: 39)

The strategies employed in postmodern texts are not dissimilar to this, as Werner Wolf (1993) explains in some detail. John Barth's texts provide good examples of this:

All the preceding except the last few sentences is exposition that should've been done earlier or interspersed with the present action instead of lumped together. No reader would put up with so much with such *prolixity*. It's interesting that Ambrose's father, though presumably an intelligent man (as indicated by his role as grade-school principal), neither encouraged nor discouraged his sons at all in any way – as if he either didn't care about them or cared all right but didn't know how to act. If this fact should contribute to one of them's becoming a celebrated but wretchedly unhappy scientist, was it a good thing or not? He too might someday face the question; it would be useful to know whether it had tortured his father for years, for example, or never once crossed his mind.

(*Lost in the Funhouse*; Barth 1981: 90)

At this point it is important to remember that metafictionality is not only generated by metanarrative narratorial comments which have a metafictional effect. It can also derive from other strategies which do not come into play at the level of narrative discourse. First among these are the plot devices of the endless loop (Möbius strip), as discussed by Brian McHale (1987); the tale within a tale within a tale (reminiscent of a Russian doll); the device of metalepsis, in other words the shifting between narrative levels (characters who desire to kill the narrator/author; third-person narrators who enter the world of the characters); as well as an overemphasis on plot, as Wolf (1993) observes: too much action as well as too little both destroy the illusion of a realistic portrayal of events. Non-metanarrative metafictionality

Perhaps it would be as well to note, in conclusion, that metanarration and metafiction are managed in a rather unobtrusive way in most novels and so do not weaken the illusion of a fictional world but intensify it. For instance, the narrator in Victorian novels, who makes moral comments and is frequently characterized as an 'intrusive' narrator, does not, in fact, shatter the realistic illusion. Rather, these narratorial comments and moral judgements on what happens lend authenticity to the events depicted, adapt the fictional world to the needs and world view of the reader, and ultimately bring together and superimpose the real and the imaginary worlds in the reader's mind. The illusionism of the realistic novel is thus extremely flexible and includes a secondary mimesis of the narrative process as well as leaving room for subtle hints about its fictionality.

7 Language, the Representation of Speech and the Stylistics of Narrative

In this chapter we shall be looking at the part played by language and traditional stylistic and rhetorical devices in narrative discourse. Scarcely any attention has been paid to this in classical narrative theory. I am primarily concerned with the status of stylistic features in relation to the quasi-universal structures which are generally assumed to underlie narrative texts.

Language

The linguistic medium

Language is by far the most common medium of narrative texts. Novels and plays consist of language, and films or cartoons include a significant percentage of language. Only ballet, mime, and, in rare instances, cartoons are purely visual and dispense with language altogether.

It is important to remember that language, as well as being the medium for narrative texts, is also a part of the fictional world created by narratives. Taking this into account, it becomes clear that in drama, film and cartoon, language is not in fact the predominant medium of representation but exists only as one element of the story world (for the moment, I shall not deal with film scripts and play texts). In conversational narrative and in novels and short stories (as well as in poetry), language is both the medium and the object of representation.

The role of speech in characterization

To put this in a different way, in the alternative world of a novel, language is the means by which characters communicate with each other. The narrator, in so far as s/he figures in the story, uses a language of her/his own. It might, in fact, be better to say that precisely because language is used here, we as readers become aware that there are characters and narrators. No language, no characters: even animal protagonists in novels make use of language, otherwise they would lack the essential quality which protagonists in narratives must have – an anthropomorphic existence.

Diegesis and mimesis

As narratives are traditionally couched in language, the dual role it plays in them has been an object of enquiry for scholars of poetics and narratology since ancient times. In his *Republic*, Plato distinguishes between *mimesis* and *diegesis*: mimesis refers to the characters' discourse and diegesis to the narrative discourse of the poet or bard.[1] By contrast, in Aristotle's *Poetics*, the use of the term mimesis (in the sense of representation, i.e. with reference to the fictional world) is not restricted to the utterances of characters but describes the process of depicting the fictional world in general.

Mimesis of speech: Genette

The disparities between these classical texts have led to a lack of precision or even confusion in formulating the concepts of mimesis and diegesis. Genette, for example, draws a distinction between mimesis of action and mimesis of language. When land-scape, actions, locations or characters are being represented, the language of a novel should be seen as the medium which, by virtue of its symbolic potential, makes it possible for the fictional world to be evoked and to take shape in the reader's imagination. If, on the other hand, we look at the direct speech the narrator uses to address her/his narratees and the actual words the characters exchange, it seems as if these were represented iconically, mirroring the actual utterances in the world of the novel in the same form. Language reproduces language verbatim.

The impression that this is the case is wrong, as spoken language can never be faithfully represented in writing. Even in conversational narrative, direct speech is often markedly different from the real thing, sometimes even entirely fictive, although we expect it to be authentic (Fludernik 1993a: Chapter 9). Characters in novels or plays do not speak in the same way as real people do when they talk to each other. Recordings of genuine spoken exchanges show that written representations of these have been stylized or 'purified'. Spoken exchanges in novels are grammatically and syntactically correct; they are more concise than real-life conversations since numerous repetitions, rephrasings, fillers and many other features of spoken conversation have been elimi-nated. We can discern a trend towards using a repertoire of recurring clichés and formulaic phrases, especially in the case of expressive utterances. Interjections such as 'Bother!' or 'Oh dear!' are much more common in the dialogue of novels than in real life, replacing meatier and possibly less acceptable expressions.

Schematic representation of language

The speech of characters is located at a level subordinate to that of the narrative discourse, which would justify the assertion that the narrative discourse is the primary level of discourse in a story. From this perspective, the utterances of the characters can only be perceived via this level, in spite of all the conventions of authenticity. The mediated nature of direct speech is more evident in the selection process which precedes its formulation than in the form it takes. In fact, the narrative discourse controls what is presented, and in which form (direct speech, speech report, indirect speech or free indirect discourse), and it also determines what is omitted, abridged or shows some kind of bias.

We can, therefore, say that utterances in narrative texts may be considered mimetic elements, in so far as these utterances can be attributed to characters at the story level or to the narrator (first-person or authorial). Nevertheless, the narrative discourse is not always clearly marked as being uttered by one person, i.e. the narrator. Several linguistically oriented narratologists, including Benveniste, Banfield and Fludernik, do not necessarily consider narration to be a speech act, above all when stories are filtered and focused through the consciousness of one character (in reflector-mode narrative or in the figural narrative situation). In such texts, one could regard the language as only a medium and not see it, mimetically, as an utterance or speech act. Here, narratologists often bring in the implied author: the narrative discourse has to be produced by someone, and when a narrator is not clearly discernible, many researchers would locate this speech act at the next higher narrative level. The 'implied author' is transformed into a persona responsible for the 'speech act' of the narration; the covert narrator is invented.

Narrative discourse as utterance

Representing speech

Speech
representation

It is even more challenging to describe speech when it is represented in an indirect or oblique way. Here, the medium and the utterance it represents merge, grammatically and stylistically. There are various ways of representing speech, ranging from the summarized, compressed and concise versions of what characters say in speech report ('Anton went on to comment about progress with the construction work and made particular mention of the problems with the foundations') – to indirect speech ('He asked if she still had a little time to spare. She replied that the shop was already closed') and free indirect discourse ('Was he in his right mind, talking like this?').

Speech report

Speech report presents the words of another person in summarized form. Here, the nature of the utterance, the kind of words uttered and the overall topic are the focus of attention. The exact propositions that make up the original are not reproduced word for word, however. Michael Short has recently made a distinction between 'NRSA' (*narrator's representation of speech acts*) and 'NRS' (*narrator's report of speech*) (Semino/Short 2004: 30) as in 'He welcomed him joyfully home [. . .]' (*Buddenbrooks* IV, x; Mann 1984: 194). In NRS, the fact of something being uttered is mentioned, but the words themselves are not reported.

Indirect speech

Indirect speech is characterized by its syntactic subordination. As a result passages of indirect speech are easiest to pick out when they fill the syntagmatic slots that follow introductory *inquit* phrases such as: *Paul claimed that . . . , Eva asked whether . . . , The Colonel ordered . . . .* Pronominal references have to be changed to fit in with the referential parameters; if the narrative tense is the past tense, then the tenses also shift accordingly. For instance, Paul reports, using direct speech:

> I went to the cinema yesterday and there was this big fat guy in front of me, so I couldn't see anything and I poked him and asked, 'Mister, can't you lean over to the right a bit?' Then up he jumps and yells at me, 'You idiot, who do you think you are? I paid for my ticket just like you did!'

Later on, Paul can retell these events in the form of indirect speech:

> *I went to the cinema yesterday and there was this big fat guy in front of me, so I couldn't see anything and I poked him and <u>asked him if</u> he couldn't lean over to the right a bit. Then he jumped up and <u>yelled at me that</u> **I was** an idiot. He shouted at me <u>asking who</u> **I thought** I was and <u>insisted that</u> he **had paid** for his ticked just as I had.*

As this is a case of first-person narrative, the first-person pronoun for Paul remains unchanged in the indirect speech ('that *I* was an idiot'), but the tense is shifted: 'that I **was** an idiot'; 'that he **had paid** for his ticket'. The mood in English (and French) is indicative. (German would require a subjunctive.) All the sentences in indirect speech are subordinated. In German, simply using the subjunctive can mark out a passage as indirect speech; no introductory verb and dependent subordinate clause are necessary then.

Free indirect
discourse

However, the passage is not very idiomatic when one tries to render it in indirect speech. A more likely, oblique version would be one using free indirect speech: *Then up he jumped and yelled at me: I was an idiot; and who did I think I was. He had paid for his ticket just like I had.* The laborious and formal syntactic introduction of indirect speech is dropped, and the expressive, emotional tone of the speech reproduced syntactically and lexically. Only the referential and temporal features of indirect speech clarify that this is not direct speech: *who **did** I think **I was.***

Free indirect discourse (Fr. *style indirect libre*; Ger. *erlebte Rede*) has been the object of a good deal of narratological research (Steinberg 1971, Fludernik 1993a). While still representing the contents of an utterance in a narrative context, it draws stylistically and syntactically on the expressive power of direct speech. Thanks to the fact that there is no syntactic frame (i.e. no *She said that . . .* or *Father wanted to know when . . .* syntagms), the stretch of speech being depicted is incorporated into the flow of the narrative. This means that it is not always easy to ascertain where speech representation begins or whether we have an instance of free indirect discourse at all. Free indirect discourse is called 'free' because the introductory verbs of saying (*He claimed that . . .*) are dispensed with; 'indirect' because the utterances represented are referentially aligned and tenses shifted in accordance with the surrounding narrative discourse. In traditional third-person past-tense narrative, sequence of tense rules apply and first/second-person pronouns of original/supposed utterances are shifted into the third person:

> Oh yes though! said Bella; *she might as well mention one other thing; Lizzie was very desirous to thank her unknown friend who had sent her the written retraction. Was she, indeed?* observed the Secretary. Ah! Bella asked him, *had **he** [you → he] any notion who that unknown friend might be? **He** [I → he] had no notion whatever.*
> (*Our Mutual Friend* III, ix; Dickens 1979: 593)

> She [. . .] bid him never let her see him more except upon a footing of the most distant acquaintance, as she was determined never again to subject herself to so unworthy a treatment. [= indirect speech] ***She was** happy that **he had** at length **disclosed** to her his true character, and **would** know how to profit of her present experience to avoid a repetition of the same danger.*
> (*Caleb Williams*; Godwin 1991: I, ii, 13)

In the first passage Bella's address to the 'Secretary' (John Harmon in disguise) is shifted from a presumably used *you* to *he* in alignment with the surrounding third-person narrative; likewise, the final sentence 'He had no notion whatever', if taken as a representation of John's answer to Bella's question, shifts an underlying first-person pronoun into a third-person pronoun. Note that in the sentence 'Was she indeed?', the *she* is not a shifted item since Lizzie is a third person both for Bella and the Secretary/John Harmon.

In the second passage, temporal shifting from present perfect to pluperfect (past perfect), present to preterite (past tense) and *will*-future to conditional tense can be observed. This, of course, corresponds to the sequence of tenses familiar from indirect speech. Simultaneity is signalled by the use of the past, anteriority by the pluperfect and posteriority by the conditional. If we were to try to reconstruct the direct speech underlying the excerpt from William Godwin's *Caleb Williams*, we would have to use 'I' instead of 'she'. In the section in italics Lady Lucretia presumably says to Count Malvesi: 'I am happy that you have disclosed your character and I shall now know how to avoid a repetition of the same sort of thing in future.' The first- and second-person pronouns are realized as *he* and *she* to fit in with the authorial narrative, and the tenses are shifted as they would be in indirect speech. Naturally Lady Lucretia would not have used exactly the same words, and she would in fact have spoken in Italian. The shifted tenses therefore refer to an imaginary utterance which is projected by the narrative discourse.

The corpora of spoken English we now have at our disposal show that the use of free indirect discourse to represent speech in oral communication is very common. But there are early instances of it, too: in English as early as the thirteenth century, and there are also similar examples in French. While the use of free indirect discourse to represent speech is widely attested before the eighteenth century, scholars are by no means of one mind as to how extensively it is employed in the representation of thought (cf. Chapter 8).

Since free indirect discourse seeks to evoke the manner of speaking and the actual words of a character, it is often, like direct speech, stylistically differentiated from the surrounding more neutral narrative discourse. Moreover, it often echoes interjections and other syntactic markers of expressivity:

> The trader was not shocked or amazed [. . .]. He *had seen* Death many times [. . .]; and so he only swore that the gal *was* a baggage, and that he *was* devilish unlucky, and that, if things *went* on in this way, he *should not make* a cent on the trip.
> (*Uncle Tom's Cabin*, xii; Stowe 1981: 130)

> [Mr Tyrrel] often commented upon [Mr Falkland] to his particular confidents [. . .]. *It was impossible that people could seriously feel any liking for such a ridiculous piece of goods as this outlandish, foreign-made Englishman. But he knew very well how it was; it was a miserable piece of mummery that was played only in spite of him.* **But God for ever blast his soul**, *if he were not bitterly revenged upon them all!*
> (*Caleb Williams* I, iii; Godwin 1991: 20)

In these extracts, the passages in free indirect speech are italicized. They contain a multiplicity of expressive and dialectal words, e.g. the curse 'God for ever blast my soul!' The same holds true for the representation of thought in free indirect discourse as can be seen from the following example, which includes a deictic *now* (in reference to Mr Tulliver's temporal location) and some colloquialisms that are to be attributed to Tulliver:

> But *to-day it was clear that the good principle was triumphant: this affair of the water-power had been a tangled business somehow, for all it seemed – look at it one way – as plain as water's water; but, big a puzzle as it was, it hadn't got the better of Riley.*
> (*Mill on the Floss* I, iii; Eliot 1980: 14)

As the italicized passages show, free indirect discourse may use exclamations, biased and pejorative expressions and other features stemming from the actual language of the characters ('this affair', 'somehow'), which would only feature in indirect speech under exceptional circumstances (cf. Fludernik 1993a: 227–8). In addition, free indirect discourse has two different ways of rendering speech: on the one hand, a neutral or empathetic version of the words or thoughts of the protagonists and, on the other, an ironic mode, which is popular in conversational narrative and satirical novels. As far as the depiction of psychological states is concerned, Dorrit Cohn opts for a distinction between consonant (empathetic) and dissonant (ironic) presentation (Cohn 1978). Before her, Roy Pascal in *The Dual Voice* (1977) likewise emphasized the satirical use of free indirect discourse in Jane Austen, among other authors. The examples given above were neutral or consonant; but the following famous passage from Thomas Mann's *Buddenbrooks* is clearly ironic. Mr Gosch exaggerates unashamedly:

> *Things were going badly with Herr Gosch.* He made a fine, sweeping gesture to wave away the imputation that he was a prosperous man. *The burdens of old age approached, they were at hand even now; as aforesaid, his grave was dug.*
>
> (*Buddenbrooks* IX, iv; Mann 1984: 479)

All these examples show the importance of stylistic features in the representation of speech and thought, which brings us to the second focus of this chapter.

Language and style

In principle, points of style are language specific, whereas phenomena like analepsis or focalization are not restricted to any one language but, theoretically, may occur in a variety of languages and cultures. To be sure, different vernacular languages and cultures can show a preference for some devices and make little use of others (for example, internal focalization may be extremely rare). The same holds true for literary periods (for example, novels with a reflector character were really only 'invented' in the late nineteenth century). *(margin: Style)*

A distinction on the stylistic level between, on the one hand, quasi-timeless narrative categories and, on the other, specific uses of language which vary from period to period, culture to culture or individual to individual is not wholly valid. Stylistics also has invariables or universals, which assume different historical, cultural and individual forms. In Chapter 5, in our discussion of the structure of conversational narrative, the point was made that narrative structure is realized differently at the surface level in German, English or French, depending on the tense system of the respective language. The different ways of marking gender and the various options available for obscuring or concealing the gender of the protagonist or first-person narrator have also been pointed out already. In such cases, we have to conclude that certain basic options might not be taken up because the linguistic system (for instance, the syntactic system) of a specific language disallows them. Disputes between narratologists about the status of the category gender in narrative theory focus on this very issue (Diengott 1988, Lanser 1986, 1988, 1992). Should narratology take into account categories that vary across time and culture or are completely random (random in the sense that a text may have been written or read by a man or by a woman)? Lanser's point of view has prevailed in this matter of gender. Nowadays most narratologists would acknowledge the fact that readers regularly perceive narrators, especially first-person narrators but also authorial narrators, as being gendered either male or female, even if they are not explicitly labelled as men or women. In this implicit attribution of gender, which is historically and culturally conditioned, the biological sex of the novel's author is highly significant; so are the narrator's style and the level of politeness of her/his verbal interaction with the narratee or implied reader.

Now we have arrived at a point where style has a significant contribution to make to narrative categories. A 'feminine' style of interaction on the part of a narrator, one that *(margin: Example: gender in narrative theory)* assumes, as Robyn Warhol has shown, an 'engaging reader' as interlocutor (Warhol 1986), tends to indicate a female narrator. Similarly, certain patterns of behaviour, tastes in clothes and so on may suggest male or female gender (although not necessarily biological sex). (See also Fludernik 1999.)

How, then, is the category of gender to be handled in narratology? The best solution would be to treat it as an optional category. Gender can be foregrounded or problematized. Often, however, it does not feature explicitly but can still be sensed, resonating, as a result of the cultural context of a particular text. Traditionally, the word 'author' has a masculine connotation (cf. the concept of *auctoritas*), which means that an authorial narrator is male by default unless, of course, the readers know that the novel was written by a woman, in which case the process of automatic male gendering will be suspended. The influence of style when attributing gender is particularly strong in texts whose authors are not identifiable as male or female. This may be the case with ambiguous first names such as Leslie, for example. It is also problematic with first names of African or Asian origin, where the initiated may be able to assign gender but ordinary Western readers will be unable to do so. I can still remember reading the novel *Ceremony* by Leslie Silko (1977) as a student, and my British English orientation led me to suppose Leslie was a man's first name. I was surprised by the sympathetic portrayal of the female point of view and by the criticism levelled at men. However, the novel I assumed to be by a male Native American author turned out to have been written by a woman.

Register and dialect

What about stylistic aspects of narrative in general? And what exactly is meant by style in this context? In the following, we shall consider style as *register* (specific to certain text types), as an indicator of social status (*dialect* versus *standard* forms), as a factor which varies according to age, and as *idiolect* (the characteristic style of one particular individual).[2]

The first aspect, register, plays only a minor role in narrative discourse, except in cases where characters are members of a particular profession. The choice between regional variety and standard language, on the other hand, is of major importance when discussing style in narrative. The opposition between dialect and standard forms of the language has regularly been exploited in novels from the eighteenth century to the present in order to distinguish the educated language used by the narrator from the various levels of language used by her/his characters. Regional forms are used for a wide variety of purposes ranging from humorous-satirical renderings of direct speech (also in drama) to the adding of local colour – a major element in historical novels and novels of provincial life (including those of Hardy and Lawrence).[3]

> 'I've not much faith i' Moses Barraclough,' said he; 'and I would speak a word to you myseln, Mr Moore. It's out o' no ill-will that I'm here, for my part; it's just to mak' a effort to get things straightened, for they're sorely a crooked. Ye see we're ill off, – varry ill off: wer families is poor and pined. We're thrown out o' work wi' these frames: we can get naught to do: we can earn naught. What is to be done? Mun we say, wisht! and lig us down and dee? Nay: I've no grand words at my tongue's end, Mr Moore, but I feel that it would be a low principle for a reasonable man to starve to death like a dumb cratur': I will n't do't.'
>
> (*Shirley* viii; Brontë 2006: 132)

Direct speech is used here to indicate social status, to add local Yorkshire colour and to represent William Farron as a reasonable working man driven to rebellion by his plight.

He is depicted in a condescending way as an unlettered person trying to come to terms with economic recession and imminent starvation. The passage tells us more about how the upper classes regard their workers than about the workers themselves.

As the twentieth century progressed, narrators (and not only first-person narrators) tended to use dialect more, which meant that once again it was not possible to distinguish between the language of the characters and that of the narrator; in some contexts standard language even seemed to be politically incorrect. This reorientation (standard forms seen as bourgeois, slang regarded as 'in') represents a reversal of the previous status quo. In nineteenth-century novels, direct speech was used to depict the social and regional roots of a character or her/his level of education in an indirect way, but we also find the same kind of representation in the narrative discourse in indirect and free indirect discourse, and in all reporting of characters' actual discourse in direct speech. Although such stylistic differences can be perceived most clearly in the rendering of dialogue, where the satirical-condescending element is also most pronounced, stylistic differences in the representation of speech permit certain aspects to be brought to the fore. In general, the use of register, idiolect and dialect is a surface-structure strategy which, at a deeper level, allows us to differentiate between the narrator's and the characters' discourses. Realistic elements in the discourse of the characters make it easier to distinguish the narrative levels. Here style is not a narratological category, for the same kind of stylistic differences can be found in reports, minutes, phone calls, etc. It is a linguistic category (like the use of tenses) which is exploited in a specific narrative context to achieve a particular effect.

The same holds true for child language, which also lends itself particularly well to the portrayal of a figural point of view since it has connotations of lack of knowledge of the world, naivety, innocence and the like. The use of language typical of children allows for a particularly convincing depiction of a young person's view of the world (cf. Henry James's *What Maisie Knew*, 1897) or for a high degree of unreliability (see Chapter 4). Of course, naivety or lack of formal education can also be conveyed by numerous other explicit and implicit narrative strategies. Style is just one strategy among many, even though it is the most strikingly obvious one.

Age and idiolect

This leaves the question of idiolect. From the narratological point of view, this is also significant in the representation of dialogue in cases where certain characters make particular use of a catchphrase, which they keep repeating. Dickens is famous for his minor characters, who are often individualized by the catchphrases he attributes to them. This was already standard practice in the drama of the seventeenth century; compare, for instance, Lord Foppington's repeated use of the exclamation 'Stap my vitals!' in Sir John Vanbrugh's play *The Relapse* (1696).

A literary critical analysis of the style of an author, on the other hand, which is the kind of investigation of individual style we meet most frequently in literary studies, is to a large extent narratologically irrelevant. Such analyses are only conducted when the aim is to date texts or attribute them to particular authors (cf. Love 2002).

Stylistic variation

Alongside register, level of style and idiolect we also have to take a brief look at that area of style which is concerned with syntactic patterns and word choice. A non-specialist would probably consider these features as coming under the heading of idiolect or stylistic variation. But syntax and lexis often correlate with narrative representation strategies, which are indeed of relevance for the narratologist. I should like to consider just two examples here: conscious variation in word order and the choice between several different types of anaphora (use of pronouns, use of proper names, use of epithets) in narrative prose.

Word order

A concern with such choices is not exclusively the preserve of a narratological analysis of texts. For instance, the exploitation of various word order options over and above their significance as a feature of individual style is clearly also the kind of text-grammatical phenomenon which is dealt with in linguistic pragmatics. In this connection, the important role of word order in the theme–rheme development of a text must be taken into account. In English and German, the usual word order generally corresponds to the sequence: theme (known information)–rheme (new information). Certain constituent parts may be emphasized by topicalizing them and placing them at the beginning of the sentence. This contravenes the usual theme–rheme pattern for the sake of emphasis and a thematic re-focalization of key arguments. The following sentences demonstrate this. Such topicalization (= theme) can be found in argumentative and narrative, in fictional and non-fictional, and in spoken and written texts (= rheme). In the previous sentence, the phrase 'Such topicalization' is the theme, the rest of the sentence makes up the rheme. In narrative discourse (= topicalization), however, it (= theme) is very frequently used to fulfil certain functions (= rheme). For example, the initial positioning of prepositional phrases of place or direction as in *Into the room it came* or *In flew a large bird* is frequently linked in narrative with the description of surprising developments, often presented from the point of view of an observer (the protagonist, who implicitly functions as an indirect focalizer, see Chapter 4).[4] The same word order options are also often found in academic writing and expository texts. Introductory prepositional phrases may, for example, help to make instructions on how to get somewhere clearer, as in *On the other side of the park, you'll find a fine statue of Lord Palmerston. To its left, there is a rotunda constructed by Humphrey Repton.* So, generally speaking, from the text-grammatical point of view, the fronting of such prepositional phrases is a focusing device. In narrative texts, it is particularly likely to occur at crucial points in the action. This means that, on a secondary level, instances of variation in normal word order are associated with surprising plot turns. Since such changes in word order frequently occur in conjunction with inversion of the subject–verb order, they are often dealt with when discussing the stylistic function of inversion (see Riffaterre 1959, 1961).

How to refer to characters

In addition to variation in word order, which is used to great effect in narrative texts, the choice of various forms of reference is also relevant from a narratological point of view. However, it has to be stressed from the outset that, in English at least, the distribution of noun phrases and pronouns is subject to strict syntactic and pragmatic rules (Kuno 1987). Once one moves beyond grammatical restrictions, it is extremely difficult to distinguish between (individual) stylistic variation and narratologically relevant phenomena. When looking at the use of pronouns versus nouns or modifying phrases (*the old man, the beaming farmer's wife, the soldier with the red beret* and so on), we can start out from two basic principles. The first has to do with the structure of the paragraph in literary (rather than non-literary) style. When references to protagonists in novels are clear and unambiguous, pronouns are usually employed to designate the characters, and mentioning a name deviates from this norm and should be seen as significant. As Catherine Emmott has shown in a seminal study (Emmott 1997), the shift between pronouns and full noun phrases plays an important part in eliciting and shaping the reader's sympathies as s/he is reading the text, and in focusing on the protagonist's thoughts and feelings. Emmott regards such strategies as being specific to particular text types. The choice between pronouns and noun phrases is particularly significant at the beginning of paragraphs or entire texts. As we saw in Chapter 5, a distinction is made, with text openings, between emic and etic beginnings (Harweg 1968). The use of etic openings corresponds to internal focalization (Genette) or reflector mode (Stanzel): in narratives told from the point of view of the main character, pronouns predominate as a way of referring to the hero or heroine as well as the other people s/he is concerned with. It is, however, much more difficult to explain why references using names or modifiers occur. Basically, these predominate in authorial narrative. It is also quite clear that when new characters are introduced they have to be described and named. We also come across modifiers with a stylistic function, designed to relieve the monotonous catalogue of names and pronouns. On the other hand, authors like Charles Dickens frequently mark their figures with descriptive modifying phrases in order to make them stand out from the multitude of minor characters and to enable the readers of the various instalments of the novel to recognize them again, even after some time has elapsed. A good deal of work remains to be done in this area since there have been no systematic studies so far that would, for example, shed light on when the use of particular modifiers can be seen as a stylistic device (in other words, the exploitation of synonyms is used to avoid repetition) and when it supports the narrative structure, for instance in order to signal a change in focalization.

Metaphor and metonymy

In the final section of this chapter we shall take a look at the part played in narrative texts by metaphor and related phenomena. This subject has not yet been investigated from a narratological perspective. In spite of the importance of metaphor, its use in narrative texts has simply been attributed to the author and regarded as part of her/his individual style, seemingly irrelevant from a narratological point of view. Nevertheless, metaphors do have an important role to play in the interpretation of novels, although they are not usually considered to be the concern of narrative theory.

Bearing this in mind, it is high time we looked at the meaning and function of metaphor in narrative texts. In the following paragraphs, we shall discuss the narratological relevance of simile, metaphor and metonymy. These remarks should be seen as a first attempt at a theoretical discussion of metaphor in the context of narrativity. It is hoped that they will contribute towards opening up this new field of research. *[Metaphor in narrative text]*

To start with, we should note that metaphor as a phenomenon must be located, like other expressive elements of text, in the category of *voice* (Fr. *voix*, Ger. *Stimme*). In a narrative text, metaphors are produced by the narrator's discourse, in the thoughts of characters or by the remarks of the main protagonist. As is the case with expressive formulations in free indirect speech, it is not always easy to attribute such metaphors to the correct source (or to any source, for that matter). In the case of similes which occur in the representation of Emma Bovary's mind, for instance, researchers have puzzled over the problem of whether to attribute them to Emma, to the narrator (or to Flaubert himself). In other cases, the source of similes is made abundantly clear. *[Problems with attributing metaphors to particular sources]*

Fielding's narrator in *Tom Jones* is indisputably the one who compares the reading process with eating:

> [. . .] we shall represent Human Nature at first to the keen appetite of our reader, in that more plain and simple manner in which it is found in the country, and shall hereafter hash and ragout it with all the high French and Italian seasoning of affectation and vice which courts and cities can afford.
>
> (Fielding 1996: I, i, 31)

In Dickens's novel *Great Expectations*, the simile of prisoners and flowers is drawn by Pip, the first-person narrator:

> It struck me that Wemmick walked among the prisoners, much as a gardener might walk among his plants. [. . .] Wemmick [. . .] looked at them while in conference, as if he were taking particular notice of the advance they had made, since last observed, towards coming out in full blow at their trial.
>
> (Dickens 1962: II, xxxii, 266)

Attributing the figurative language to the appropriate people in the examples given above poses few problems. But things look different when the figures of speech transcend their micro-context and become relevant for the entire work. In Dickens's novel *Little Dorrit* (1855–57), the prison metaphor is extended to cover so many areas that ultimately all the characters in the novel seem to be prisoners; one could even say that life itself is a prison. This impression derives from the accumulation of metaphors of imprisonment that we find throughout the book. For example, London and the house in which Mrs Clennam lives are described as prisons (Chapter iii). Yet the pervasive prison metaphor is also the result of a metonymical juxtaposition of prison-like settings and situations within the novel. There are only two genuine prisons; yet Mrs Clennam's house, her life, the Merdles' marriage, the excessive care lavished on their daughter by the Meagles family, Tattycoram's relationship to Mr and Mrs Meagles and to Miss Wade – these are all implicitly portrayed as metaphorical prisons, too. In such a situation (which would also apply to other novels like Richardson's *Clarissa*, 1747–48), the prison metaphor turns out to be the structuring principle of the novel and thus must be a strategy employed by the implied author. The metaphor assumes narratological importance because it creates, on the linguistic level of the whole text, powerful and all-embracing structures which not only feature in the discourse but are also crucial to the overall symbolism of the novel, operating at the level of the story (plot and setting) as well.

Narratological approaches to attributing metaphors

The point at issue here is the significance of this for narrative theory. On the one hand, macro-structural metaphors in texts can be seen as clues to the nature of the implied author (and so to that of the whole text as a construct). Most of the features that are located at this level are to do with story and plot: character grouping, focalization through one character, etc. If we take the relationship of the narrator to the characters into account, however, we begin to bring in the level of style.

At this point, I should like to suggest that the occurrence of metaphors in the discourse of the narrator be included in narrative theory as a separate, optional level, much in the same way as the question of gender is. Metaphor can, but need not, be narratologically relevant. It is a well-known fact that certain authors and works are particularly 'metaphorical'. In the case of literature in English this would certainly be Dickens, in German, Elfriede Jelinek and in French, Honoré de Balzac. A comprehensive account of the distribution and development of the use of simile, metaphor and metonymy in the English, German and French novel would be highly desirable but has not been attempted yet. So far only some individual authors' predilection for metaphor has been analysed.

Having dealt with metaphor, I should now like to add a few words about metonymy. Recent (cognitive) studies of metaphor show that metaphor and metonymy are closely related phenomena (Kövecses/Radden 1998, Barcelona 2000). Every image generates a series of associations which can be traced back to metonymical aspects of the source domain (for instance, the growing and flowering of plants in the extract from *Great Expectations* cited above to refer to the 'development' of the prisoners in custody). Just as a plate conjures up images of cutlery, a tablecloth or food – all objects belonging to the same cognitive frame – flowers evoke the ideas of buds and blossoms, thorns, watering cans and so on. Metonymy focuses on a prominent feature of a whole (sail for boat, steering wheel for car) and these striking features (cognitive scientists use the notion of *salience* here) also serve as starting points for fully worked-out metaphors. Over and above this, metonymy seems to have a structural function as Michael Riffaterre points out in connection with the English novelist Trollope (Riffaterre 1982). The correlation of behavioural patterns with psychological states, in Riffaterre's example, is related to the symbolization process involved in metonymy. According to him, the behaviour of skinflint old ladies who are anything but generous when they entertain visitors symbolizes their intellectual desiccation, their narrow-mindedness and their insensitivity, but it also stands for village life, which stifles all emotions and represents spiritual impoverishment, a first step on the way to (spiritual) death.

The standard treatments of the relationship of metaphor to metonymy are, of course, Roman Jakobson's superb essay 'Two Aspects of Language' (1956) and, later, David Lodge's contribution in his book *The Modes of Modern Writing* (1977). Both authors argue in favour of a strict division, a radical differentiation between metaphor and metonymy. Lodge maintains that metonymy is the norm in prose, whereas poetry is predominantly metaphorical. However, as I have shown in the preceding paragraph, metonyms are transmuted into metaphors, at least in the work of a number of authors, just as in poetry, according to Jakobson, the paradigmatic axis is projected onto the syntagmatic one. Furthermore, many novels are predominantly metaphorical, or at least metaphor is as strongly present in them as metonymy is.

In recent work on metaphor, many visual metaphors have been examined and discussed. Visual metaphors, for example in cartoons or in advertising posters on billboards (Forceville 1996), are often characterized by the fact that the target domain (tenor) is present as a visual image, but the source domain (vehicle) is in the caption or slogan: in other words, it is linguistic. An image can also function as a source domain. For instance, a picture of two scorpions squabbling over their prey captioned 'Pillow talk' is an ironic depiction of problematic personal relationships (marriage is like a battle between scorpions). Yet this is an anthropomorphic metaphor, drawn from the animal kingdom (the mating of scorpions). As Jan Alber shows in his dissertation (Alber 2007), many cinematic depictions of two parallel but incompatible situations (one usually diegetic and the other non-diegetic[5]) have metaphorical connotations. A sequence showing workers streaming into the subway followed by another showing images of a flock of sheep being herded along suggests that the workers are sheep that

Metonymy (margin note)

Metaphor versus metonymy (margin note)

are to be 'slaughtered' (exploited) in a factory (cf. Chaplin's *Modern Times*, 1936). It would be worthwhile investigating whether such strategies are also employed in novels. It could, for instance, be argued that novels like *Little Dorrit*, which feature a series of portrayals of prison-like rooms and situations, depict the world as a kind of prison by means of metonymy rather than by the use of a metaphor in which several disparate, but in this case comparable, spaces or situations are juxtaposed. In such cases, as in the diagram to Jakobson's explanation of the poetic function, similarity and equivalence are projected onto the axis of contiguity (sequence of scenes). All the scenes described in *Little Dorrit* form part of an overall picture of London, so one could say that there is a network of underlying metonymical references.

Besides metaphor and metonymy, simile should also be taken into consideration. For instance, in Chapter 11 we will discuss a passage from Fielding's *Joseph Andrews* in which Mrs Slipslop tries to seduce poor Joseph and is compared to a tiger or pike pouncing upon its prey. Although similes are better known from the genre of the epic, some novelists are very adept at employing simile for the purpose of characterization or of describing a situation in a memorable phrase that echoes throughout the text. Above we looked at the passage from *Great Expectations* in which Wemmick 'walked among the prisoners, *much as a gardener might walk among his plants*' (II, xxxii, 266). 'Much as' introduces an extended simile which evolves into a straightforward metaphor ('coming out in full blow at their trial'). Equally memorable is a passage from Charlotte Brontë's *Shirley*, in which the heroine is contrasted with her stupid and boring companions who cherish etiquette and cannot develop an idea of their own:

> On leaving the instrument, she [Shirley] went to the fire [. . .] The Misses Sympson and the Misses Nunnely looked upon her, as quiet poultry might look on an egret, an ibis, or any other strange fowl. What made her sing so? They never sang so. Was it proper to sing with such expression, with such originality – so unlike a schoolgirl? Decidedly not: it was strange; it was unusual. What was strange must be wrong; what was unusual must be improper. Shirley was judged.
>
> (2006: xxxi, 510)

The striking image converts Shirley into an exotic bird looked at with envious disfavour by common hens. Brontë's sarcastic narrator underlines the mental distance between these two categories of fowl by adding the hens' comments on Shirley's superior singing in free indirect discourse, reducing the hen-centred world view to ridicule.

In sum, one could say that metaphor (metonymy, simile) can play a decisive role in structuring novels and that, consequently, the inclusion of imagery into narrative typologies is well worth considering. Nevertheless, it may well be difficult to distinguish the specifically narrative qualities of such metaphorical patterns from more general ones that are not actually exploited for narrative purposes. Perhaps these aspects of novels and dramas would best be treated as a sub-set of lyrical structures in narrative which may or may not be activated by individual writers.

Conceptual networks

In addition to the use of metaphor, in many novels (but also plays) we come across a strategy of repeating keywords and word fields for structuring purposes. To the best of my knowledge, there is no technical term for this. I have demonstrated the existence of such networks of words and word fields in Sherwood Anderson's *Winesburg, Ohio* (1919), William Godwin's *Caleb Williams* (1794) and Eugene O'Neill's *A Touch of the Poet* (1957) (Fludernik 1988, 1990, 2001). In texts like these, certain key words keep recurring, like leitmotifs. As a result of the associations which they conjure up in the context of characters and plot, they become symbols which suggest connections and arguments at a higher level. The network of references to the sublime in Godwin's political novel *Caleb Williams* will serve as an example here. Despite all the usual very positive connotations of sublimity, all in all, in this novel, the references to the sublime suggest that both Lord Falkland and his servant Caleb Williams have been dazzled by its false glamour, and that despotism is the political correlate of an aesthetic built upon it. The web of recurring mentions and repetitions gives rise to a kind of symbolism, which, in my view, should definitely not be seen as metaphorical. Rather it functions metonymically: a sequence of key ideas is associated with particular characters and situations. At the same time, there is some similarity to metaphor, in so far as these ideas are correlated syntagmatically, are compared and then create meaning equivalences (but also contrasts). Similarities are to be expected as the ideas stem from word repetitions or are drawn from the same word fields. They are not exploited to create sensory impressions but are used, instead, to generate arguments, contrasts and interpretations: in other words a conceptual network of meaning is created on a higher level.

Here, too, the definitive status of these conceptual networks cannot be determined from a theoretical point of view before the extent of their use in various national literatures has been investigated. Is this a phenomenon which only occurs in a handful of texts in English, or can we find something comparable in a number of national literatures, and in works from various periods?

With my remarks on language and style, I have sought to incorporate these levels of analysis into narratology, while at the same time not regarding them as constitutive since they play an important role in all literary as well as non-literary and non-fictional texts. Still, the specific aspects of language and style described in this chapter are of special relevance for narratology, which would seem to justify including a consideration of stylistic questions in the discussion of narrative theory.

Summary

8 Thoughts, Feelings and the Unconscious

Characters and
their inner lives

In the previous chapter, we looked at the discourse of narrators and characters. Even more important than their spoken or written utterances, however, are their minds, their thoughts, their reflections, their feelings and desires. In her classic study written in 1957 (*The Logic of Literature*, 1993), Käte Hamburger pointed out that fictional narratives alone offer a perspective on the mental world of the actants – only fiction can successfully represent each person's inner world. Since 1957, interior monologue (Erwin R. Steinberg 1969), free indirect discourse (Güntner Steinberg 1971) and the representation of consciousness in general (Cohn 1978, Palmer 2004) have been the focus of studies that are concerned with the various ways in which thought can be expressed through the medium of language.

Käte Hamburger

Hamburger based her argument on the theory of language of Karl Bühler (1934) and, more specifically, on his theory of deixis. The important point here is that Bühler's work allows one to identify linguistic signals of subjectivity (i.e. the deictic centre of the individual located in the here and now) in free indirect discourse. This kind of speech representation (for example: *God, he loathed that slimy fellow* or *For Chrissake, now the guy had spilled the beans!*) retains expressive vocabulary and word forms which reflect the perspective of the characters whose thoughts or words are being reported. Hamburger's example sentence: 'Tomorrow was Christmas' (Hamburger 1993: 72) shows us – from little Hanno Buddenbrook's perspective – how impatiently he is looking forward to the events of that day ('Morgen kam der dritte Weihnachtsabend an die Reihe [. . .]', Mann 1991: 547; 'Next day [lit. 'tomorrow'] there would be a third Christmas party [. . .]' – Mann 1984: 442). Deictically speaking, *morgen* ('tomorrow') refers to Hanno's time frame, not that of the narrator or reader. Consequently, as we share the point of view of the child, we become keenly aware of his excitement. But even more important here is the fact that literature routinely provides insight into the hearts and minds of characters, in contrast to real life, where we can only speculate about the thoughts and motives of our fellow human beings. Literary texts, then, offer us glimpses into other people's psyches: thus characters become as familiar to us as we are to ourselves. The sympathy we feel towards the protagonists in novels is, to a large extent, the result of this magical ability of narrative discourse to grant us insight into characters' inner worlds.

Consciousness
and motivation

Admittedly, not every story provides us with this privilege. This is only an option which is not always taken up. On the other hand, literature is not the only source of insights into the minds of others. As discourse analysts like Deborah Tannen and Wallace Chafe have shown, in conversational narrative it is quite normal to attribute thoughts to the people who feature in the stories although the first-person narrator cannot, of course, know what they are really thinking (e.g. Chafe 1980, Tannen 1984). What we have here is a verbal rendering of thoughts which have been deduced from outward signs like the body language or the facial expressions of the protagonists. There are parallels here with film and drama, where feelings are usually hinted at indirectly by means of facial expressions, postures and gestures on the part of the actors. Be that as it may, the similarities between conversational narrative and the novel lead us to conclude that the thoughts and feelings of the characters have an important role to play in narratives: they help to put across the intentions and underlying motives of the actants as well as their reactions to outside influences. There is a very good reason why E. M. Forster's example of a plot – *The king died and then the queen died of grief* – is a sentence in which the key element that transforms the *story* (sequence of events) into a narrative or *plot* consists in pointing out the connection between the events; it can be gathered from the queen's emotional response to what happens. Our sympathy for the queen in her grief makes the story worth reading; we can understand the how and why of what happened. In other action-oriented stories, an understanding of the intentions or expectations of the protagonists will enable the reader to interpret the story in a more rewarding way.

In history books (with the exception of traditional histories that concentrate solely on political decisions, and here, more specifically, on the person of the king or emperor responsible for those decisions), the world of the thoughts and feelings of the actants is scarcely significant. Not only anthropomorphic actants, but also tribes or ethnic groups, states, institutions and other trans-human or non-human entities function as decision-makers, or feature as quasi-protagonists or 'quasi-characters' in historical accounts (Ricoeur 1988: I 182). This means that consciousness does not play a major role at the story level. On the level of the narrative discourse, too, academic history eliminates all traces of individuality, especially the personal feelings and opinions of the author. In the novel and in conversational narrative, on the other hand, the emotions and opinions of the narrator are revealed which, in some novels, leads to the phenomenon of 'secondary mimesis' (Nünning 2001) whereby the narrator comes across to the reader in the same finely differentiated way as the actants. After a careful consideration of all these points, Monika Fludernik in *Towards a 'Natural' Narratology* (1996) suggested taking consciousness as the central defining feature of narrativity and excluding academic history from the group of genres classified as narratives. *Historiography*

As well as considering the centrality of consciousness to narrative, and in particular to narrative fiction, narratology has mainly concerned itself with the presentation of thought in the novel. This topic has been of perennial interest in narrative theory because of the rise of the so-called *novel of consciousness* (Ger. *Bewusstseinsroman*[1]), which marked a significant step in the history of the novel as a genre. This type of narrative emerged at the end of the nineteenth century and reached its zenith in the works of literary modernists like Virgina Woolf, James Joyce, Marcel Proust, Franz Kafka and Hermann Broch. Narratologically speaking, the novel of consciousness can be allocated to Stanzel's category of figural narrative or the so-called reflector mode (cf. Stanzel 2001: 190–96). Genette and other theorists see the novel of consciousness as the purest example of internal focalization. That narratologists focus on the novel of consciousness is understandable, but this fact has obscured other important aspects of the representation of thought in the novel as a genre. *The novel of consciousness*

As Alan Palmer noted in his much acclaimed book *Fictional Minds* (2004), narrato-logy has fallen into the trap of assuming that thought is always verbal. An overemphasis *Psycho-narration* on the modernist novel and a concentration on interior monologue and free indirect discourse have obscured the fact that the great majority of representations of thought in novels are not formulated as free indirect discourse or interior monologue, but take the form of *psycho-narration* (or *thought report*) (Fr. *discours intérieur narrativisé* [Genette]; Ger. *Gedankenbericht*). Psycho-narration is extremely flexible and totally independent of the verbal content of the mind being represented; it lends itself extremely well to rendering characters' feelings, fears, wishes and motivations. Interior monologue and free indirect discourse, on the other hand, tend to privilege verbal structures.

> The thirst for action, for power and success, the longing to force fortune to her knees, sprang up quick and passionate in his eyes. He felt all the world looking at him expectantly, questioning if he would know how to command prestige for the firm and the family and protect its name.
>
> (*Buddenbrooks*; Mann 1984: V, I, 212)

In this extract, Thomas's expectations, his personal propensities and his feelings are described for us, but they obviously do not exist in his head in verbal form, or do so only hazily. Note the preponderance of nouns and verbs of emotion and cogitation: 'The thirst for action ... the longing ... sprang up ... He felt'. Such passages can often describe characters' inner mental states and processes much more compellingly than would be the case with interior monologue. Large stretches of Trollope's, George Eliot's or Hardy's work comprise various manifestations of psycho-narration, and even Virginia Woolf's *Mrs Dalloway* features more psycho-narration than interior monologue.

Quoted internal speech and interior monologue

> The Frau Consul took the announcement with discreet calm; Tony put on an adorable expression of pride and ignorance, and then could not repress an anxious mental query: Is that a lot? Are we very rich now?
>
> (*Buddenbrooks*; Mann 1984: V, I, 211)

In the above extract, Tony's internal speech is clearly marked as fictive; a facial expression is described in verbal form, and these words are then presented as being what a character thinks. Later, Thomas Buddenbrook's struggle as his death draws near is told in free indirect discourse, alternating with quoted interior monologue, which results in a certain artificiality, deriving from the implied verbalization of the ideas:

> And behold, it was as though the darkness were rent from before his eyes, as if the whole wall of the night parted wide and disclosed an immeasurable, boundless prospect of light. 'I shall live!' said Thomas Buddenbrook, almost aloud, and felt his breast shaken with inward sobs. 'This is the revelation: that I shall live! For *it* will live and that this *it* is not I is only an illusion, an error which death will make plain. This is it, this is it! Why?' But at this question the night closed in again upon him. He saw, he knew, he understood, no least particle more; he let himself sink deep in the pillows, quite blinded and exhausted by the morsel of truth which had been vouchsafed.
>
> (X, v, 526; original emphasis)

Quoted and verbalized interior monologue predominates in this passage, with a shift to psycho-narration occurring towards the end: 'He saw, he knew'. It is characterized by the use of full sentences with verbs in the first person singular and the present tense. When the surrounding narrative discourse is in the third person and the past tense, internal speech stands out sharply. Most passages of interior monologue, however, are less formal. Indeed, they attempt to reflect the feel of the character's incoherent musings and often represent snatches of thoughts, visual impressions or spontaneous reactions in incomplete sentences, random words and phrases or in repetitious language. Formally, these extracts from the character's mind are unquoted, hence: free interior monologue. If the mental world is rendered as a flow of thoughts and associations, with one incomplete sentence tumbling out after the other, then the interior monologue turns into a so-called *stream of consciousness* (Fr. *courant de conscience*; Ger. *Bewusstseinsstrom*). Such a stream of consciousness can, at least as far as the form is concerned, blend in with free indirect thought. Sentence fragments may be treated as interior monologue (direct speech) or regarded as part of an adjoining stretch of free indirect speech.

Interior monologue may also contain traces of non-verbal thought. While more formal interior monologue uses the first-person pronoun and finite verbs in the present tense,

> Verbal and pre-verbal thought

> He [Stephen] lifted his feet up from the suck [of the sand] and turned back by the mole of boulders. Take all, keep all. *My* soul *walks with me*, form of forms. [...]
> The flood *is following me. I can watch* it flow past from here.
> (*Ulysses* iii; Joyce 1993: 37; my emphasis)

in *Ulysses* James Joyce conducts more radical experiments with the form of the interior monologue, especially in his representation of the thoughts of Leopold Bloom and his wife, Molly. He eschews full sentences with finite verbs in favour of incomplete, often verbless syntagms which simulate Bloom's mental leaps as he associates ideas:

> Hynes jotting down something in his notebook. Ah, the names. But he knows them all. No: coming to me.
> — I am just taking the names, Hynes said below his breath. What is your christian name? I'm not sure.
> (vi, 92)

In this example, Bloom's impressions and speculations are confirmed by Hynes's remarks. Note also the phrase 'Take all, keep all' in Stephen's musings in the previous quote. In the next extract, Bloom helps a blind piano tuner across the road. Although many of the half-sentences could well be verbalized in his mind, the sequence of syntagms mainly serves to express the erratic nature of his perception of reality and places less emphasis on the verbal as such than on his capacity for making associations:

> He touched the thin elbow gently: then took the limp seeing hand to guide it forward.
> Say something to him. Better not do the condescending. They mistrust what you tell them. Pass a common remark:
> — The rain kept off.

No answer.

Stains on his coat. Slobbers his food, I suppose. Tastes all different for him. Have to be spoonfed first. Like a child's hand his hand. Like Milly's was. Sensitive. Sizing me up I daresay from my hand. Wonder if he has a name. Van. Keep his cane clear of the horse's legs: tired drudge get his doze. That's right. Clear. Behind a bull: in front of a horse.

— Thanks, sir.

Knows I'm a man. Voice.

(viii, 148)

At the beginning of this extract it seems as if we were reading a recording of Bloom's thoughts; as the passage goes on (from "stains on his coat"), however, visual impressions, intuitions and subconscious premonitions are presented which Bloom would never have formulated in this way.

Molly Bloom: stream of consciousness

In his presentation of Molly Bloom's stream of consciousness, Joyce tries dispensing with punctuation altogether, in order to suggest a non-stop torrent of colloquial speech, which in its turn simulates the flow of Molly's thoughts. In this case, the monologue is extremely verbal; in spite of this, the rapid sequence of sentences captures the buoyant yet vulgar nature of Molly's mind to perfection. It gives us access to Molly's way of thinking:

Mulveys was the first when I was in bed that morning and Mrs Rubio brought it in with the coffee she stood there standing when I asked her to hand me and I pointing at them I couldnt think of the word a hairpin to open it with ah horquilla disobliging old thing and it staring her in the face with her switch of false hair on her and vain about her appearance ugly as she was near 80 or a 100 her face a mass of wrinkles with all her religion domineering . . .

(xviii, 624)

Molly's run-on sentences reflect her scatterbrained, illogical and spontaneous stream of consciousness; her easy and loose, yet very humorous view of the world, her energy and vitality.

Three basic categories of thought representation

To sum up briefly and concisely: we can make a formal distinction between

a) a quasi-direct representation of thoughts in *free direct thought*, also referred to as *interior monologue* (Fr. *monologue intérieur*; Ger. *direkte innere Rede/innerer Monolog*), which is characterized by the use of first-person pronouns and finite verbs (present tense);

b) the representation of thought in *free indirect thought/discourse*[2] (Fr. *discours indirecte libre*; Ger. *erlebte Rede*): *What a shame she could not keep the cat. She'd so loved to stroke it*; and

c) *psycho-narration* (Fr. *discours narrativisé* [Genette]; Ger. *Gedankenbericht*), in which the verbs and nouns used indicate mental processes: *His head was buzzing with ideas; She weighed up her options.*

When it comes to content, this formal tripartite categorization on a scale from directness to indirectness is undermined by the distinction between verbal and non-verbal mind content. This provides for an alternative sliding scale that does not completely coincide with the formal scale from narratorial language to characters' internal discourse. Even from the point of view of grammar, the division into three formal categories is by no means clear and unambiguous. Exclamations and other syntagms without finite verbs, or without any kind of verb, are often found in both interior monologue and free indirect speech (cf. Bloom's reaction to the blind man quoted above). Traditionally such passages have been assigned to interior monologue or attributed to the adjoining stretch of free indirect speech (as we saw in Thomas Buddenbrook's deathbed scene). Here is another instance of free indirect speech which is laced with comments and sentence fragments ('a real mistress, in fine'):

> Léon, sur le trottoir, continuait à marcher. Elle le suivait jusqu'à l'hôtel; il montait, il ouvrait la porte, il entrait . . . Quelle étreinte! [. . .]
>
> Il savourait pour la première fois l'inexprimable délicatesse des élégances féminines. Jamais il n'avait rencontré cette grâce de langage, cette réserve du vêtement, ces poses de colombe assoupie. Il admirait l'exaltation de son âme et les dentelles de sa jupe. D'ailleurs, n'était-ce pas *une femme du monde*, et une femme mariée! *une vraie maîtresse enfin?*
>
> > (*Madame Bovary* III,v; Flaubert 1972: 313–14;
> > italics original emphasis; bold italics my emphasis)

> Leon walked along the pavement. She followed him to the hotel. He went up, opened the door, entered – What an embrace! [. . .]
>
> He for the first time enjoyed the inexpressible delicacy of feminine refinements. He had never met this grace of language, this reserve of clothing, these poses of the weary dove. He admired the exaltation of her soul and the lace on her petticoat. Besides, was she not "a lady" and a married woman – a real mistress, in fine?
>
> > (http://www.online-literature.com/gustave-flaubert/madame-bovary/28/)

From 'He had never met' on this can be categorized as free indirect speech. The final sentence is particularly expressive, employing several locutions and ideas directly ascribable to Léon's world view.

Distinguishing the various forms is more difficult when the narrative discourse is in the present tense and even more so when we are dealing with a first-person narrative in the present tense. Döblin's *Berlin Alexanderplatz* (1961/1980) is a third-person narrative – for which we can be grateful – but written in the present tense. The fact that Franz Biberkopf 'infiltrates' the narrative discourse with his Berlin dialect makes it much more difficult to pick up on the stylistic difference between narration and thought presentation:

First-person narrative

> And when Franz has pushed his way through the crowd, till he gets up in front, who do you think is fighting there with whom? *Two lads, why, he knows 'em, they're Pum's boys. Now what do ye think o' that!* Bang, the tall fellow's got the other in a stranglehold; bing, he's got him eating dirt. Boy, you let that fellow kick you around like that; why, you're no good. What's this pushin' here, heh there! Oh baby, the cops, the bulls. Cheese it, the cops, the cops, beat it. Two coppers in their rain-capes are making their way through the crowd. Wow! one of the pugilists is on his feet, in the crowd, off he flies. The other one, the tall chap, he can't get up right away, he's got a punch in the ribs, and a good one, too. At that moment Franz

Mixture of forms

pushes himself through, right to the front. Why, we can't leave that man lying around here, what a bunch of boobs, nobody touches 'im! So Franz takes him under his arms, and walks right into the crowd. The cops are looking around. 'What's the matter here?' 'Two guys've been fighting.' 'Get a move on, now beat it!' They're always bawling and just the same they're always a day too late. Move on, we're going all right, sergeant, only don't get yourself all worked up.

(*Berlin Alexanderplatz* V; Döblin 2004: 163–4; italics added for FID passage)

Und wie Franz sich durchgedrängelt hat bis vorn, wer haut sich da mit wem? *Zwei Jungen, die kennt er doch, das sich welche von Pums. Wat sagste nu.* Klatsch hat der Lange den im Schwitzkasten, klatsch schmeißt er ihn in den Matsch. Junge, von dem läßt du dir schmeißen; bist ja minderwertig. Wat soll denn det Gedrängele, Sie. Au weih, Polente, die Grünen. Polente, Polente, verdrückt euch. Die Regencapes über, schieben sich zwei Grüne durch den Haufen. Schubb, ist der eine Ringer auf, im Gedränge, macht Beine. Der zweite, der Lange, der kommt nicht gleich hoch, der hat ne Wucht in die Rippen gekriegt, aber ne ordentliche. Da pufft sich Franz ganz vorn durch. Werd doch den Mann nicht liegen lassen, ist das ne Gesellschaft, keener faßt an. Und schon hat Franz ihn unter die Arme und rin zwischen die Leute. Die Grünen suchen. "Was is hier los?" "Haben sich zwei gehauen." "Auseinandergehen, weitergehen." Die krähen und kommen immer einen Posttag zu spät. Weitergehen, machen wir schon, Herr Wachtmeister, nur keene überflüssige Uffregung.

(*Berlin Alexanderplatz*; Döblin 1980: V, 223; italics added for FID passage)

The passage is a mixture of psycho-narration, direct speech, free indirect speech and interior monologue. This makes it difficult to distinguish the various characters from each other or to decide what is said and what is only thought. Thus, the clause 'who do you think is fighting there with whom?' can be something that Franz is thinking (direct thought) or what the crowd is saying (collective direct speech), or even collective direct speech echoed in Franz's mind. After the passage of free indirect discourse – clearly marked by the 'shift' from *I* to *he* – the continuation of the text can be an exclamation which is still part of Franz's internal thought, but it might also be anybody's utterance. (I have taken it to still be part of Franz's free indirect discourse.) This is followed by Franz's narrated perception of the fight, but could also be what everybody perceives, or the narrator's emotive and empathetic depiction of events. Further down in the passage, the questions and orders on the parts of the police and the crowd's various responses (first in direct citation, later without quotation marks) are all juxtaposed with the narrative report and with Franz's thoughts before he rescues the pugilist ('Why, we can't leave that man . . .') and his sarcastic remarks (internal?) about the police always arriving too late.

First-person present tense narratives are especially tricky. They make it often impossible to recognize whether a passage represents the narrator's comment, a character's interior monologue or free indirect discourse:

But in some way I do feel that the house has suddenly become a glamorous, glittering place, a place where unexpected, fascinating people could turn up at any moment. [. . .] None of this happens, but for some reason I feel as if it might.

And where do I fit in to all this?

('The Russian'; Seymour-Ure 1998: 108; my emphasis)

Is the final question spoken by Anna, is the narrating self speaking? Or is this what she is thinking at that moment (as experiencing self) in free indirect discourse (or in interior monologue)? In the following passage from Duncan McLaren's 'Soap Circle', internal focalization predominates so that the italicised clauses can more confidently be read as free indirect discourse:

> Back in the gallery, a second glance at the list of exhibits tells me that the eighteen soaps refer to the artist's order of washing himself in London on 23 March 1994. I'm now doubting if I went along the row in the right direction. *Sure enough, the reverse order makes more sense given the effect of gravity on soap water. So:* ARMPITS, CHEST, BELLY, PRICK, BALLS, ARSE, BACK, HANDS . . . I stop at hands as before, puzzled.
>
> I can still smell vinegar. I raise my left hand to my nose and confirm the scent of acetic acid. How come? . . . I suppose the handle of my bag and the pocket of my jacket were contaminated by the vinegar before I washed my hands, and that contact with handle and pocket subsequent to the wash has . . . *oh, it's obvious enough. So what I have to do now is return to the loo and soap my hands again, as well as washing the tainted parts of jacket and bag. Wrong. After all I haven't been kicking up dust for a week along the Rio Grande; I am relatively clean and the best thing would be simply to move on to a different part of the building and another artist altogether.*
>
> (1997: 117; my emphasis)

The experiencing self in these passages is clearly puzzling over the art installation (first paragraph) and debating with herself how to deal with the smelly fingers and bag. Since the highlighted passages are not a realistic rendering of quoted interior monologue, they are a good candidate for the first-person narrator's echoing of her ongoing thoughts in first-person present-tense free indirect discourse.

What is true of speech representation also holds true for the representation of thought: a definitive categorization of stretches of text is only possible if the narrative is realistic. If the narrative discourse adopts the style of the protagonists, as in Anthony Burgess's *A Clockwork Orange* (1962) or as in the paragraph from Döblin cited above, there will be many grey areas which cannot be identified unambiguously as either narrative discourse or speech representation or representation of thought.

Besides the three categories of thought representation (psycho-narration, free indirect speech, interior monologue), narratological research has also introduced the term *mind style* (Ger. *Mentalstil*). This concept characterizes a way of writing in which the protagonists' use of specific lexical and syntactic features suggests a characteristic way of thinking which is revealed when their minds and mental processes are represented in the text. This can best be observed with a character like the mentally retarded Benji in William Faulkner's *The Sound and the Fury* (1956), or in a novel like William Golding's *The Inheritors* (1955), which is told from the point of view of a Neanderthal. In both novels we can find typical syntactic and lexical deviations and ambiguous references which can be attributed to the limited mental horizons of the protagonists.[3]

Mind style

To round off this chapter, I want to take a look at that part of the human mind which, since Freud, has been termed 'the subconscious' and which it is not easy to accommodate in a discussion of the representation of thought. There is general agreement

Representing the subconscious

that what is subconscious cannot be verbalized although, according to Freud, it does include verbal elements. Lacan even suggests that the subconscious may be structured in the same way as language (Lacan 1977: 147). In point of fact, representing the subconscious (or unconscious) seems to be beyond the scope of narrative discourse. On the other hand, we do find a great many psychoanalytic interpretations of narrative texts, dealing with the unrecognized and unacknowledged wishes, impulses and obsessions of narrators and characters. Typical subjects for psychoanalytic interpretation are unreliable narrators, for example, like the obviously insane first-person narrators in Edgar Allan Poe's 'The Black Cat' or 'The Tell-Tale Heart'. Their insanity is clearly discernible in the discourse strategies they use: protestations, unnecessary repetitions and obfuscation. The behaviour of characters in novels can also be scrutinized for symptoms of unacknowledged mental states. Contradictions between actual behaviour and expressed intentions, usually discussed under the heading of hypocrisy, are often found in satirical texts, and neatly demonstrate the breakdown of the continuum presumed to exist between thought and deed.

The subconscious (or unconscious) also plays an important role in non-satirical contexts in cases where characters are not aware of (or ignorant of) the true reasons for their behaving as they do. Emma Bovary in Flaubert's famous novel is a good example of this. She longs to break out of her monotonous life as a housewife, to escape from the provincial life that holds her prisoner. The discourse of romantic love used by her and by her seducers is clearly escapist and feeds off illusions. The reader recognizes the narrow confines of Emma's life and can understand that she is frustrated, but s/he will also see that Emma is deluding herself, that she is letting herself be deceived by Léon and that, above all, she ignores or suppresses the real problem: her unrealistic expectations of the world in which she lives. Which means that she will never find a solution. Emma's actions always achieve the opposite of what she intended, something that even holds true for her suicide at the end of the novel.

Narratology and psychoanalysis

Psychoanalytic methods have only influenced narrative theory in the analysis of reader response, and then only in so far as the act of reading is seen as *jouissance* (pleasure, delight) and the ins and outs of the plot and its unravelling as a metaphorical equivalent to sexual excitement and satisfaction (Chambers 1984; Brooks 1985). Not only is this model strongly male-oriented and, to stick with the metaphor, not only does it take no account of the pleasure women might derive from the act of reading (Winnett 1990) but, in concentrating on reading as an act of love, it obscures the fact that psychoanalytic interpretations would require a more systematic narratological analysis. Admittedly, it is the case that psychoanalytic as well as post-colonial readings of texts regard the surface level of the text or the plot as merely symptomatic of concealed ideological or psychological phenomena. This is why narrative theory seems to want to have nothing to do with such strategies of interpretation; it investigates precisely that part of a narrative (novel), namely the text itself, which such methods marginalize. Yet, psychological approaches can be of particular interest as they prioritize the need, given a realistic frame of reference, to make a careful distinction between story level and the level of the narrative discourse. (What actually happens on the plot level, and what do the narrator and the character perceive to happen or believe happens?) Generally speaking, psychoanalytic or post-colonial approaches draw attention to the fact that this supposedly realistic distinction between story and discourse is only valid in limited areas and circumstances. At the level of plot or narrative discourse, psychological phenomena on the story level are accessible only indirectly. Furthermore, a psychologically unstable first-person narrator may undermine the normal continuum we automatically assume to exist between narrating and experiencing selves.

Thus psychoanalytic interpretations show that even texts which seem totally 'realistic' contain the germ of postmodern ambiguity, uncertainty and variability. The fantastic anticipates many postmodern schemata of uncertainty. According to Todorov (1970), the fantastic does not lend itself to being defined as an exclusively mental (imagined) or an exclusively supernatural phenomenon; this ambivalence is seen as a key feature of the text. Masters of such uncertainty are, for instance, Henry James with stories like 'The Turn of the Screw' (1898) or Joseph Conrad in 'The Secret Sharer' (1912). In the former, the first-person narrative allows for the possibility that the uncanny is not necessarily the result of supernatural forces, that everything was only an illusion conjured up by a mentally unstable protagonist. It is precisely the frame story refracting the governess's tale through the prism of Douglas's introduction and the peripheral first-person narrator's scene-setting of Douglas's storytelling that illustrate the modern vs. postmodern wavering between epistemological and ontological dominance (see McHale 1987).[4] So, as it turns out, there is a direct link between the representation of the subconscious and of the fantastic and the problems of illusion and authenticity discussed in Chapter 6.

9 Narrative Typologies

Structuralist
narratology

Classical narratological theories are concerned with universal aspects of narrative, with the basic options available and with narrative instances and categories which can be found in (almost) all texts. The structuralist roots of contemporary narratology show up clearly in the predominance of binary oppositional pairs: deep/surface structure; competence/performance; first-person/third-person narrative; extra-/intradiegetic, and so forth. But in addition to this, a structuralist approach presupposes a system within which these various options and categories can be positioned. Many early works on narrative theory simply took one or two distinctions as being constitutive of narrative, but for Franz Karl Stanzel and Gérard Genette the question was rather how to reconcile the many different aspects within one coherent system, and how these same aspects combine and interweave in individual narrative texts. These scholars, like Chatman, Prince, Lanser and Bal who came after them, were in search of a descriptive model which would embrace the whole range of options available to the storyteller. They proposed taxonomies (or typologies) consisting of categories into which individual narratives could be fitted. A typology is just such a schema or framework which encompasses a number of types, arranged on systematic principles. The individual texts, in linguistic terms, would then be *tokens*, in other words concrete manifestations of the abstract, theoretical *types*. The two best-known narratologists, Stanzel and Genette, approached this problem in very different ways. In the 1950s, Stanzel, following in the footsteps of German scholars, constructed a 'morphology' of texts, while, in the 1970s, Genette had recourse to an abstract, metaphorical structure, that of grammar.

Stanzel and the
morphological
tradition

Stanzel's morphological model goes back to Goethe and Robert Petsch (Darby 2001; Herman 2005) in that he takes botany and the evolution of plants as his starting point. He postulates three types of narrative, three *narrative situations*, as he calls them, which are organically designed rather than being a random combination of features: *first-person narrative*, *authorial narrative* and *figural narrative*. In each of these three basic types we find various aspects of narrative combining with each other in different ways. First-person narrative and authorial narrative both throw into relief their narrator figures, featuring a distinct teller persona, but the first-person narrator also figures as a protagonist in the story whereas the authorial narrator stands apart from, as if above, the world of the characters. An authorial narrator has an external perspective on the events of the story while the perspective of a figural narrative is an internal one. The organic design of Stanzel's narrative situations also becomes apparent in the so-called typological circle (Ger. *Typenkreis*), around which the narrative situations are arranged (see Figure 9.1). The three narrative situations 'naturally' morph into one another. We shall return to the idea that this morphological approach is actually a concealed metaphor later in this chapter.

Gérard Genette's *Discours du récit* (1972), one part of a three-volume study of rhetoric, *Figures I–III*, situates his insights into narrative, and in particular his ideas about Marcel Proust's *A la recherche du temps perdu* (1913–27), within a rhetorical-grammatical framework. Genette distinguishes between *voix*, *mode* and *temps*, three categories which have to do with the verb. In Latin grammar, verbs are inflected in these three ways: *voice* (active, passive), *mood* (indicative, subjunctive) and *tense* (present, past, future, etc.). Many subsequent narrative typologies start out from narrative levels or with quasi-ontological/existential assumptions (like *setting* or *characters*). Not so Genette, who lists the three levels of *récit* (*narrative*) as story, discourse and narration (cf. Chapter 1) and then presents his three basic categories (voice, mood, tense), which reflect the way in which the narrative levels intersect, and here more especially the way in which the story is configured at the level of the narrative discourse. This terminology based on the categories of the verb is actually a metaphorical framework: for instance, the *genus* or voice (active, passive, medium) of the verb has actually got very little to do with narrative voice. What Genette successfully demonstrates with his metaphors is that each and every narrative is inflected by voice, mood and tense just as each verb can be categorized in relation to this triad. (*She would not have been killed*, for instance, is passive voice, indicative mood and past conditional tense.) Analogously, narratives are either homo- or heterodiegetic; they have a particular perspective (type of focalization) and a particular time structure. But, as is also the case with grammar, there is no connection between a narrative's tense, perspective or 'voice'. In the case of the verb, too, the third-person plural can be found together with the past tense or the future, with the subjunctive or the indicative mood. Combinability is at its maximum.

Genette and grammar

Franz Karl Stanzel's theory of narrative

Let us now take a closer look at Stanzel's theory.[1] In *A Theory of Narrative* Stanzel radically revises his 1955 typology. He fleshes out and illustrates many of his ideas by having recourse to text linguistics and adds a number of binary oppositions.

Stanzel follows the traditional German division of literary texts into lyric, epic and drama. In this approach, lyric poetry is a meditation on the part of the speaker of the poem, and in drama the dramatis personae are on the stage, before the audience's very eyes. Only epic has a story that is told, one which is mediated by a narrator. Starting out from this crucial distinction between drama and epic, Stanzel sees the key defining feature of narrative as mediacy. But this mediacy does not necessarily manifest itself in a personalized or even embodied narrative instance, a *teller*. In figural narrative, mediacy by means of telling can be replaced by an illusion of im-mediacy. In this case, the reader has the impression that there is no narrator: events and actions are represented as in drama, directly from the perspective of one particular character. In actual fact, according to Stanzel, there still is a narrator/teller, concealed behind the perspective of the character in the story and responsible for reportative sentences like *He turned to the window*. The focal character is *not* a narrator (s/he does not tell or narrate), but we seem to see the events through his/her eyes. The protagonist through whose mind the narrative is focalized (as Genette would say) is therefore called a *reflector* (*character*), a term originally coined by Henry James. Narratives which convey

Mediacy

an illusion of immediate access to the fictional world through the medium of a reflector's consciousness are called reflector mode narratives. Thus, because of the prominence given to mediacy in Stanzel's work, mode and the oppositional pairs sub-sumed in it (*telling vs. showing; teller mode vs. reflector mode*) can be argued to be constitutive of narrative.

Although the figural narrative situation is located within the confines of the reflector mode on the typological circle, there are areas of overlap between the three narrative situations. This does not mean, as is often claimed, that it is the case that there are two kinds of teller-based narrative situations (authorial and first-person narratives) and only one type of reflector mode (figural narrative situation). There are also reflector mode first-person texts, often present-tense stories, for instance Ernest Gaines's 'The Sky is Gray' (from *Bloodline*, 1976) or Judith Small's 'Body of Work' (1991).[2]

First-person narrative

Let us now consider the narrative situations one after the other. The **first-person narrative situation** is predicated on the fact that one of the characters in the story also functions as the narrator. In this respect it simulates autobiography; most first-person novels are pseudo-autobiographies. On Stanzel's typological circle, if we take the axis which concerns the identity/non-identity of the worlds of the narrator and of the protagonist(s), first-person narrative is so positioned that it has the identity pole as its defining feature. An interesting aspect of fictional first-person narratives is that the focus can be either on the so-called *narrating self* or the *experiencing self*. For instance, when events and actions are reported from the perspective of a now older and wiser narrator, this narrating self often indulges in retrospection, evaluation and the drawing of moral conclusions. Conversely, the text may eschew retrospection and concentrate on the action as it takes place, at any one particular moment in time. In such cases, the focus is on the narrator as protagonist, the experiencing self. There is a kind of dynamic at work here: ideally, experience and evaluation should be in equilibrium. In the twentieth century, however, first-person narratives increasingly concentrated on the experiencing self, alluding only vaguely to the telling of the story. These narratives seem to be entirely located in the experiences of the protagonists. They often make use of the present as their narrative tense. When, in addition, the emphasis is on the protagonist's consciousness, Fludernik (1996: 253) assigns them to the figural narrative situation (in which the reflector mode predominates).

Peripheral first-person narrators

It is also interesting to note that the narrator need not necessarily be the story's main protagonist (the standard form of first-person narrative, for which Genette coined the useful term autodiegetic). The first-person narrator can also be a minor character. Such peripheral first-person narrators, as Stanzel calls them, are also of taxonomical interest as they mark the transition to the authorial narrative situation (cf. the typological circle, Figure 9.1). Peripheral first-person narrators frequently recount what happens from a naive and uninformed perspective. Famous examples are Nick Carraway in F. Scott Fitzgerald's *The Great Gatsby* (1925) and Serenus Zeitblom in Thomas Mann's *Doctor Faustus* (1947). This is why peripheral first-person narrators may also be unreliable, and their naivety becomes a source of amusement to us. At the same time, introducing such a narrator is an ideal way of making the main protagonist seem unapproachable, impenetrable or mysterious.

First-person narrative in Stanzel's account is the equivalent of Genette's homo-diegetic narrative (see below). Isolating its distinctive features does not pose any problems – there is overall consensus among narratologists regarding this form of narrative. Only Mieke Bal has drawn attention to new aspects of focalization or voice

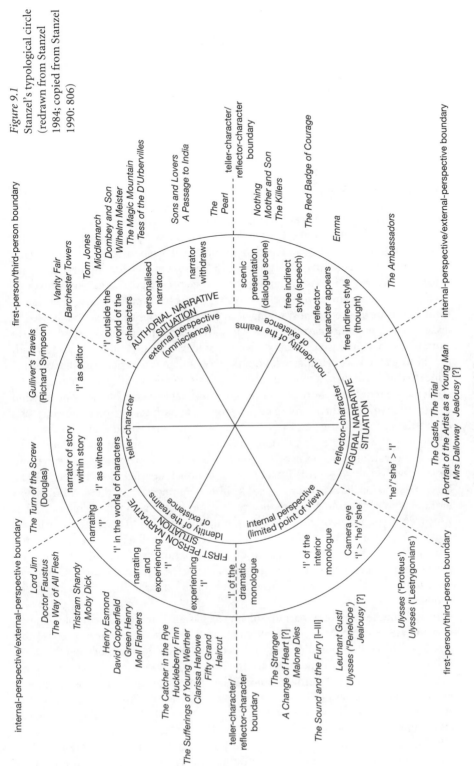

Figure 9.1
Stanzel's typological circle
(redrawn from Stanzel
1984; copied from Stanzel
1990: 806)

first-person/third-person boundary

internal-perspective/external-perspective boundary

internal-perspective/external-perspective boundary

first-person/third-person boundary

internal-perspective/external-perspective boundary

teller-character/
reflector-character
boundary

first-person/third-person boundary

teller-character/
reflector-character boundary

AUTHORIAL NARRATIVE SITUATION
external perspective
(omniscience)

'I' outside the world of the characters

personalised narrator

narrator withdraws

scenic presentation
(dialogue scene)

free indirect style (speech)

reflector-character appears

free indirect style (thought)

non-identity of the realms of existence

FIGURAL NARRATIVE SITUATION
internal perspective
(limited point of view)

reflector-character

'he'/'she' > 'I'

Camera eye
'I' > 'he'/'she'

'I' of the interior monologue

'I' of the dramatic monologue

'I' experiencing

'I' narrating and experiencing

'I' in the world of characters

narrating 'I'

narrator of story within story

'I' as witness

'I' as editor

teller-character

Identity of the realms of existence

FIRST PERSON NARRATIVE SITUATION

THE TYPOLOGICAL CIRCLE

Vanity Fair
Barchester Towers

Tom Jones
Middlemarch
Dombey and Son
Wilhelm Meister
The Magic Mountain
Tess of the D'Urbervilles

Sons and Lovers
A Passage to India

The
Pearl

Nothing
Mother and Son
The Killers

The Red Badge of Courage

Emma

The Ambassadors

The Castle, The Trial
A Portrait of the Artist as a Young Man
Mrs Dalloway Jealousy [?]

Ulysses ('Proteus')
Ulysses ('Lestrygonians')

Leutnant Gustl
Ulysses ('Penelope')
Jealousy [?]

The Sound and the Fury [I–III]

The Stranger
A Change of Heart [?]
Malone Dies

The Catcher in the Rye
Huckleberry Finn
The Sufferings of Young Werther
Clarissa Harlowe
Fifty Grand
Haircut

Henry Esmond
David Copperfield
Green Henry
Moll Flanders

Tristram Shandy
Moby Dick

Lord Jim
Doctor Faustus
The Way of All Flesh

The Turn of the Screw
(Douglas)

Gulliver's Travels
(Richard Sympson)

in first-person narration by suggesting that there is a kind of 'authorial first-person narrator' (see also Nielsen 2004). The basic idea of this line of research is to parallelize the functions of the narrating self and the narrator in authorial narrative. The narrating self becomes a kind of extradiegetic narrative voice outside the world of the fiction.

First-person narrative as a form not only correlates with the traditional 'birth' of the novel in the work of Defoe but also provides the key constituent of the epistolary novel which preceded Defoe (in English from Aphra Behn onwards) and which played such a large role at the beginning of the history of the genre. Stanzel points out that the first-person form only emerged relatively late in literary history. In the Middle Ages we only come across rare, late examples of first-person narratives (that is, if one takes narrative dream poetry to be a separate genre). The first real first-person texts in English literature are the picaresque novels and criminal autobiographies of the early modern period.

Authorial narrative

Stanzel's second narrative situation, the **authorial narrative situation**, is the most problematic. It deviates from other typologies (only Lanser partly agrees with Stanzel and uses his terminology) and is based on the notion of perspective, which is one of the most controversial concepts in narratology. In Stanzel's model, the authorial narrative situation is defined by its position at the external perspective pole of the perspective axis on the typological circle. Authorial narrative is fairly common and quite easy to identify; it is its theoretical positioning at the external perspective pole that has led to disagreement with other narratologists. Moreover, some literary scholars find the term 'authorial' problematic since many students tend to confuse the authorial narrator with the (historical) author her/himself. Both the term and the concept have even led some critics to discern in them a touch of authoritarianism in the politico-ideological sense.

Non-identity of the world of the characters and that of the narrator

The concept of the authorial narrative situation enables Stanzel to describe the kind of narrative which features a more or less prominent narrator persona, someone who enjoys the narratee's trust and who tells about a fictional world that s/he does not belong to, one which s/he – in a certain sense – stands aloof from. Such a narrator often assumes the role of an historian or a chronicler. S/he floats above things, as it were, and looks down on them knowledgeably. All traditional storytelling – Homer's *Iliad*, Virgil's *Aeneid*, medieval romance – is, like history, 'authorial'. All these works share a narrator who is far removed from the events depicted and who reports on a world in which s/he (and frequently the narratees, too) does not live. This distance makes it possible for the narrator to drop hints about events that will happen in the future (a retrospective first-person narrator can do this, too, however), and also to compare several settings, periods of time and groups of characters. S/he can switch from one of these options to the other and focus on it (or not) in the narrative discourse as s/he chooses.

Omniscience

In addition, the authorial narrator of a novel has the privilege of being able to look into the minds of the characters, although s/he need not necessarily exercise this privilege. Thus the authorial narrator is located, godlike, above and beyond the world of the story; s/he sees and knows everything even if s/he does not reveal all s/he knows – at least, this is how it seems to the reader. Not surprisingly, such a narrator is described as *omniscient* (Fr. *omniscient*; Ger. *allwissend*). This godlike distance of authorial narrators is often acted out or performatively displayed by them, but it can also be breached for the sake of irony. Think of Denis Diderot's novel *Jacques le fataliste* (1778–80), Thackeray's metaphor of the puppeteer in *Vanity Fair* (1847–48) or Flaubert's and Joyce's comments on the author as a persona who lords it over the story world and sits manicuring his nails, seemingly expressing indifference or unbiased objectivity: 'The artist, like the God of the creation, remains within or behind or beyond or above his handiwork, invisible, refined out of existence, indifferent, paring his fingernails' (Joyce 1993: 187); 'L'artiste doit être dans son oeuvre comme Dieu dans la création, invisible et tout-puissant; qu'on le sente partout, mais qu'on ne le voie pas' (Flaubert 1927: 164).[3]

Due to the fact that the great novels of the nineteenth century all have authorial narrators – Goethe's *Elective Affinities*, most of the novels of Dickens, *Middlemarch* by George Eliot, Balzac's novels, the works of Theodor Storm, Tolstoy's *War and Peace* – it can certainly be said that this kind of novel is very important. The problem is not, then, that experts disagree about whether such a novel exists; even Genette admits that the narrators of *Tom Jones* or *War and Peace* stand above and beyond the world of their protagonists, are able to switch to and fro between various locations and time frames and have the option of informing the narratee what the characters are thinking. The problem has to do with terminology and with the constraints that apply when any theory is worked out systematically.

The term 'authorial'

Let us begin with a brief defence of the term 'authorial' before we turn to the tricky question of perspective. When we refer to an authorial narrator, we mean to say that the narrator takes a role resembling that of the author of the narrative in question. S/he is reliable, in total control (holds the puppets' strings in her/his hands, as it were) and 'manages' the arrangement of time frames, settings and the characters themselves. The term therefore expresses metaphorically the idea that the narrator, like the author, is cast in an 'author role', which is why the authorial narrators in Dickens or Thackeray are often referred to as 'Dickens' or 'Thackeray', since the implied author and narrator seem to be one and the same person. In the narratorial persona the real author assumes the role of 'author'. However, this author role of the narrator is not consistent between texts, as can be noted, for instance, in the case of Dickens, whose authorial style undergoes a radical transformation between, say, *Bleak House* and *Hard Times*. The term *authorial* characterizes very precisely the affinity which the reader perceives between narrator and author role. One could certainly contend that the phrase 'authorial narrator' is not a good choice of term since it actually obscures the difference between author and narrator. Yet, one can also argue that the authorial novel commonly has that kind of narrator whose authoritative presentation of the narrative world and whose trustworthy dependability for the reader constitutively align the narrator with the image of the author, in fact the implied author. In first-person or figural narrative, by contrast, there is no room for confusion of this kind: the first-person narrator is a distinct fictional character, who tells his or her own story. In reflector mode narrative, no narratorial persona exists to be confused with the author.

The figural narrative situation

The third type of narrative situation proposed by Stanzel is the so-called **'figural' narrative situation** (Ger. *personale Erzählsituation*). Stanzel's choice of terminology has led to a great deal of confusion since the word *figural* is widely misunderstood, particularly in the German original in the context of the notion of the *personalized narrator.* Stanzel's placing of the figural narrative situation in the domain of the reflector mode, on the other hand, is much clearer and uncontested. The 'person' or figure referred to by the term *figural* is a *reflector figure*, and the story is reflected, so to speak, through her/his consciousness. In the revised version of Stanzel's theory of narrative, the figural narrative situation is governed by the reflector-mode end of the mode axis, while in first-person and authorial narrative the *teller mode* is dominant.

Signs of teller or reflector modes

Stanzel's *A Theory of Narrative* contains a list of the typical features of teller and reflector modes which is particularly student-friendly and which is intended to make it easy to ascertain whether the narrative situation is figural from the very beginning of a work of fiction (1984: 169–70). Texts that are written in the teller mode usually have an emic beginning (see Chapter 5), as suggested by Harweg (1968). The early stages of the narrative will include a detailed exposition, tailored to the needs of the narratee, so that important basic information (setting in time and space; social status and background of the protagonists) is conveyed. The narrative discourse tends to consist of synopses, abstractions and generalizations. Logic, or at least something approaching logic, underlies the various choices made with regard to presentation. The here and now of the narrative discourse stands in contrast to the there and then of the story. As the first-person pronoun of the narrative discourse refers only to the narrator, the opposition between first- and third-person reference is a distinguishing feature.

Texts in the reflector mode, on the other hand, have etic beginnings: we start off in the thick of things. The reader knows as much (or as little) as the reflector figure, whose knowledge or perception determine what is presented on the page. The text assumes prior knowledge of the people the protagonist sees (pronouns without antecedents), of where we are, what can be observed and what remains invisible to the reflector. In contrast to the organized view of a narrator writing in retrospect, the account of events offered in figural narrative is often disjointed and incoherent. The protagonist is only experiencing the events at this very moment and so is not able to grasp them fully or impose any kind of order on them. This is why the criteria for selecting what is perceived are spontaneous and unsystematic. The mind of the reflector figure is rooted in the here and now, without there being any distance from the events depicted. Moreover, the prevailing internal perspective is fleshed out by expressive elements in the language used by the characters and in the emotions of the protagonist. Thanks to the reflector figure the reader has the impression that s/he is directly involved in the action, albeit through the filter of the protagonist's consciousness.

Reflector mode vs. figural narrative situation

Complications arise, however, because the term figural narrative situation does not cover exactly the same ground on the typological circle as the reflector mode. As the typological circle is divided into three segments, the authorial narrative situation on the right-hand side of the circle extends into the reflector mode. Novels located on the so-called *authorial-figural continuum*, in which many passages rendering thought processes are presented from the perspective of the characters in spite of there being an authorial narrator, are to be found in this transitional area (see Figure 9.1), for instance, the novels of Thomas Hardy, e.g. *Tess of the D'Urbervilles* (1891). We also find some overlap in the segment of first-person narrative; in other words, there are first-person narratives in the reflector mode. Here the experiencing self ousts the narrating self. Given the substantial number of modern first-person narratives in the present tense which are written from the perspective of the protagonist, we can say that this segment of the typological circle, still quite empty in Stanzel's versions, is beginning to be filled.

Criticisms of Stanzel's model

Stanzel's model has met with a good deal of criticism. In a review in *Poetics Today* (1981), even Dorrit Cohn, who was responsible for disseminating Stanzel's ideas in the United States, suggested improving the model by having only two axes – person and mode – instead of three (voice, person and mode). In this case, there would only be four segments in the circle (Figure 9.2).

Cohn

According to Cohn, first- and third-person narratives carry the same weight. In first-person narrative, she distinguishes between *dissonant* and *consonant* modes.

Retrospective first-person narrative with a pronounced narrating self is, so to speak, the equivalent of the authorial narrator, and consonant first-person narrative is equivalent to first-person narrative in which the experiencing self predominates. Cohn takes the terms consonant and dissonant from her study *Transparent Minds* (1978), in which she makes a distinction between ironic (dissonant) and empathetic (consonant) thought report or free indirect discourse. In Stanzel's model, placing pure interior monologue on the typological circle had been problematic since the figural narrative situation, where there is no narrator, is situated at the 'South Pole' of Stanzel's circle, where there is non-identity of the worlds of characters and the narrator. This inconsistency is eliminated in Cohn's revision, in which interior monologue texts easily go into the south-west quadrant.

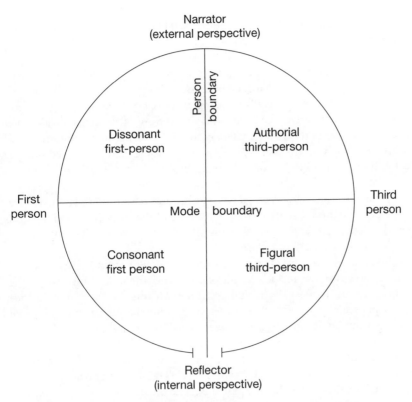

Figure 9.2 Cohn's model (after Cohn (1981: 179))

Last but not least, Stanzel in his revised typological circle eliminated his earlier so-called 'neutral' narrative situation. This term was used to characterize two types of narrative. On the one hand, it referred to third-person texts with an external perspective but without an overt narrator, or to first-person narratives which do not represent the consciousness of this first-person narrator. Examples of such texts are Hemingway's first-person novels and some of his short stories written in the third person, as well as the crime novels of Raymond Chandler. The label 'neutral' here is a misnomer: such narratives do not actually come across as either neutral or objective. This technique, which is also known as 'camera-eye', conveys a sense of apathy and stunted emotional

The neutral narrative situation

development, of being transfixed by fear, or of a pathological lack of emotional involvement (often the case in the novels of Raymond Chandler). On the other hand, Stanzel classifies dialogue novels, such as the works of Ivy Compton-Burnett's, which have no narrators and no internal perspective, as neutral texts. In fact, dialogue novels are close to being dramatic texts in which the stage directions have the form of minimal reportative sentences (*The bell rang*). In later re-conceptualizations of his theory, Stanzel abandoned the idea of the neutral narrative situation and now considers such texts to be, in principle, positionable anywhere on the typological circle, depending on whether the framing reportative clauses are first-person or third-person, and on whether they allow for a reflectoral reading. In Genette's model, with its three forms of focalization, the neutral narrative situation is a totally unproblematic case (see below). Within the framework of Stanzel's model, however, the neutral camera-eye narrative remains an awkward problem.[4]

Further important aspects of Stanzel's theory of narrative

Before turning to the work of Genette, I should first like to focus on other aspects of Stanzel's theory of narrative which, it seems to me, provide valuable insights but have largely been ignored in subsequent narratological research.

In both authorial and first-person novels, the presence of the narrator (that is to say, the personalized narrator) does not always make itself felt to the same extent as the text unfolds. We can observe that, generally speaking, there is a marked narrator presence at the beginning of the narrative, which tails away, apart from a few climaxes within the story, only to re-emerge at the end.

Narrative profile and narrative rhythm

De facto, individual texts naturally show different *narrative profiles*, which means that typical narrative profiles can be worked out for individual authors or periods. Stanzel distinguishes between the ratio of narrative passages to dialogue (narrative profile) and *narrative rhythm*, which characterizes the sequence of narrative passages, dialogue, comment and description. The narrative process may become more dynamic when the telling of the story is the main focus, or it may develop a more schematic quality if the narrative profile flattens out (dynamization/schematicization; 1984: 63–78).

Synoptic chapter headings

Stanzel also looks into the use of tenses in synoptic chapter headings. He notes that, in general, the present tense in such headings underlines the lack of mediacy of the paratext: headings do not usually include references to the narrator, nor do they incorporate a particular perspective. Nevertheless, synoptic chapter headings may well present things from an authorial point of view, and in this case they can be either narrative (using the past tense) or discursive (in the present tense). For instance, the second type of chapter heading is rather like summary: 'Agathon arrives in Smyrna and is sold' (*Agathon* I, xi: Wieland 2001: 47; trans. Patricia Häusler-Greenfield). Narrative chapter headings, on the other hand, use past tenses and often include *verba dicendi* and subordinate clauses or phrases:

> *Relates that* Mr. Jones continued his Journey . . .
> > (*Tom Jones* XII, xii; Fielding 1996: 663)

> *Comment* Pantagruel trouva Panurge, lequel il aima toute sa vie.
> > (*Pantagruel* II, ix—Rabelais 1962: 262; 'How Pantagruel found Panurge,
> > whom he loved all his life'—Rabelais 1987: 196)

> *How* Captain Dobbin bought a piano.
> > (*Vanity Fair* xxvii; Thackeray 1994: 169)

As we already noted in Chapter 4, one can even find metanarrative chapter headings.

In Chapter 5 (1984: 117–25) of *A Theory of Narrative*, Stanzel puts forward an interesting idea, namely that, in classical authorial narrative, fictional space is not described from a perspective which would enable one to draw a plan, for instance. Only in figural narratives, where one character's perspective dominates, does the description of the furnishings of a room follow the gaze of this character as s/he enters it. This enables the fictional setting to be reconstructed in the mind of the reader. Manfred Jahn (1999: 95–7) has provided some criticism of this thesis. He demonstrates that aperspectivism is not a lack of perspective but – by analogy with zero focalization – actually a particular way of handling perspective, which he terms 'ambient focalization'. This enables a focalized object to be considered from all or many angles, so that the focalizer need not be bound to a particular point in time or space. Of course, Jahn's model also implies that the narrator functions as a focalizer here and so 'sees' as well as 'tells'. This view is controversial, and I myself do not share it.[5] What is commendable about Stanzel's thesis is that it points out that the representation of locations in space in older texts, in which the authorial mode predominates, does not reflect the perspective of just one character and, in general, does not admit of any high degree of visual reconstruction. (This is also true of first-person narratives such as Defoe's *Moll Flanders* (1722).) Stanzel's is, therefore, predominantly a diachronic analysis. On the other hand, Jahn is correct in asserting that descriptions of rooms in authorial novels are not perspective-less; rather, it is the case that the narrator's gaze roves to and fro and focuses on individual objects, without imposing any specific pattern on them.

> Perspectivism and aperspectivism

In Section 4.8 Stanzel addresses the question of *alternating first- and third-person narrative*. He shows very clearly that in modernist figural narratives a switch from first- to third-person pronouns in reference to the reflector figure is not significant; the opposition between first- and third-person narrative is neutralized. This can be explained by the fact that the sole point of reference for locating consciousness is the reflector figure who occupies the stage – all personal pronouns have to refer to her/his point of view. An example of this type is analysed in Chapter 11, John McGahern's *The Dark* (1965). However, the neutralization of the first-person/third-person opposition can only take place in texts in which the reflector does not interact with other characters (cf. also Nischik 1994). Stanzel's example, Ingeborg Bachmann's short story 'Paestum' (Stanzel 1981), overcomes this difficulty by making the second protagonist involved a man, so that both the first-person pronoun and the third-person singular feminine pronoun (Ger. *ich; sie*) clearly refer to the female protagonist. In other cases, the alternation of first- and third-person narrative tends to be psychologically motivated. In the case of Thackeray's *Henry Esmond* (1852), the shift from first to third person, as Stanzel shows (1984: 100–104), goes hand in hand with perspectivization, with something approximating to the representation of consciousness and even emergent reflector mode. More radical postmodern texts use shifts in person (pronouns) in order to illustrate protagonists' dissolving identities (cf. Fludernik 1996: 236–44).

> Alternating first- and third-person narrative

As a final point, I should like to expound on Stanzel's discussion of the narrator. He introduces the notion of the personalized narrator in order to account for the kind of narratorial persona who figures as a character on the discourse level. Every first-person narrator is personalized by definition, but authorial narrators, too, may come across as personalities in their own right. Thackeray's acid-tongued narrator in *Vanity Fair* acts like a puppet master; the narrator of Fielding's *Tom Jones* is an ironic moralist. If the authorial narrator is presented in such concrete detail that s/he makes

> The embodied self

comments about the writing process or her/his physical and social circumstances while writing, then we are confronted with an embodiment of the narrator, an embodied self (Ger. *Ich mit Leib*) (Stanzel 1984: 90–4). We find an extreme instance of this embodiment when an authorial narrator suddenly 'descends' to the level of the fictional world. For example, in Chapter 62 of *Vanity Fair*, we learn that the narrator was himself in the village of Pumpernickel and got to know the main protagonists personally (Stanzel 1984: 202–5).

Narrative
situations as
prototypes

Thus, summing up we can say that F. K. Stanzel's theory of narrative has a sound historical basis and concerns itself particularly with intermediate and borderline cases in narratology. His three narrative situations are conceived of as prototypes, in other words they are fuzzy categories. It follows from this that we find more and less typical manifestations of them in token texts. The strong points of Stanzel's theory are that the categories are open-ended and transitional, and in-between categories are not excluded. A novel need not be allocated a fixed place on the typological circle in its entirety, but parts of it can be situated at different points. (As an extreme example of this one can mention James Joyce's *Ulysses*, where each chapter has its own narrative situation.) Stanzel's theory is also attractive for another reason: the way in which it takes the historical dimension of narrative forms into account. Of course, in creating universal categories of narrative, his model is descriptive and therefore static, but it is certainly compatible with diachronic lines of inquiry. All the narrative situations need not necessarily have been in existence from the early beginnings of narrative on. On the contrary, according to Stanzel, the typological circle is gradually being completed as time goes by. These are points on which Stanzel radically differs from Gérard Genette, to whose ideas we shall now turn.

Gérard Genette's theory of narrative

Gérard Genette's narrative theory is based on structuralist principles. He identifies, as we have already noted, three levels of *narrative* (Fr. *récit*; Ger. *Erzählung*): *narration*, *discourse* and *story* (Fr. *narration, récit* or *discours, histoire*), and by analogy with these he postulates three categories in which the relations between these three levels can be classified: *voice* (Fr. *voix*; Ger. *Genus/Stimme.*), *tense* (Fr. *temps*; Ger. *Tempus*) and *mode* (Fr. *mode*; Ger. *Modus*).

Genette's categories are summarized in Figure 9.3.

Homodiegetic vs.
heterodiegetic

Genette makes a first distinction between voice and mode: voice is concerned with 'Who speaks?' (the narrator? a character?) and mode with 'Who sees?' (or the perspective from which the story is presented). His term for perspective is *focalization* (Fr. *focalization*; Ger. *Fokalisierung*). The most crucial binary opposition in the category of voice is the distinction between *homodiegesis* and *heterodiegesis*, in other words, first-person vs. third-person narrative. The major advantage of this termi-nological innovation is that there is no confusion about the use of the first-person pronoun. Homo/heterodiegetic defines the relationship between the narrator and the fictional world – the narrator is (or is not) part of that world. By contrast, the standard term 'first-person narrative' ostensibly indicates that the first-person pronoun refers to the central protagonist on the story level just as third-person narrative uses a third-person pronoun, *he, she* or *they*, in referring to the main protagonist(s), or second-person narrative refers to the central protagonist by means of *you* or an equivalent address pronoun. In practice, many texts have first-person

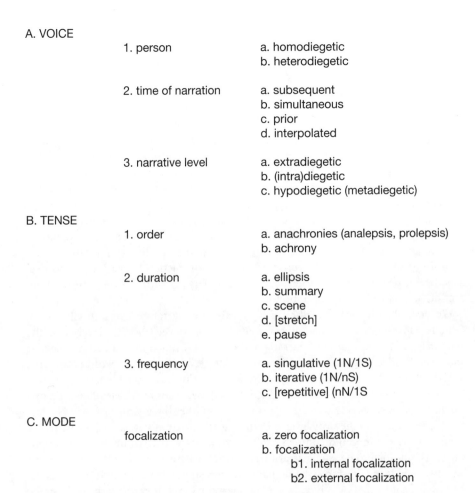

A. VOICE

	1. person	a. homodiegetic
		b. heterodiegetic
	2. time of narration	a. subsequent
		b. simultaneous
		c. prior
		d. interpolated
	3. narrative level	a. extradiegetic
		b. (intra)diegetic
		c. hypodiegetic (metadiegetic)

B. TENSE

	1. order	a. anachronies (analepsis, prolepsis)
		b. achrony
	2. duration	a. ellipsis
		b. summary
		c. scene
		d. [stretch]
		e. pause
	3. frequency	a. singulative (1N/1S)
		b. iterative (1N/nS)
		c. [repetitive] (nN/1S

C. MODE

	focalization	a. zero focalization
		b. focalization
		b1. internal focalization
		b2. external focalization

Figure 9.3 Genette's major categories

pronouns that refer to the 'speaker', the narrator figure who is not a protagonist (the phrase *As I mentioned above*, for instance, can be found extensively in heterodiegetic narratives), so the term 'first-person narrative' tempts readers to concentrate on first-person pronouns in the text, whose presence misleads them into assuming a reference to a protagonist.

As we have already seen, however, Genette does not integrate second-person narrative in a satisfactory way since some second-person narratives are homodiegetic as far as the narrator is concerned and heterodiegetic as far as the 'you' is concerned. Thus the narrator in Paul Zech's *Geschichte einer armen Johanna* (1925) lives in the same world as Johanna: 'I don't know how often we passed each other by' (1925: 6). However, he is a kind of peripheral first-person narrator as the main protagonist (the referent of *you*) is Johanna, and it is her fate which is the focus of attention: 'Dawn was breaking by the time you returned home. [. . .] You were happy to be home, for you could not help thinking: Oh, it's the witching hour' (67).[6] What we have is, therefore, a (second-person) heterodiegetic narrative with a peripheral first-person narrator. *The*

Great Gatsby, by way of comparison, would be a (third-person) heterodiegetic narrative about Gatsby, with a peripheral first-person narrator, Nick Carraway.

The relationship between telling and experiencing

As a second sub-category of voice, time of narration, Genette proposes a division into four types of telling: (a) subsequent, (b) simultaneous, (c) prior and (d) interpolated. He hereby makes a distinction between traditional retrospective narration (the narrator reports at a later point in time on events which took place earlier); concurrent report (for example in sports reporting, but also in many twentieth-century stories); the less frequently found forms of prophetic/visionary discourse (the fortune teller tells what will happen, the narrator uses the future tense), and the writing of letters and diary entries, where episodes of experiencing events and episodes of recounting what happened alternate with each other. (In fact, variant (d) is also retrospective, the difference being that there is no great distance between the time of narration and the events related.)

Initially, it may seem somewhat confusing that Genette does not situate this second subcategory of voice as a fourth subcategory under the heading of tense. But we should take account of the fact that the subcategories under that heading all refer to the relationship between story and discourse, whereas the distinction between retrospective, concurrent, prospective and interpolated telling has primarily to do with the relationship between story and narration.

Narrative levels

We have already looked at the third subcategory, narrative levels, in Chapter 4. Genette introduces a distinction between the story level (diegetic level) and the extradiegetic level of the act of narrating, as well as a distinction between the diegetic and an embedded diegetic level, in other words the level of the 'story within the story'. Mieke Bal coined the useful term *hypodiegetic* to describe this embedded level, whereas Genette's term *meta*diegetic is easily misconstrued. By analogy with *metalinguistic*, one would expect *metadiegetic* to refer to a story *about* rather than *within* a story. The fact that Genette refers to the story level as both diegetic and intradiegetic is likewise rather confusing. The compound conforms to the symmetrical patterning of binary oppositions (homo/heterodiegetic, extra/intradiegetic), whereas the morph *diegetic* is the basic stem with the meaning 'story' that underlies all the contrastive compounds. As we saw in Chapter 4, the distinction between narrative levels is particularly useful in the analysis of frame stories and of metalepsis.

Metalepsis

The concept of metalepsis, which Genette uses to describe crossovers between narrative levels, has gained wide currency owing to its popularity in much postmodern writing. Basically, metalepsis is a narrative technique in which ontological axioms, e.g. that authorial narrators live in a different world from that of their characters, are undermined with the result of destroying one's impression that the narrated world is real. When characters gang up against their author as in Flann O'Brien's *At-Swim-Two-Birds* (1939), or, as in Luigi Pirandello's *Six Characters in Search of an Author* (1927), set off to find their maker, or when the male narrator suddenly spends the night with his female protagonist (also O'Brien), these are all instances of a metaleptic transgressing of the boundaries between telling and told, and destroying the fictional illusion. Metalepses can also be generated at the discourse level when the narrator projects him/herself (at least empathetically) towards the level of the characters and becomes involved in what happens, as if s/he were standing there in the flesh. Marie-Laure Ryan calls this second kind of metalepsis 'métalepse rhétorique' (2005: 205–12).[7] The following extract from Fielding's *Tom Jones* (1749) is a typical example of discursive or rhetorical metalepsis:

As we have now brought Sophia into safe hands, the reader will, I apprehend, be contented to *deposit her there awhile, and to look a little after other personages*, and particularly poor Jones, whom we have left long enough to do penance for his past offences, which, as is the nature of vice, brought sufficient punishment upon him themselves.

> (*Tom Jones* XI, x; Fielding 1996: 538)

In the discourse here, the narrator descends to the same level as the characters – it is as if he had literally carried Sophia to safety before going off in search of Tom Jones. Ryan also discusses the logical contradictions of metaleptical structures.

Genette's category 'tense' is made up of the subcategories of order, duration and frequency. This is by far the longest of Genette's chapters and it offers a detailed account of the temporal devices on the discourse level which reorder events in the story (temporal ordering), shorten or lengthen them (duration) or manipulate how often they occur in the text (frequency). Here we should note that, barring a few narratives such as the *Odyssey* and Laurence Sterne's *Tristram Shandy* (1759–67), such reorganizations only become really significant with the advent of literary modernism. Most canonical narratives begin at the beginning and present the events described in chronological order, starting from a particular point in time. The only exceptions to this are found in flashbacks, which are necessary when new characters appear on the scene (to fill in the background to these characters), or in embedded stories told by protagonists. At the threshold of the twentieth century and in the great novels of consciousness, where the memory of the protagonist plays a crucial role, these rearrangement techniques that Genette describes in such meticulous detail come into their own. Indeed, these narrative strategies even begin to impact on first-person narrative. An example of this is Evelyn Waugh's *Brideshead Revisited* (1945), a novel in which the narrator begins his story with his visit to Brideshead as a soldier during the Second World War and then moves back to his student days, recounting all the events linking him with the country house and its occupants until that moment. The relative extent of analepsis in first-person and third-person novels has not yet been investigated from a narratological perspective. Among more recent texts which make very striking use of temporal reordering one could note Christa Wolf's *A Model Childhood* (*Kindheitsmuster* 1976) or Michael Ondaatje's *The English Patient* (1992), the film version of which takes over the analeptic sequence in which events are depicted in the novel.

Tense

Playing with order is for the most part a modernist and postmodernist technique (see Chapter 4 for a complete account), but the modulation of the subcategory of duration is quite common in traditional narratives – after all, who would be capable of depicting events one-to-one with the time they take to happen, or of doing so without driving the reader (and him/herself) insane? Since antiquity, ellipsis, pause, scene and summary have been recurring elements in every narrative. It could, however, be the case that the extended representation in the narrative discourse referred to by Seymour Chatman as *stretch* is a modernist phenomenon, too. This technique may have developed as the result of the detailed depiction of states of mind and thought processes in modernist texts and in imitation of the filmic technique of *slow motion*. The same holds true for the manipulation of frequency. Whereas recurring events have always been condensed into one telling, the deliberate multiple narration of an event that has already been told is a peculiarity of (post)modernist texts.

Duration and frequency

Mode

Genette's third category, mode, includes the subcategories of distance and focalization. Under the heading *distance* he draws a distinction between different types of mimesis. In the narrative discourse of the novel, language can represent verbal utterances much better than actions, colours or feelings, for example. The point at issue here is how far the *symbolic* medium of language can be used to achieve *iconic* or quasi-iconic effects. This is the point at which Genette discusses speech and thought representation.

A word of explanation about the terminology may be in order in this connection. In semiotics, we distinguish between three kinds of signs: deictic, iconic and symbolic. Deictic signs point from one spot to an object or in a specific direction (the index finger points to the right, for example, meaning 'This way, move to the right.'). Iconic signs are characterized by the fact that the sign (*signifier*) resembles the *signified* in some way (for example, the road sign for a roundabout has a circle on it). Gestures in film are iconic as they reflect and reproduce gestures in the real world. Symbolic signs, on the other hand, are arbitrary – they show no referential link to the signified nor are they in any way similar to it.

Genette did not concern himself with narratives in other media as he (like Stanzel) insists on narrative being solely the product of an act of narration. However, the subcategory of distance opens up a particularly promising avenue of research, if one includes film and drama in the study of narrative. In these forms of narrative, iconic representation can be extended to cover actions, gestures, movement, appearance, facial expression, costume, sets, etc. On the other hand, film cannot represent thought (or, when it does, it has to resort to language to express it), although visual impressions and the facial expressions indicative of thought and emotion certainly play a significant role. Similarly, time is easy to handle in a novel (*On a warm summer's day in August 1956...*), but film and drama have to rely on language to make their references to time explicit. Because they are essentially visual media, film and drama are restricted to scenic representation. On stage, an actor performing a dance represents a character doing precisely those steps. The occasional use of slow motion and condensation (and in film, *fast motion*) can be effective, but too frequent use of such techniques would become ridiculous. Repeated fast motion sequences even become metafilmic since they focus attention on the form of the film, thereby destroying the mimetic effect.

Focalization

This brings us to the probably most controversial and hotly disputed category in Genette's typology: focalization.

According to Genette there are three kinds of focalization: zero focalization (Fr. *focalisation zéro*; Ger. *Nichtperspektivierung, unbeschränkte Fokalisierung*) and focalization, which can be either internal or external (Fr. *focalisation interne, focalisation externe*). Genette thus characterizes the authorial novel, in which focalization is not restricted to any one point of view, as zero focalization; the figural novel, in which the perspective of one character dominates on the diegetic level, *focalisation interne*; and the 'neutral' narrative situation, in which characters are described from the outside only without any inner view, as *focalisation externe*.

Bal

As Mieke Bal (1985) explained in her by now classic reformulation of Genette's model of focalization, Genette's threefold division is illogical. Zero focalization is situated on the extradiegetic level whereas internal focalization is located on the (intra)diegetic level, and external focalization may be encountered on either the (intra)diegetic or the extradiegetic level. Secondly, we should note that, in the term *external focalization*, *external* means 'from outside' whereas in the term *internal focalization, internal* means 'from within'. External focalization therefore implies that the focalized (Fr. *le focalisé*; Ger. *das Fokussierte*) is visible; invisible things, for instance thoughts, cannot be focalized from outside. Conversely, the focalizer (Fr. *le focalisateur*; Ger. *Fokalisierungsinstanz*) is sometimes a character and sometimes the narrator. In the case of internal focalization, the focalizer is the character from whose point of view we 'see', so this person's own thoughts are transparent to him/her, while those of the other characters are a closed book. So, even with internal focalization, the perspective on other people is external, since their thoughts are not perceptible to the reflector figure.

Bal's model is more systematic than Genette's but it is, nevertheless, not unproblematic. It forces us to specify who the focalizer is. This means that an authorial narrator always functions as a focalizer, as a narrator-focalizer (Fr. *narrateur-focalisateur*). However, this flies in the face of Genette's binary distinction between 'speaking' and 'seeing' – the narrator speaks, but does s/he also see? Narratologists do not see eye to eye here. Seymour Chatman, for instance, distinguishes between *slant* and *filter*: narrators can *report* from their own point of view in a biased way; reflectors are the medium through which the fictional world is seen, thus they are filters.

At this point it becomes apparent that ideological and visual approaches to perspective are becoming intermingled. The traditional position on *point of view* (Percy Lubbock and Jean Pouillon) is that it is mainly a matter of visual perception, and both Genette's and Bal's categories are also rooted in this approach. Pouillon (1946) makes a distinction between 'vision from without' (Fr. *vision sur*), which corresponds to external focalization and 'vision with' (Fr. *vision avec*), i.e. from within a character's mind, which would be equivalent to internal focalization. Manfred Jahn's more recent theoretical proposals also start out from the sense of sight (Jahn 1996, 1999). By contrast, Boris Uspensky (1973) and V.N. Vološinov (1929) already included the ideological level in their discussion of perspective. Uspensky differentiated between points of view on the ideological, phraseological, spatio-temporal and psychological levels. These four levels can intersect. In this manner, Uspensky comes up with a solution to the fundamental problem of point of view: we always talk of focalization and of seeing, but the issue at stake is, usually, access to the consciousness of characters in novels. Uspensky's model is far too complex to enable one to sum up the narrative situation of a whole novel in just two words, but it lends itself particularly well to the analysis of individual text passages. *[margin: Uspensky]*

In sum, Genette's typology succeeds admirably in making useful distinctions, in terminology which is both readily remembered and precise. As elements from his model may be freely combined, we find no restrictions governing the compatibility or incompatibility of the categories. This is a great advantage vis à vis Stanzel, who has problems in placing the 'neutral narrative situation' on the typological circle because of the arrangement of the axes. On the other hand, the advantage of Stanzel's model is that he locates recognized and historically relevant types of the novel on his circle: the quasi-autobiography of the typical first-person novel; the peripheral first-person narrator; the authorial narrator such as we find in Fielding; the authorial-figural continuum; the figural novel. Even the transitional forms between the narrative situations are actually well-known novel types. Stanzel's model relies on organic wholes – narrative situations which are prototypical and merge into one another along a scale on the circumference of the typological circle. The intention is partly to show how certain aspects of narrative do not merely combine but depend on each other for certain *[margin: Genette vs. Stanzel]* overall effects and constellations. In the tradition of the novel, certain types arise like species – hence the morphological basis of Stanzel's work.

While Genette's key metaphor relates to the grammar of the verb, and is therefore analytic, Stanzel's organicist metaphors are synthetic. Genette is also able to combine various categories, which are 'crossed' in diagrammatic form.

His model has the advantage that it provides the tools for careful, detailed analyses, which do not require conclusions to be drawn about the text as a whole. Ultimately, it should be stressed that Genette's book, despite offering a theoretical account of narrative, is really a study of Proust's magnum opus and so does not, in fact, lay claim to offer a theory which would be valid for narrative from classical antiquity through to postmodernism. In theory, additional categories could be added to complete the picture and account for newer types of narrative.

focalization / person	authorial (zero focalization)	actorial (internal focalization)	neutral (external focalization)
heterodiegetic	Goethe's *Wilhelm Meister*	Kafka, *The Trial*	Hemingway, "The Killers"
homodiegetic	Sterne, *Tristram Shandy*	Goethe, *Werther*	Camus, *The Stranger* (*L'Etranger*)

Figure 9.4 Genette's 'narrative situations' (after Martínez/Scheffel 1999:94)

Neither Stanzel nor Genette consider drama or non-verbal narratives as part of their object of analysis. Another disadvantage of both models is their inability to integrate second-person fiction. Stanzel's model is unable to position you-narrative or we-narrative anywhere on the circle since the potential continuity of worlds is limited to that of narrator and fictional world, but cannot terminologically embrace the positioning of narratees in the world of the story or of multiple characters as narrators and protagonists. Genette's polarity between homo- and heterodiegesis likewise makes it impossible to focus on the position of the narratee both inside and outside the fictional world. This failure in the two models is, however, a clear reflection of the (lack of) knowledge about second-person narrative available when Stanzel and Genette wrote their studies. Owing to the discovery of a wide variety of second-person texts, newer narrative theories had to be developed. It is to these that we will now turn.

Recent theories of narrative

After this detailed account of the models of Genette and Stanzel, we shall take a brief look at other narratologists who have made significant contributions to narrative terminology.

Mieke Bal

Mieke Bal's *Narratology* (1985; with additional material 1997) is an introduction to narratology which starts out from Genette's ideas but introduces some important modifications. One of these is the reconceptualization of the types of focalization as explained above. Narrative media is another area in which Bal has made a significant contribution. In contrast to traditional approaches, Bal's theory includes film and ballet among narrative genres: '*Narratology* is the theory of narratives, narrative texts, images, spectacles, events; cultural artefacts that "tell a story"' (Bal 1997: 3). This makes it necessary to de-anthropomorphize the narrator: Bal uses the neuter pronoun 'it' when she refers to the narrative instance (Bal 1997: 16). Although this idea has not been universally accepted, it does come up in discussion again and again.[8]

The opening chapter of Bal's book is particularly impressive. Here, for instance, in the section dealing with time, she presents basic plot types: plots based on *development* and those which concentrate on a *crisis*. Furthermore, she discusses several novels, among them Alain Robbe-Grillet's *The Voyeur* (1955) and Gabriel García Márquez's *One Hundred Years of Solitude* (1967). In these texts, it is impossible to work out a storyline (*fabula*) since we know too little about what happens, or, in the case of Márquez, we have conflicting accounts of events. Such cases of achrony have rarely been discussed, and the logical conclusion that there is no story here, only narrative discourse, has been brushed aside far too often. Bal's groundbreaking remarks on description in narrative have already been discussed in Chapter 5.

Together with Gerald Prince, the 'inventor' of the narratee (Fr. *narrataire*; Ger. *Leserfigur*) and the author of the *Dictionary of Narratology* (1987), Seymour Chatman can be ranked among the most important narratologists. Chatman's *Story and Discourse* (1978) offers an excellent basic account of narrative theory, which uses refreshingly 'normal' terminology. What is new in this book is, first, the analysis of film as a narrative genre and, second, the basic definition of narrative as consisting of story and discourse. In other words, only artefacts which have a story level and a level of communication are narratives. This early book also introduces the terms *overt* and *covert narrator*, which correspond to the notions of personalized and neutral narrator respectively. Chatman

Chatman's second important book, *Coming to Terms* (1990), offers a detailed account of filmic narrative and introduces the term *cinematic narrator*. Whether narrators exist in film or not is highly controversial, especially as Chatman's cinematic narrator is not to be understood as a character but as an instantiation of the medium of film. This being the case, Manfred Jahn (2003) has proposed the alternative term *filmic composition device* (FCD), which would more or less correspond to the notion of an implied author of the film. As well as introducing the notion of the cinematic narrator, Chatman suggests adding the innovative concepts of *filter* and *slant* to focalization theory. He takes the same position as Genette: the narrator only 'speaks' and does not 'see'. This is why ideologically charged perception is attributable to the bias of the narrator (slant). If a character perceives things in a biased way, this is apparent to the reader from the distorted vision of the character, whose consciousness acts like a filter in internal focalization:

> I propose *slant* to name the narrator's attitudes and other mental nuances appropriate to the report function of discourse, and *filter* to name the much wider range of mental activity experienced by characters in the story world – perceptions, cognitions, attitudes, emotions, memories, fantasies, and the like.
>
> (1990: 143)

Chatman's most significant contribution in *Coming to Terms*, however, has to do with embedding narrative in a framework which accommodates *all* types of text. According to Chatman, there are three main text types: argumentative, descriptive and narrative. Descriptions have no temporal ordering or plot elements; arguments build on logical connections and links; only narratives have temporal structure and a discourse level. Individual sentences or passages may belong to the other text types (there can be descriptive or argumentative passages in narrative, or narrative and descriptive passages in argumentative texts, for example). However, narrative texts proper are based on the combination of story and discourse, a dyad which description and argument do not have, just as they have no 'story'. Although the number of text types should be increased (see Fludernik 2000), Chatman's is an inspired proposal which also allows the notion of narrative to be extended to intermedial contexts (Nünning/Nünning 2002c: 1–22). In this manner, Chatman manages to connect literary genre theory with linguistic text-type theory.

Lanser   Another influential publication which pointed in new directions was Susan Lanser's second book, *Fictions of Authority: Women Writers and Narrative Voice* (1992). Lanser had been strongly influenced by structuralist thought and, in her first book, *The Narrative Act: Point of View in Prose Fiction* (1981), she attempted to tease out the notion of focalization in more detail than either Stanzel or Genette, drawing in part on the work of Uspensky. Her model identifies the categories of *status*, *contact* and *stance*. Various kinds of diegetic and mimetic authority come under the heading of status – here an important aspect for Lanser is the social background of the narrator: gender, ethnicity, social class. Under the heading of contact (borrowed from Jakobson's six-function model of communication [Jakobson 1958]), we find the subcategories of mode (direct vs. indirect contact), attitude (for example, respect/scorn, informality/formality) and the realization of the narratee as an individualized, passive or active counterpart to the narrator. Under stance, Lanser lists Uspensky's four kinds of perspective, which in their turn, are divided into further subcategories. Lanser's model is too complex for me to do it justice here. Suffice it to say that it is still regarded as an outstanding contribution to point of view studies.

In her next book, *Fictions of Authority*, Lanser addressed the problem of gender both from a feminist and from a general ideological perspective. The study includes many interpretations and has three sections devoted to authorial voice (among others in Austen, George Eliot and Woolf), first-person-singular novels, and *we*-novels. It starts with a theoretical chapter discussing the significance for a feminist approach of 'voice' (Genette's category of *voix*). The questions are how is the gender of narrators represented, implicitly or explicitly, in narrative texts, and how – even if there is no textual evidence – do readers assign gender to an authorial narrator? The three sections mentioned above illustrate in a practical way how women adopted various feminist positions in their writing, positions which they had to get across in spite of the traditional associations of the male authoritative discourse inherent in the type of novel they were writing.

Ryan   Marie-Laure Ryan is another narratologist who has made an important contribution to research. Ryan established possible-worlds theory in the United States and has worked extensively on narrative in computer games, in film and in other media (Ryan 1991, 1999, 2001a). She has not devised her own typology, at least not in the sense that the theorists we have discussed so far have done, but her theoretical and terminological contributions have been extremely fruitful. In addition to her monographs, *Possible Worlds, Artificial Intelligence, and Narrative Theory* (1991) and *Narrative as Virtual Reality* (2001a), she has also written a number of seminal essays, for example on present-tense narration in the reporting of baseball games (1993), on degrees of narrativity (1992), on frame stories (1986, 1990, 1991: 175–200), on the functions of the narrator (2001b) as well as on metalepsis (2005).

In *Possible Worlds*, Ryan demonstrated how to derive fictional worlds from semantic logic, including virtual scenarios (Chapter 8). With the introduction of the terms *immersion* and *interactivity*, *Narrative as Virtual Reality* extends the scope of this approach to reception-related issues. Ryan situates aspects of narrative texts that were hitherto discussed at the level of communication in a binary relationship of reader-text interaction and contrasts this interaction with readerly immersion in the fictional world. Many of Ryan's ideas have been taken up by Hilary Dannenberg (2004a, b, 2008) and applied to the analysis of plot.

In *possible-worlds theory* a basic distinction is made between the actual world and a series of alternative possible worlds, which may be fictional, visionary or speculative. Thus possible-worlds theory unites the fictional and the fictive (see Chapter 6). Within the framework of the *textual actual world*, in other words of (fictional or non-fictional) reality – described, for instance, in *Madame Bovary* as the world of Emma and Léon and Charles Bovary – characters in texts also have privately imagined alternative worlds in their minds (*wish-worlds*, *obligation-worlds* and *knowledge-worlds*). These alternative, private worlds offer an explanation for the conflicts which arise in many narratives. They are conflicts between the textual actual world and one of these private worlds, or conflicts within the private worlds (cf. Wenzel 2004: 36). Ryan puts forward a masterly explanation of the way in which the wishes and desires of characters sketch out alternative storylines, which are often prevented from materializing by the realities of the textual actual world (cf. Ryan 1987).

In his 2002 book *Story Logic*, David Herman sets out to use the cognitive sciences to describe the logical mainspring of narrative, i.e. plot. In a previous essay, which appeared in *Narrative*, he defines the term he uses in the book title as follows:

> *Story logic*, as I use the term, refers both to the logic that stories *have* and the logic that they *are*. [. . .] But narrative also *constitutes* a logic in its own right, providing human beings with one of their primary resources for organizing and comprehending experience.
>
> (Herman 2001: 130–1)

According to Herman, the inherent logic of narrative is constituted on a micro-level which includes various categories: distinctions between various kinds of events (cf. Chapter 1 'States, Events and Actions'); the means of representing actions and events (cf. Chapter 2 'Action Representations'); basic theoretical questions to do with cognitive frames (cf. Chapter 3 'Scripts, Sequences and Stories'); the developing/ formation of actants (cf. Chapter 4 'Participant Roles and Relations') and the representation of verbal interactions (cf. Chapter 5 'Dialogues and Styles'). The macro-level of story has four parameters: time (Chapter 6), space (Chapter 7), the anchoring of the action in perspectival orientation (Chapter 8), and incorporating the story into the context at the level of communication (Chapter 8, 'Contextual Anchoring').

The most prominent German narratologist at present is Ansgar Nünning. Nünning began his career in narratology with a dissertation on narrative discourse in the novels of George Eliot (Nünning 1989). This piece of work contains an in-depth review of all the important narratorial functions and modifies the notion of narrator in the communication model by introducing a scheme in which the implied author is

Herman

Nünning

replaced by a further narrative level, N3 (*Niveau* 3). After this, Nünning turned to the analysis of the British novel after 1945 and, in his post-doctoral (habilitation) thesis, examined five types of historical novel, with particular emphasis on *historiographic metafiction*, a postmodern variant of the historical novel. His distinction between the documentary historical novel (e.g. Thomas Keneally's *Schindler's Ark*), the realistic historical novel (Walter Scott), the revisionist historical novel (e.g. Adam Thorpe's *Ulverton*), the metahistorical novel (e.g. Peter Ackroyd's *Hawksmoor*) and historical metafiction (e.g. Julian Barnes's *Flaubert's Parrot*) has been extremely influential already (Butter 2007).[9]

In addition to authoring a wide variety of student textbooks and works of reference, Nünning has edited a series of seminal volumes of essays which provide a wealth of new insights into a variety of narratological questions. His contribution to the study of unreliable narration is of particular interest. He rejects Booth's notion of the implied author and replaces the description of unreliability with a reader-oriented model that relies on the different textual signals that can be found in narratives (Nünning 1998). The neglected phenomenon of multiperspectivity was the focus of his next book (Nünning/Nünning 2000), and a work on transmedial narrative theory followed (Nünning/Nünning 2002a). A second study published in the same year and dealing with new directions in narratology might also be of interest to readers of the present volume (Nünning/Nünning 2002b).

The characteristic features of Nünning's work are a concentration on the communicative model of narrative, an approach which draws on reception theory (and is therefore reader-oriented) and a gift for describing and categorizing narratological phenomena. For instance, Nünning succeeds in providing highly useful typologies of the historical novel, the functions of the narrator, textual signals of unreliability, various kinds of metanarrativity (Nünning 2001) and of many other things besides, and he does so in clear and accessible models, which are mostly based on binary oppositions. The fact that such models are available makes the business of text description and analysis a good deal easier than it would be otherwise. Of the younger generation of narratologists, Nünning is the one whose method is most structuralist, although his approach draws on the cognitive sciences and reception theory.

Fludernik

To conclude this chapter, I should like to give a brief account of my own narrative theory. My starting point was, on the one hand, the desire to establish conversational narrative as prototypical of narrative and, on the other, to provide a historical perspective on the development of narrative forms.

I moved into narratological theorizing from my study of speech and thought representation, especially of free indirect discourse (*The Fictions of Language*, 1993). In the course of my research, it emerged that passages of free indirect discourse required readers to exert a good deal of interpretative effort since they had to determine whether a given clause should be read as narrative report, as the representation of a character's reflections or as a rendering of what that person actually uttered aloud. This insight led to the general view that formal elements do not always allow for a definitive understanding of a passage. Secondly, analyses of conversational British English at the Survey of English Usage in London demonstrated that a good deal of direct speech was not a faithful rendering of what was said but an invented utterance put in to liven up the discourse and give it an emotional edge. This gave rise to the schematic language theory which I proposed in the book, and also provided the germ of the theses set out in the following study.

The central thesis of my book *Towards a 'Natural' Narratology* (1996) is therefore   Experientiality
that narrativity should be detached from its dependence on plot and be redefined as the
representation of experientiality. Actions, intentions and feelings are all *part* of the
human experience which is reported and, at the same time, evaluated in narratives.
(This corresponds to the categories of *tellability* and *point* in Labov/Waletzky 1967.)
Experientiality is filtered through consciousness, thus implying that narrative is a
subjective representation through the medium of consciousness. By contrast, academic
historiography, which represents facts and arguments but not experientiality, is not
entirely narrative. Historiography focuses on the reporting of events, which do
not necessarily express narrativity in the sense given above. The model therefore
emphasizes that conversational narrative shares more essential features with the novel
than with historical academic discourse, though traditional historiography from
antiquity up to the nineteenth century much resembled fiction and even focused on
historical protagonists' minds. The model also embraces modernist fiction as the
ultimate realization of the narrative potential for representing consciousness, rather
than criticizing this type of writing for its lack of plot.

In spite of its somewhat controversial theses, *Towards a 'Natural' Narratology* has
generated a lively response, perhaps due to its cognitive and constructivist principles.
The book is premised on the fact that readers narrativize texts as they read, in other
words they also read postmodern anti-novels in such a way that these may be
interpreted as narrative. Hence, narrativity is not something that is simply present in
or absent from texts but rather something that is recognized by readers or sometimes
projected onto the text by them. The narrativization of reluctant story material in the
reading process thus reinforces or even creates narrativity for certain texts.

Towards a 'Natural' Narratology moreover examines hitherto neglected areas of   Diachronization
narrative more closely: conversational narrative, medieval and early modern narrative,   of narratology
postmodern narrative. Another major focus is grammatical and linguistic innovation
(second-person narrative, present-tense narrative). I shall not attempt to give a full
account of the cognitive bases of my model here. I would, however, like to emphasize
that the study also represents the first stage on the way towards a diachronic theory of
narrative. Fludernik (2003a) put forward tentative proposals for a history of narrative
structures from the Middle Ages until the rise of the novel; my current work is moving
towards a narratological history of English literature, including an account of the rise
of the novel from a narratological perspective.

We have come to the end of this account of the most significant theories that   Summary
currently serve as models in narratology. As can be seen from the position of this
chapter in the whole book, and from the discussion in previous chapters, knowledge
about the various typologies themselves is not as important as familiarity with the
categories of narratological analysis and a grasp of the semantic and functional
properties of narrative texts. Asking how the various categories fit together in a system
only becomes important when one starts to adopt a scholarly approach. Only then do
the typologies treated here come to be relevant. It is when one tries to explain how
narrative works and how all the pieces fit together that the issues outlined by the
theories discussed in this chapter move to the forefront of one's attention.

10 Diachronic Approaches to Narrative

Narratology and its corpus

Although individual aspects of narrative texts have often been treated from a historical point of view (for instance, the 'history' of free indirect discourse), narrative theory has, for the most part, concerned itself with the universal structures found in narrative. Typologies have been devised which include and classify every conceivable kind of narrative, and historical matters have been regarded as the domain of genre theory or non-narratological literary studies. Classical narratology of the French school (Genette, Greimas, Bremond, Todorov) such as it developed in the late 1960s and early 1970s concentrated on the novel as the prototypical form of literary narrative. This has meant that the theoretical concepts applied in narrative theory derive from a body of novel (and also short-story) texts dating from the eighteenth to the early twentieth century. Postmodern texts and, above all, narratives originating before the eighteenth century were only discussed as exceptions to the rule, and medieval narrative was almost entirely ignored.

The canon

At the same time, narratological research tended to concentrate on the traditional literary canon. Popular fiction, conversational narrative, newspaper reports and, initially, also historical writing were not subjected to narratological analysis since literary texts in all their intricacy seemed to shed more light on complex features of narratological interest.

As a consequence of developments in pragmatics, text linguistics, and conversational analysis as well as a renewed interest in historical studies of narrative (Paul Ricoeur, Hayden White), this state of affairs has meanwhile changed radically. There is a growing body of narratologically influenced research into popular fiction (Warhol 2003). In addition to this, conversational narrative has attracted the attention of scholars in French Studies (Stempel 1987), German Studies (Quasthoff 1980; Ehlich 1980) and English Studies (Fludernik 1996, Herman 1999).

Historical approaches in Germany

However, this diachronic approach to the study of narrative is almost exclusively the preserve of research conducted in the German-speaking world. The reason for this may be the nature of the 'habilitation', an advanced post-doctoral dissertation which qualifies the writers as candidates for professorships. Typically, these studies treat a broad topic within a theoretical framework, and then the argument is substantiated by drawing on a wide selection of texts. The texts in this corpus are often drawn from different periods, which makes it necessary to adopt a historical perspective on matters of theory. Studies of this type include Barbara Korte's work on representations of the body in the novel and Werner Wolf's book on anti-illusionism (Korte 1993, Wolf 1993). Both scholars discuss texts dating from the Renaissance to the eighteenth century and on into the present and trace developments in narrative forms and functions through the centuries.

In his theory of narrative, F. K. Stanzel pioneered historical considerations, for example in the observation that the pace at which the typological circle was filling up accelerated in the twentieth century; due to the relatively late 'discovery' of figural narrative, the lower half of the circle had long remained empty. Fludernik also devotes considerable space to historical topics such as medieval narrative and published a programmatic essay on diachronic narratological research (Fludernik 2003a).

In the following, we shall take a look at some developments which could be regarded as part of a diachronic theory of narrative. The focus will be on three main aspects. Firstly, there is the matter of development in narrative form, above all in connection with the shift from oral storytelling to the medium of writing; secondly, there is the part played by innovation in bringing about change; the third aspect is the question as to when the first evidence of these forms or structures can be found. Historical analyses are relevant because they provide additional information about how specific narrative techniques originated and when they came to predominate or fell out of favour. But this is not all: such analyses can sometimes lead to a significant revision or modification of the theoretical, especially the typological, bases of narrative theory.

Diachronic narratological research

From speech to writing

We tell each other stories every day, and such stories are the means by which we first come into contact with narrative. So, it can be claimed that conversational narrative is the prototypical form of narrative: it is the form we first listen to, then learn to employ ourselves, and it accompanies us on our way through life, day in day out. Learning to tell stories can be included under the overall heading of language acquisition (cf., for instance, Broeder 1995). The presence of conversational narrative all around us explains why elements of this everyday, oral storytelling find their way into literary narratives. Dialogue and free indirect discourse are quite often used in conversational narrative, for example, and the fact that they occur in literary texts can be interpreted as a reflection of the tradition of oral storytelling. Postmodern narratives, too, imitate certain aspects of spoken narrative for ideological reasons or in order to show how different they are from established literary models. We find texts, for instance, written entirely in a regional dialect or a particular sociolect. Many literary genres intentionally exploit the structures of oral storytelling; Russian *skaz* is one such example, in which 'fingierte Mündlichkeit' (Goetsch 1985) or pseudo-orality has been brought to near perfection.[1]

Oral storytelling as prototype

For all languages which only had an oral tradition to begin with, which was then set down in writing at some later date, it is the case that structures taken from oral narrative predominate in early written texts. This could be accounted for by the fact that structures going back to conversational narrative are used unwittingly as texts are produced. We can even find 'oral' narrative structures in genres, particularly prose genres, that do not go back to traditional forms of oral storytelling. What is of particular interest here is the way in which these narrative structures continue to evolve, leaving the oral model way behind them. In English, this change took place in the fourteenth and fifteenth centuries, when the style of French and Latin models was adopted. At the same time, the increasing length of the texts was also responsible for changes in the structure of narratives. Regrettably, there has so far been surprisingly little research into the way in which narrative structure changed with the shift from verse form to prose.

The shift to prose

Kittay and Godzich (1987) show that interesting changes in narrative structure can be found in this transition in French, but, as far as I am aware, there are no comparable studies for English or German.

The development of new narrative modes and their cognitive bases

As I suggested in *Towards a 'Natural' Narratology* (1996) and Fludernik (2003c), a change of narrative models always results in changed horizons of expectation on the part of the addressee. As reception theory has shown, pressure to be innovative in contemporary writing keeps generating new solutions to old problems. The popularity of *you*-narratives can be attributed to the fact that the second-person pronoun is well suited to involving the reader more closely in the fictional world. Then again, *you*-narrative and generic pronouns such as *one* work in a similar way, which heightens the reader's empathy. Thus, *you*-narrative perfects postmodern strategies of reflexivity, culminating in transferential metalepsis (the reader appears to participate in the action on the story level), while at the same time such texts can present internal perspective more effectively than reflector texts in the figural first- or third-person form.

Authorial narrative

The best example of the naturalization of 'un-natural' narrative situations is authorial narrative, which offers an internal perspective on the characters. Authorial narrative provides what each and every reader wants: insights into the motives behind the protagonists' behaviour. This is why the development of the omniscient narrator should not be regarded as an anti-illusionist or anti-mimetic breach of convention, but rather as the refining of an ideal narrative technique whose inherently un-natural quality fails to be consciously noted by readers.

Interior monologue

The same holds true for interior monologue. This may be conspicuous because of its form, but, in creating the illusion of being able to access the mind of a character directly, it delivers something that, though actually impossible, represents a further refinement of the Victorian novel of consciousness. The same is true of texts which give accounts of 'dying in the first person', as Stanzel called it (Stanzel 1984: 229–32), and of the recent spate of combinations of first-person narrative and authorial knowledge. Examples of the latter are Salman Rushdie's *Midnight's Children* (1981) and Jeffrey Eugenides' *Middlesex* (2002) (see Heinze 2008). Both of these narrative strategies seek to satisfy very basic desires on the part of the reader: who does not wish to hear something about what it feels like to die; who would not like to hear someone's life story from the point of view of this person, but with the first-person narrator not being entirely dependent on what s/he can perceive directly or remember?

Simultaneous narration

Similar arguments can be put forward in defence of present-tense narrative. The first novels written in the present tense attracted a good deal of attention and seemed to be very 'un-natural', but in the meantime, readers cannot actually remember if a novel they have just read was written in the present or the past tense. In this case, too, the increasing use of a narrative form that does not 'naturally' occur (one cannot experience something and tell about it at the very same time) paved the way for a technique which is now quite common. Telling in the present tense is now quite widespread in third- and first-person texts (as well as in *you*-texts), particularly in novels with figural narrative situations, where the traditional past-tense verb forms had a final illusion-destroying quality.

Narratological firsts

The investigation into the origin of various narrative techniques and stylistic elements is a particularly attractive avenue of inquiry in diachronic narratology. With regard to indirect discourse, for instance, the specific questions would be: Do we find any instances of this before the eighteenth century and, if so, from when onwards? Contrary to the traditional account of this type of speech and thought representation, there is evidence of the use of free indirect discourse in the legends of saints and in romances dating from the thirteenth century onwards. Admittedly these instances are rare, and it is mainly speech that is represented, not thought. In the fifteenth century, passages of free indirect discourse representing thought become more common, but, until Aphra Behn and, later, the eighteenth-century English novel, free indirect discourse is used primarily as a means to represent spoken utterances. It is only with the Gothic novel that more attention begins to be paid to characters' thoughts. Naturally, these findings regarding English must not be generalized and applied to other national literatures. According to Fleischman (1990), there are numerous examples of free indirect discourse being used for the representation of thought in Old French, far more, in fact, than we find in Middle English texts. (See also Marnette 1996.) Diachronic analysis of how consciousness is depicted in narrative has recently become a more prominent focus of narratological research (Herman, forthcoming).

Free indirect discourse

You-narrative is another strategy that appears to be a brand-new postmodern technique but in fact turns out to have existed for quite a while. After the turn of the twentieth century there did indeed emerge increasing numbers of *you*-texts, but we can also find isolated examples in the seventeenth century (Behn, Sully) and there is even a text from the fifteenth (!) (cf. Fludernik 1994a). Such early evidence is not only of interest because of the time when it was produced but also because it throws some light on the questions of how new narrative forms originate, in which contexts they first appear, and which forms are able to establish themselves successfully and why.

You-narrative

Unreliable narration is a good example of how complex these matters are. One would think that unreliable narration must always have existed, but then again, all the texts whose narrators are classics of this type date from the period between 1800 and 1950.[2] As Zerweck (2001) already suggested, this could mean that unreliability is only recognizable in realist novels in cases where the reader's expectations of a reliable narrator are not fulfilled. Where non-parodic allegory and homily predominate, the narrator is raised up on a kind of ideological platform, without necessarily becoming unreliable – it is not the intention of the author that the reader should doubt the narrator's credibility behind his/her back. Nor is unreliability common in postmodern texts since the lack of a realistic representation of the fictional world undermines the application of possible criteria of (un)reliability. In the light of the above remarks, one may be justified in asking if attributing unreliability to texts like Goldsmith's *The Vicar of Wakefield* (1766) or Defoe's *Moll Flanders* (1722) is not an inappropriate imposition of twentieth- or twenty-first century methods of interpretation on earlier periods (Vera Nünning 1998). On the other hand, I have no doubt that the way in which the Wife of Bath in Chaucer's *Canterbury Tales* presents herself clearly marks her out as unreliable. What we have here is a kind of satirical self-exposure on the part of this good lady, five times married, who with her scandalous views unites in one person all the worst stereotypes of negative femininity. In this context, as in many others, Chaucer may, to a great extent, have anticipated the 'realistic' novel.

Unreliable narration

New media

Film

The new media pose a real challenge to narratology. In this section we shall just take a detailed look at two problems arising in connection with film and with interactive computer narratives. These days, film is widely recognized as a narrative medium, although its affinity with drama cannot be completely denied. In earlier chapters, I made my position on filmic narrators and the attendant problems clear (cf. Chapter 4). At this point, I should like to pursue the question of what corresponds to the narratological concept of focalization in film. A discussion of this issue demonstrates very clearly how film has moved away from purely verbal narrative.

Focalization

In novels and conversational narrative the notion of 'perspective' (point of view, focalization) is a metaphor. The reader 'sees' events, as it were, from the point of view of a character in a novel. In actual fact, though, the reader only sees letters on the page. The metaphor of sight and seeing is intended to convey the mimetic illusion achieved by the narrative technique. Things are described in such a way that an impression of seeing everything from the point of view of the protagonist is created. In verbal narrative, after all, the visual can only be evoked through the power of suggestion – it cannot be directly or properly expressed in the linguistic medium. This is why describing things in words must be regarded as a form of art.

With film, the situation is quite different. Here there is no place for the written word, and even conversational narrative becomes boring if it is overused. Sight and sound are the media of film. Photography makes it possible to reproduce things extremely accurately, and this in turn calls for a high degree of precision on the part of a film director. What is recorded on film is perceived as reality and has to be consistent with it. Authors can be accused of having poor styles or criticized for the improbability of their plots, but we do not require of them that what they portray should correspond one hundred per cent to our experience of reality. By contrast, a film set in the 1950s will have to portray the characters in that era's fashions and show interior design and contemporary cars.

Hence the question arises as to what might correspond to perspective/focalization in film. Film theorists see perspective in film as being the expression of a subjective point of view – one which has to operate *against* the medium, against the basic setting of the movie camera. We get a subjective view in film by filming what a character sees, usually after a prefatory shot of the character or the character's face (*shot-reverse shot*). Subjective vision can also be conveyed by low-angle settings – a character sees from below something large and threatening coming at him. Subjectivity is also frequently evoked by means of close-ups.

In narrative, objective narrative discourse is the 'default' position; in film this would be filming as if one were seeing things through one's own eyes, i.e. the camera is positioned at eye level. Shots taken from higher than this are nothing unusual either, in expositional sequences, for example. Film actually combines the angle of vision from the fictional world with so-called camera-eye angles from above, which supply overviews similar to those we find in emic novel openings. Films shot from the point of view of a single character are very rare since this would make it difficult to provide any kind of exposition or to help the spectator to orientate him/herself visually. Summing up, we can say that film often makes use of the external view of a protagonist as a signal for a subsequent focalization using his/her point of view, or else unusual camera angles are used to create point of view. Hence, from the example of film we can see that the transfer of traditional categories from narratology to other media may be problematic. If one takes different media into account, it may become necessary to rethink current narrative typologies.

Aspects of narrative structure which relate to the medium of transmission play an even more important role in the study of interactive computer games. This kind of narrative, in which the reader/PC-user interacts with the programme while playing, has been the object of extensive narratological study (cf. the various contributions in Nünning/Nünning 2002a and Ryan 2004). Whereas with film it is the visual nature of the medium that necessitates interesting adjustments to the way things are presented, with computer games the modification results from the lack of a predetermined plot. The plot only partially exists in the shape of episodes which the reader can arrange as s/he wishes. It goes without saying that this kind of structure lends itself particularly well to adaptations of action films, and that less attention is paid to the depiction of mental states than in verbal narrative or in film. So the medium in which a narrative is transmitted not only determines the categories which can be used to analyse it but also the type of subject that can be treated.

> Computer games as interactive narrative

Changing functions and theoretical readjustments

Perhaps the most interesting aspect of historical narratology is the analysis of the various categories of stylistic technique, their transformation over time and the impact of this on already existing narrative typologies. One could argue, for instance, that certain accepted notions in narratology are only valid for certain periods. If this is so, can one still justifiably regard these categories as universals, or are they only special features which may come into play in particular historical periods? Monitoring how certain techniques change and develop over the centuries and whether they are modified in form or function during this time is also very revealing. To provide an example of this, let us return to free indirect discourse. Here we can see a shift in function from a predominant use in speech representation to a predominant use in the representation of thought. This change of function is mirrored on the formal level by a shift from short *for*-clauses to longer passages, which may extend over several pages. Free indirect thought emerges in contexts in which a character begins to ponder the cause of events and her/his own feelings. Such musings are frequently opened by *for*-clauses, which render the character's deliberations in free indirect discourse.

> Universal or historical categories

The third case I referred to above, the possible need to modify narrative typologies, has hitherto not been recognized, particularly for the study of medieval narrative. Nor have analyses of conversational narrative so far led to typological readjustment. One can cite the 'discovery' of so-called *you*-narrative as an example of a development that made modifications in the theory of narrative necessary. As long as only a few instances of this type of narrative had been identified (Butor's *La modification* (1957; *Second Thoughts*), Calvino's *If on a Winter's Night a Traveller* (1979)), narratologists did not need to consider the phenomenon more closely or rethink their theoretical assumptions. In the 1990s, however, the list of known *you*-texts began to lengthen (cf. Fludernik 1994a, 1994d). As a consequence, the need arose to account for these texts and to clarify the relationship between these texts and first- and third-person narrative. When this happened, it became clear that the hitherto satisfactory dichotomy first-/third-person narrative (which was also able to accommodate *we*-narratives and *they*-narratives) was

> Modification

no longer adequate for the purposes of interpretation. *You*-narratives are often mixed with first-person narrative since the first-person narrator does not only represent an authorial speaker but is also part of the story (an experiencing self). Thus, for example, in Günter Grass's *Cat and Mouse* (1961), the *I* and the *you* share experiences, which are reported by the first-person narrator. Then again, there are *you*-narratives in which the *I* only narrates and only the *you* acts; and *you*-texts cast in the figural narrative situation (reflector mode) in which the *you* only features as reference to the protagonist. (An example here would be Rumer Godden's 'You Need to Go Upstairs'.)

These facts led me to reformulate the first/third-person narrative dichotomy (homo/ heterodiegesis) as what I called homo/hetero-communicativity (Fludernik 1993b, 1994b: 447). In the case of homo-communicative narratives, narrators and narratees are also active on the level of communication (as *I*, as *you* or as *I-and-you*). In hetero-communicative narratives, there is a strict separation between the level of communication and the plot level. *I* and *you* 'live' or rather 'communicate' on a level which has no connection with the story; they are both extradiegetic, as is the case for the narrator and narratee in authorial novels.

Revision of narratological categories

The revision of narratological axioms and orthodoxies is a popular area for research in narrative theory. For example, the notion of omniscience has recently received extensive criticism and reappreciation: Jonathan Culler criticized the theological notion of omniscience on the part of the authorial narrator (Culler 2004), whereas Meir Sternberg criticizes both Culler's proposals and the 'package deals' which the concept of omniscience involves (Sternberg 2007). Sternberg also draws attention to the fact that, in accounts of the representation of speech and thought, the role of listening/ hearing as a complex aspect of the narrative process has been neglected (Sternberg 2005); and I myself have called into question the author/narrator dichotomy in medieval texts and suggested introducing a new category of 'narrative performance' (Fludernik 2005, 2008).

Open research questions

Collectives

Many other areas could be mentioned in which a modification of the traditional categories and schemata would be appropriate. For instance, the collective or group has been somewhat neglected in narrative research. It is only recently that studies on *we*-narrative and analyses of the representation of collective mental worlds have come to the fore (Lanser 1992, Margolin 2000, Palmer 2004, 2005a,b). Narrative, in many respects, is a schema which is applied to individual fates and the often subjective interpretation of one's own experience or that of a group of characters who are presented as individuals. How these individual destinies are situated in relation to various collectives (nation, village, 'men', 'women', etc.) is a central concern of the Victorian novel. This area might also be a fascinating field for narratological enquiry: one could not only examine the representation of rumours and gossip but also the way in which certain individuals are presented as ideologically dissident in relation to their communities. This could be done by looking at the narrative techniques which make a protagonist stand out from his/her neighbours, or by analyzing the workings of public opinion.[3] How exactly does the narrative draw attention to a character we confidently expect to turn out to be a hero or a heroine? How far is resistance to prevailing norms a prerequisite for narrativity?

Another largely underexplored area in narratological research is description in novels   Description
(but cf. Hamon 1972, Bal 1982, Wolf/Bernhart 2007). Passages of description are often
regarded as non-narrative (*non-diegetic*): nothing happens while the narrator describes
a fair, a landscape or a character. Having said that, we also have to concede that
description is actually central at the story level since the fictional world through which
the actants move is only created through and by it. Even some aspects of actions have
to be described, for instance the order in which they happen and what they are like, and
what this contributes to the meaning: *He raised his arm <u>in a threatening gesture</u> and
<u>swung</u> himself up onto the table from where he began to speak, <u>brandishing his fists wildly</u>.*
In this sentence the protagonist's movement is characterized by the adverbial phrase *in
a threatening gesture*, which makes its meaning quite clear. In addition, the expressions
swung and *brandishing his fists wildly* help to specify the nature of the action (and the
feelings of the protagonist in a visually impressive manner).

Over and above this, the way description is located in separate paragraphs would also
repay study. Early Middle English literature contains hardly any extended passages of
description, and those descriptions we do find are very stereotypical:

> He [Murry] hadde a sone that het Horn
> *Faire ne mighte non beo born,*
> [. . .]
> Fairer nis non thane he was:
> *He was so bright so the glas;*
> *He was so whit so the flur;*
> *Rose-red was his colur.*
> *He was fair and eke bold*
> *And of fiftene winter old.*
>
> (*King Horn* ll. 9–10, 13–18; Sands 1986: 17; my emphasis)

It was only in the fourteenth century and increasingly so in the fifteenth that characters
began to be described as individuals and in much more detail. But even then
information about countryside, towns or castles was minimal while people, clothes,
armour and the like were depicted in more detail. A history of description in English
narratives before the Gothic novel, for example, would provide information on when
the first descriptions of landscape can be found, or when rooms begin to be described
in more detail and what kind of perspective is adopted in such passages (cf. Chapter 9
on perspectivism and aperspectivism). When do we first come across descriptions of
rooms which treat the narratee as a virtual character entering the described setting and
provide, as it were, orientation clues? (An example of this is e.g.: *To the left there were
two chairs near the fireplace, to the right one could see a large table, laid for eight people.*)

Extended passages of description may also be analysed in other ways. Birgit Haupt
in Peter Wenzel (2004), in the section about rooms (Wenzel 2004: 70–77), lists three
phenomenological types of room in novels: rooms presented as subjective experience
(rooms that evoke private associations in the character who enters); rooms serving as
backdrops to the action (for instance, a church as the setting of a wedding); and
rooms presented as objects of visual appreciation. It is the last type of room that serves
as an indicator of perspectivism or aperspectivism and deploys ample descriptions.
In the case of mood-setting rooms, the role of description in creating the desired
atmosphere and impression is paramount. Since Haupt's contribution Ansgar Nünning

has presented a typology of description (2007) which distinguishes several types of description in novels. Descriptions are categorized according to the narrative level at which they occur, their implicit – or explicitness, their objective or subjective nature, their literal or metaphoric quality, their placing in the text (position, extent, frequency, intermingling with action reports and textual shape – interspersed or isolated block description), and their motivational load (for instance, their plausibility within a given context). Especially interesting are Nünning's references to self-reflexive descriptive passages in fiction (2007: 99). Finally, the essay also deals with reception-oriented or functional aspects of description, for instance with the question whether a particular passage serves merely as an *effet de réel* (compare above in Chapter 6), or carries key metaphoric information relevant to the semantic structure of the novel.

Psycho-narration   As far as the representation of speech and thought are concerned, psycho-narration and speech report have so far not received much attention, either. Diachronic studies have already noted that the fifteenth century saw a marked increase in the number of passages containing psycho-narration (Fludernik in Herman, forthcoming). This is frequently associated with the motives of the actants:

> [. . .] thus departed fferant the senesschall . . . til that he approched the Reaunme of Sizile, auisyng alwey his newe seruant *considerying withyn hym self* his persone, his beaute his maner, his humbles whereof he was moche *ameruailed* for he *wende* not that yn the body of any one man might haue ben so many vertues togedir *So thought he wele that if he had* as muche worthynesse and prowes as he had persone & maner, *he shold be the moost perfit thinge* that euer god made sith tyme of his pasion.
>
> (*The Three Kings' Sons* 13.39–14.9; Furnivall 1895: 13–14; my emphasis)

As Palmer (2004) notes, psycho-narration is the most common form of thought representation in the Victorian novel and, even more so before the nineteenth century. More research could be done on a history of psycho-narration in the novel.

Referring to   The way in which characters are referred to in narrative texts would also merit more
characters   attention. It might, for instance, be possible to establish a connection between 'realistic' tendencies in the novel and the introductory *first name + surname* formula. It would also be interesting to find out when phrases like *the man in the brown hat, the lady with the lorgnette*, etc., first appear as an alternative way of referring to protagonists (instead of the use of names: *Toby Smith, Mrs Margery* or *Susan*). A great deal remains to be done in this area. The topic could be a fruitful field of research at doctoral level.

Although it would be possible to enumerate countless other topics which would lend themselves to diachronic analysis, it is time for me to conclude. One last comment, however, seems appropriate: an extension of narratological research to the periods before the eighteenth century and a focus on questions of diachronic development and change promise to open up new perspectives in narrative theory. Such research reflects questions and insights that tend to emerge in the reading of texts. Moreover, they are extremely well suited to being combined with text interpretation and thematic analysis. Since thematic issues have traditionally been neglected in narratological research, the expansion of methods and approaches resulting from diachronic research should also prove to be a welcome development in narrative studies in general.

11 Practical Applications

In this chapter I will look at a number of texts and illustrate what a narratological analysis of these might look like. In choosing the novels for discussion, I have tried to cover basic narratological types and to use examples from different regions and periods.

Great Expectations and *Mister Pip*: childhood selves

Charles Dickens's *Great Expectations* (1860–61) is one of Dickens's two first-person novels (the other being *David Copperfield*, 1849–50). It tells the story of little Pip (Philip Pirrip) from his childhood days as an orphan living in the household of Joe Gargery, the blacksmith, and his wife, Pip's elder sister, to his middle age. This novel of development or *Bildungsroman* narrates how Pip comes into an unexpected inheritance, which he incorrectly ascribes to the benevolence of Miss Havisham. It relates how he encounters his real benefactor, a convict to whom he had given food. He gets involved both with the fate of the convict, Magwitch, and Miss Havisham's ward, Estella, who turns out to be Magwitch's daughter.

One common way of reading the novel focuses on Pip's unfortunate conversion into a 'gentleman' – unfortunate because he becomes a snob and looks down on his friend Joe Gargery and the village as a whole – and on his eventual moral reformation and maturation when he starts to feel sympathy for Magwitch and recognizes and laments his alienation from Joe and Biddy, his childhood sweetheart. Another reading of the novel might foreground the psychological relevance of violence, threat and cruelty to young Pip (Pip is terrorized by his sister, by Magwitch, by Estella), and his surviving a major trauma when the convict returns like a nightmare to claim him just as he thought himself safe from the terrors of his childhood. Only by actively confronting the situation is Pip able to lay to rest the demons of the past. A possible reunion with Estella (the ending leaves it open whether or not they will marry in the end) becomes a viable solution only because Estella, too, has had to suffer in her loveless marriage and has emerged chastened and humbled from the experience. Both Pip and Estella are therefore survivors of traumatic events. Both have, to start with, been victims of abuse (cruelty and deliberate, perverse miseducation), as a result turning arrogant and losing touch with reality, and both emerge from their trauma as better, saner and more sympathetic, people. The abuse and traumas to which they are subjected are typical of an abusive social and legal system with its inherent cruelties, its harsh retributive law and its pitiless discrimination against women, who often turn into monsters when their legitimate sexual or emotional desires are frustrated (see Mrs Joe Gargery, Miss Havisham and Estella).

In what follows, I will contrast Dickens's novel with Lloyd Jones's New Zealand novel *Mister Pip* (2006), which to some extent is a post-colonial and feminist rewriting of Dickens's text. Yet this rewrite retains central features of the Victorian model: it is a first-person narrative that also focuses on a child's perspective (more consistently so since the novel concentrates on the events of one particular year and then jumps forward to the narrator's reworking of her early adult experience). Moreover, the novel can also be read as a *Bildungsroman* and as a nearly Naipaulian nostalgic appreciation of the cultural benefits of colonialism, while it simultaneously acknowledges the ravages of nativist revolutions, their human cost and their marked disregard for cultural achievements.

Both novels start with a retrospective analysis of the general situation in which the protagonists find themselves at a significant moment in their early lives. In language steeped in his childish perspective and his (mis)conceptions of the world, Pip opens his account with an explanation of his name and how he learned about his family – his parents and his five brothers – from their graves in the village churchyard. The narrator bemusedly notes how his childish imagination elaborated on the position of the brothers' corpses:

> To five little stone lozenges, each about a foot and a half long, which were arranged in a neat row beside their grave, and were sacred to the memory of five little brothers of mine – who gave up trying to get a living, exceedingly early in that universal struggle – I am indebted for a belief I religiously entertained that they had all been born on their backs with their hands in their trousers-pockets, and had never taken them out in this state of existence.
>
> (I, i; Dickens 2002: 5)

He then moves on to an appreciation of the significance of the particular day on which the convict pounced on him: 'My first most vivid and broad impression of the identity of things seems to me to have been gained on a memorable raw afternoon towards evening' (5). Yet even before Magwitch emerges from hiding, the day affords Pip an epiphany since he recognizes the full implications of his orphaned state, his loneliness and forelornness:

> At such a time I found out for certain, that this bleak place overgrown with nettles was the churchyard; and that Philip Pirrip, late of this parish, and also Georgiana wife of the above, were dead and buried; and that Alexander, Bartholomew, Abraham, Tobias, and Roger, infant children of the aforesaid, were also dead and buried; and that the dark flat wilderness beyond the churchyard, intersected with dykes and mounds and gates, with scattered cattle feeding on it, was the marshes; and that the low leaden line beyond, was the river; and that the distant savage lair from which the wind was rushing, was the sea; and that the small bundle of shivers growing afraid of it all and beginning to cry, was Pip.
>
> (I, I; 5–6)

Not only does this passage allow us some insight into Pip's naive childish equation of external visual data with social and geographic realities (churchyard, parish, marshes, river, sea) as named by linguistic convention; it also affords a curiously alienated perspective on Pip's surroundings and on himself. He becomes Pip by placing himself in the scheme of things as a shivering bundle of humanity exposed to the widening circles of marsh, river and sea; he accedes to his own identity, but to an identity that is defined by an absence of human warmth and by passivity and suffering. At this point, the retrospective quality of the account already begins to disperse in favour of Pip's perspective, and this emphasis on the experiencing self will be maintained throughout most of the novel. Yet the experiencing self, at least in this opening, is already divided since it finds itself bewildered by the contradictions between the norms of society (linguistic, legal, social) – stable, named, apparently orderly – and the appearances of things which are shape-shifting, foggy and threatening, like the marshes. As a consequence, the yet unformed character and identity of Pip are imprinted by the random forces of life.

Lloyd Jones presents us his Pip from the outside. One of the post-colonial rewriting strategies he employs is the attribution of the name to an adult white person observed from the perspective of the Pip-equivalent Dolores Laimo, a teenage girl from the Pacific island of Bougainville. In fact, Mister Pip (Mr Watts) acquires his sobriquet only during the climactic events in the village when the rebels, having found the name Pip scratched in the sand on the beach, believe there is a villager of that name, and the name gets applied to Mr Watts, also known to the children as Pop Eye.

> Everyone called him Pop Eye. Even in those days when I was a skinny thirteen-year-old I thought he probably knew about his nickname but didn't care. His eyes were too interested in what lay up ahead to notice us barefoot kids.
>
> (Jones 2008: 1)

The narrating self, Matilda (her name is not mentioned until page 16), uses a strategy similar to the one employed by Dickens. Her account is retrospective but resistant to an orderly presentation of setting and circumstances in a logical manner. Thus we find out on page 7, in a dialogue, that the first-person narrator is female ('What do you think, girl?'); the absence of the father, who works in Australia, is explained only gradually; and the setting and temporal placing of the story is first indicated on page 10:

> It was three days before my fourteenth birthday when the redskins came into our village for the first time. Four weeks later the rebels arrived. But in the time leading up to those calamitous events, Pop Eye and his wife, Grace, came back into our lives.
>
> (10–11)

In this prolepsis, the climax of the story is aligned with the narrator's personal chronology; later, the vague depiction of government troops (the redskins) and native rebels is dated in relation to the children's reading of *Great Expectations* during the winter of 1991/1992 (19).

In addition to the text's concentration on the experiencing self, the novel also highlights the life of the village community and the children's and adults' views, lack of understanding and prejudices. Although this is a first-person novel, it is also at times a novel about a collective, the native village community, and how it is at the mercy of political forces outside its control and beyond its grasp.

At the same time, the novel echoes *Great Expectations* to the extent of being a female *Bildungsroman*: Dolores manages to escape from the island, becomes an academic and a writer, and eventually meets Mrs Watts, Mr Watts's divorced wife. She is able to solve the puzzle of why Mr Watts had always drawn Grace (his partner) about on a trolley – they had performed that act in the theatre. Matilda identifies with Pip in Dickens's novel, although her trauma is not one caused by a Magwitch but brought about by the civil war on her island and the absurd cruelties it generates.

When the whites have left Bougainville and the civil war has broken out, the village is bereft of amenities, hospitals, schools and the like. Pop Eye becomes Mr Watts when he starts teaching, and he wins the hearts of the children by reading them one of his books, *Great Expectations*. When the government troops find the name Pip on the seashore, where Matilda has traced it in the sand, they want to know who this Pip is and are told it is a person in a book. But the book is not in the schoolroom, where it was supposed to be, and the troops punish the villagers for lying by burning all their possessions except for those of Mr Watts, the white man. Then Matilda finds the missing book hidden in a mattress that her mother Dolores has put on a raft of their tent and which therefore survived the destruction of the villagers' property. She is ashamed of the devastation caused in Mr Watts's house and the burning of all his books by the villagers in retaliation for his supposedly being responsible for their losses. When the rebels arrive, Mr Watts says he is called Mr Pip and entertains the rebels with his life story, partly cribbed from Dickens. Then the government troops return and kill Mr Watts as well as everybody who says they have witnessed his murder. Matilda's mother is raped and killed; Matilda survives thanks to a flood that carries her into the arms of friends. In this novel, therefore, Mr Pip becomes a kind of benevolent Magwitch; Magwitch's rescue from drowning in *Great Expectations* is transferred to Matilda-Pip. Matilda and her mother also echo the figures of Miss Havisham and Estella.

Great Expectations consistently maintains Pip's perspective – the experiencing self predominates. This happens most clearly in Pip's famous exclamation in what must, with hindsight, be read as free indirect discourse: 'My dream was out; my wild fancy was surpassed by sober reality; Miss Havisham was going to make my fortune on a grand scale' (I, xviii, 141). Pip here assumes that the money he has received comes from Miss Havisham, who eventually intends to marry him to Estella. This belief, of course, turns out to be mistaken. The exclamation reflects Pip's exultant thoughts at a moment in the past; the narrator Pip does not enlighten the reader that he had indulged in fantasy; the narrating self does not step in to provide a sober retrospective evaluation of young Pip's illusions. A similar moment of delusion occurs at the end of the book when Pip returns to Rochester to visit Joe and Biddy with the intention of marrying Biddy:

> The June weather was delicious. The sky was blue, the larks were soaring high over the green corn, I thought all that countryside more beautiful and peaceful by far than I had ever known it to be yet. Many pleasant pictures of the life I would lead there, and of the change for the better that would come over my character when I had a guiding spirit [i.e., Biddy] at my side whose simple faith and clear home-wisdom I had proved, beguiled my way. They awakened a tender emotion in me; for, my heart was softened by my return, and such a change had come to pass, that I felt like one who was toiling home barefoot from distant travel, and whose wanderings had lasted many years.
>
> (III, lviii, 485)

Pip's fantasy of leading a pleasant life with Biddy at his side receives a rude jolt only a few paragraphs on when it turns out he has arrived on the day of Biddy's marriage to Joe (486).

By contrast, when Pip meets two convicts going down to Rochester on the coach and remembers their destination, the hulks, he experiences a resurgence of a fear that he cannot at that point explain but reinterprets with the benefit of hindsight as 'the terror of childhood':

> In my fancy, I saw the boat with its convict crew waiting for them at the slime-washed stairs, – again heard the gruff 'Give way, you!' like an order to dogs – again saw the wicked Noah's Ark lying out on the black water.
>
>   I could not have said what I was afraid of, for my fear was altogether undefined and vague, but there was great fear upon me. As I walked on to the hotel, I felt that a dread, much exceeding the mere apprehension of a painful or disagreeable recognition, made me tremble. I am confident that it took no distinctness of shape, and that it was the revival for a few minutes of the terror of childhood.
>
> (II, xxviii, 235)

Another evaluative passage occurs when Pip is visited by Magwitch. On the one hand, the narrator describes how, at the realization that his money came from the convict and not Miss Havisham, Pip begins to feel that it is evil money and that he is no gentleman. At the same time, he deeply regrets the snobbish manner in which he has treated Joe and Biddy:

> I would not have gone back to Joe now, I would not have gone back to Biddy now, for any consideration; simply, I suppose, because my sense of my own worthless conduct to them was greater than every consideration. No wisdom on earth could have given me the comfort that I should have derived from their simplicity and fidelity; but I could never, never, never, undo what I had done.
>
> (II, xxxix, 329)

Here the experiencing self is evaluating its earlier conduct; especially the first and the final clause in the extract render Pip's immediate reaction to the revelation. But before that point we come across a passage discussing Pip's analysis of his feelings towards the convict; these – although this is not expressly clarified – seem to detail a later evaluation of the situation, a moment in which the initial horror has passed and an assessment of the significance of Magwitch's appearance within the larger picture of Pip's life has become possible. After Magwitch has informed Pip that he must not be caught or he will be hanged, the text continues:

> Nothing was needed but this; the wretched man, after loading wretched me with his gold and silver chains for years, had risked his life to come to me, and I held it there in my keeping! If I had loved him instead of abhorring him; if I had been attracted to him by the strongest admiration and affection, instead of shrinking from him with the strongest repugnance; it could have been no worse. On the contrary, it would have been better, for his preservation would then have naturally and tenderly addressed my heart.
>
> (II, xxxix, 328)

The opening sentence of this passage may still reflect Pip's current realization of yet another obligation placed upon him by the convict; but the sentence that follows ('If I had loved him . . .') reads like an analysis of Pip the narrating self about his present clearer sense of what his failings had been and how the situation might have been alleviated.

As is well known, *Great Expectation* does not conclude with a summary of Pip's life since Magwitch's death, but with an open-ended meeting with Estella; the narrating self therefore does not return to pronounce on his earlier self; in fact, in the published version, his inveterate tendency to chase after elusive hopes emerges with a vengeance: '[. . .] so, the evening mists were rising now, and in all the broad expanse of tranquil light they showed to me, I saw the shadow of no parting from her' (III, lix, 492). By contrast, the narrating self of *Mister Pip* becomes a dominant force in the final sections of the novel. Matilda now evaluates her love of Dickens and puts it in perspective, commenting on her own text:

> I have tried to describe the events as they happened to me and my mum on the island. I have not tried to embellish. Everyone says the same thing of Dickens. They love his characters. Well, something has changed in me. As I have grown older I have fallen out of love with his characters. They are too loud, they are grotesques. But strip away their masks and you find what their creator understood about the human soul and all its suffering and vanity. When I told my father of my mum's death he broke down and wept. That is when I learned there is a place for embellishment after all. But it belongs to life – not to literature.
>
> (Jones 2008: 217)

Whereas throughout the novel until this point the narrator has been focusing on her limited childish perspective, it is at this moment towards the end of the book that her autobiography acquires some distance and seems to put forward a retrospective analysis of the events. It is obvious that Matilda is still too immersed in her trauma to be able to judge her behaviour, or to find a neutral viewpoint from which to put the horrors of her experience in perspective. The role of the narrating self therefore dominates as a purveyor of her recent fact-finding mission (visiting Rochester and taking a tour), but her present narrating self and earlier experiencing self are still closely linked, too closely to allow for a dissociation of the two selves.

Authorial narrative: the perspective from above

Let us now turn to an example of that common type of novel in which we encounter a prominent narrator persona who tells us quite explicitly what is what, introducing scenario and setting, evaluating the dramatis personae with no uncertain strokes of the pen, and maintaining an ongoing bantering exchange with the reader in the form of exhortation. This type of narrator is not part of the fictional world, but stands above it; in Genette's terminology, this is a heterodiegetic and extradiegetic narrator figure. The narrator frequently displays what has somewhat imprecisely been called *omniscience*: he functions like the Lord of Creation surveying his world, knows the past, present and future of his characters, can move between locations at different ends of the fictional world, and has unlimited access to characters' minds. He is, in other words, an *authorial narrator* in Stanzel's typology.

Authorial narrative often opens with a broad sweep of the world of the novel, with a historical abstract or a sociological analysis of a district or period:

> In the days when the spinning-wheels hummed busily in the farmhouses – and even great ladies, clothed in silk and threadlace, had their toy spinning-wheels of polished oak – there might be seen in districts far away from the lanes, or deep in the bosom of the hills, certain pallid undersized men, who, by the side of their brawny country-folk, looked like the remnants of a disinherited race. [. . .] In the early years of this century, such a linen-weaver, named Silas Marner, worked at his vocation in a stone cottage that stood among the nutty hedgerows near the village of Raveloe, and not far from the edge of a deserted stone-pit.
>
> (*Silas Marner* I, i; Eliot 1996: 3, 4)

Authorial narrative often comments on human nature (gnomic sententious utterances):

> It is a trite but true observation, that examples work more forcibly on the mind than precepts: and if this be just in what is odious and blameable, it is more strongly so in what is amiable and praise-worthy. Here emulation most effectually operates upon us, and inspires our imitation in an irresistible manner. A good man therefore is a standing lesson to all his acquaintance, and of far greater use in that narrow circle than a good book.
>
> (*Joseph Andrews* I, i; Fielding 1986: 39)

The narrator often addresses the narratee or comments on the process of narration. Sometimes these remarks are metafictional in tone:

> I would it were possible so to tell a story that a reader should beforehand know every detail of it up to a certain point, or be so circumstanced that he might be supposed to know.
>
> (*Is He Popenjoy?* I, i; Trollope 1986: 1)

> Before the reader is introduced to the modest country medical practitioner who is to be the chief personage of the following tale, it will be well that he should be made acquainted with some particulars as to the locality in which, and the neighbours among whom, our doctor followed his profession.
>
> (*Doctor Thorne* i; Trollope 1990: 1)

> If you think, from this prelude, that anything like a romance is preparing for you, reader, you never were more mistaken. Do you anticipate sentiment, and poetry, and reverie? Do you expect passion, and stimulus, and melodrama? Calm your expectations; reduce them to a lowly standard.
>
> (*Shirley* i; Charlotte Brontë 2006: 5)

The authorial narrator persona can be elusive, or covert, disappearing behind the panorama that it is sketching: in George Eliot's *Silas Marner* and often in the novels of Thomas Hardy such a neutral, impersonal teller is at work. Other authors deploy an obtrusive narrator figure, one that keeps addressing the narratee and metanarratively comments on the telling of the story, as is the case above in *Shirley*. In fact, some Victorian novels undermine the extradiegetic position of the narrator persona even further in a playful manner. The narrator of *Shirley* asks readers to 'shake hands' at the end of the novel:

> Yes, reader, we must settle accounts now. I have only briefly to narrate the final fates of some of the personages whose acquaintance we have made in this narrative, and then you and I must shake hands, and for the present separate.
>
> (xxxvii, 594)

More impossibly still, in the opening the reader is invited into the fictional world to look at the three curates: 'You shall see them, reader. Step into this neat garden-house on the skirts of Whinbury, walk forward into the little parlour – there they are at dinner' (i, 6). At one point in the narrative, the narratee is even encouraged to read a letter from within the fictional world; this absurdity sums up metaphorically just what omniscient authorial narrative is capable of: 'Come near, by all means, reader: do not be shy: stoop over his [Louis'] shoulder fearlessly, and read as he scribbles' (xxix, 487).

Some authorial narrators are 'engaging' (Warhol 1986) in the extreme: they not only banter with their '(dear) reader' (in *Jane Eyre* and *Shirley*), they even address characters:

> Yes, Caroline; you hear the wire of the bell vibrate: it rings again for the fifth time this afternoon: you start, and you are certain now that this must be him of whom you dream. Why you are so certain you cannot explain to yourself, but you know it. You lean forward, listening eagerly as Fanny opens the door: right! that is *the* voice – low – with the slight foreign accent, but so sweet, as you fancy: you half rise: Fanny will tell him Mr Helstone is with company, and then he will go away. Oh! she cannot let him go: in spite of herself – in spite of her reason she walks half across the room; she stands ready to dart out in case the step should retreat: but he enters the passage. 'Since your master is engaged,' he says, 'just show me into the dining-room; bring me pen and ink: I will write a short note and leave it for him'.
>
> (*Shirley* vii; Brontë 2006: 117)

This passage is notable not merely for its address to Caroline but for the marked shift of focalization. It can be regarded as an anticipation of second-person reflector-mode narrative. We see Caroline's hopes and her love for Moore from her own perspective – note the definite article in '*the* voice'. The narrator does not use the *you* to harangue or exhort Caroline but to step into her mind, metaphorically speaking, adopting the role of her alter ego. Compare this with a similar passage in Trollope's *Doctor Thorne*, where Frank, one almost wishes to say, 'poor Frank', becomes the subject of the narrator's dismay and ridicule. In fact, Trollope does not actually address Frank from within the fictional world – he merely exclaims at him as an example of stupidity. (The passage is therefore much less metaleptic than it might otherwise appear to be.)

> 'Well, I am going,' said he [Frank]; 'but look here, Augusta, if you say one word of Mary —'
>
> Oh, Frank! Frank! you boy, you very boy! you goose, you silly goose! Is that the way you make love, desiring one girl not to tell of another, as though you were

three children, rearing your frocks and trousers in getting through the same hedge together? Oh, Frank! Frank! you, the full-blown heir of Greshamsbury? You, a man already endowed with a man's discretion? You, the forward rider, that did but now threaten young Harry Baker and the Honourable John to eclipse them by prowess in the field? You, of age? Why, thou canst not as yet have left thy mother's apron-string!

(viii; 1990: 115)

In many authorial texts, the narrator's extradiegetic status is further undermined by the narrator inadvertently stepping down into the penumbra of the fictional world. For instance, the clearly authorial narrator of Dostoevsky's *The Brothers Karamazov* often talks about 'our district', thus becoming a narrator who is peripherally present in the world of his narrative (e.g. 2003: I, i, 9). Such lapses serve as authentification devices, and they may occur also in novels that are more openly playful and more explicitly fictional. Thus, at the end of *Shirley*, the narrator claims to have visited the scene of the fictional events: 'The other day I passed up the Hollow, which traditions says was once green, and lone, and wild; and there I saw the manufacturer's day-dreams embodied in substantial stone and brick and ashes [. . .]. I told my old housekeeper when I came home where I had been' (xxxvii; Brontë 2006: 607). This is the first we learn of the narrator living in the village and having a housekeeper.

The perhaps most striking instance of the same device occurs in Thackeray's *Vanity Fair*, where the narrator who had taken the role of a puppet master earlier in the text suddenly announces that he, too, was at Pumpernickel and met Becky in person (Chapter lxii; cp. Stanzel 1984: 202–5).

The omniscience of the authorial narrator is also a controversial issue. Clearly, the narrator is not all-knowing, and certainly not all-telling.[1] Authorial omniscience is highly selective: it includes reading the minds of some characters but not of others; it holds back information in order to create suspense; it produces ellipses that will be filled later, and so on. In fact, many authorial narrators admit to not knowing things, or play with the topos of withholding information. Fielding's deliberately unknowing narrator has even become the subject of a famous narratological essay (Füger 1978/2004). Here is an example:

Mr Joseph Andrews, the hero of our ensuing history, was esteemed to be the only son of Gaffar and Gammer Andrews, and brother to the illustrious Pamela, whose virtue is at present so famous. As to his ancestors, we have searched with great diligence, but little success: being unable to trace them farther than his great grandfather, who, as an elderly person in the parish remembers to have heard his father say, was an excellent cudgel-player. Whether he had any ancestors before this, we must leave to the opinion of our curious reader, finding nothing of sufficient certainty to relie [sic] on.

(I, ii; 1986: 41)

In view of the extensiveness of the narrator's knowledge elsewhere, his inability to provide details of Joseph's ancestors is a humorous touch, particularly since we know that the whole story is invented anyway. The inconsistency of an authorial narrator's lack of knowledge arises precisely from the tension between the authenticating attempts of the narrator (claiming his narratives to be true to life) and the quite opposite role of the narrator as authorial spokesperson, as a substitute for the author himself. It is for this reason that the term *authorial narrator* is a handy one, since it perfectly describes the authority to which an authorial narrator lays claim as a guarantor of the fictional world.

Both *Shirley* and *Doctor Thorne* belong to that category of authorial narration which employs a reliable, moralizing narrator figure, a personality that comments on the fictional world and its inhabitants and assumes the role of a moral historian. This type of narrator is in sympathy with (most of) the characters and often presents their emotions and musings, frequently deploying internal focalization. *Joseph Andrews*, by contrast, represents a different type of authorial novel, one in which the narrator persona puts himself forward (such a narrator is usually considered to be 'male'), comments ironically on the characters and even on the reader (narratee), with whom he is maintaining a humorous conversation. He clearly characterizes the text as an invention of his, strewing it with numerous metanarrative and metafictional comments. This type of narrator is also quite commonly highly ironic, more so than the narrators in George Eliot's novels or in *Shirley*. Compare this extract from *Shirley*:

> When a food-riot broke out in a manufacturing town [. . .], some local measures were or were not taken by the local magistracy [. . .]. As to the sufferers, whose sole inheritance was labour, and who had lost that inheritance – who could not get work, and consequently could not get wages, and consequently could not get bread – they were left to suffer on; perhaps inevitably left: it would not do to stop the progress of invention, to damage science by discouraging its improvements; the war could not be terminated, efficient relief could not be raised: there was no help then; so the unemployed underwent their destiny – ate the bread and drank the waters of affliction.
>
> (ii; 2006: 30)

with the following from *Joseph Andrews*:

> As when a hungry tygress [sic], who long had traversed the woods in fruitless search, sees within the reach of her claws a lamb, she prepares to leap on her prey; or as a voracious pike, of immense size, surveys through the liquid element a roach or gudgeon which cannot escape her jaws, opens them wide to swallow the little fish: so did Mrs Slipslop prepare to lay her violent amorous hands on the poor Joseph, when luckily her mistress's bell rung, and delivered the intended martyr from her clutches. She was obliged to leave him abruptly, and defer the execution of her purpose to some other time.
>
> (V, vi; 1986: 52–3)

Whereas, in the first passage, the irony appears in the section of free indirect discourse that renders the opinions of the village folk, but does so mutedly by echoing current convictions about the inevitability of working-class starvation in times of economic recession, the extract from *Joseph Andrews* foregrounds an openly ironic narrator who incongruously compares the old maid Mrs Slipslop with a predatory animal and Joseph, the object of her amorous desires, with a martyr. Not only are Joseph and Mrs Slipslop made to look ridiculous (they are the butt of the irony), the narrator is clearly being ironic and facetious in his comparisons. By contrast, one cannot say that there is a definable target for the irony in the passage from *Shirley*. The line between these two types of irony, naturally, is thin; there is a sliding scale between them, and George Eliot's *Mill on the Floss* has a number of ironic comments on Mrs Tulliver that are as scathing as those of Fielding's narratorial voice. Fielding also likes to deploy irony at several levels. For instance, when Joseph Andrews has been left naked beside the highway, some of the passengers in the coach passing by object to helping him for reasons of decency (the horrors of nakedness):

> [. . .] it is more than probable, poor Joseph [. . .] must have perished, unless the postillion, (a lad who hath been since transported for robbing a hen-roost) had voluntarily stript off a great coat, his only garment, at the same time swearing a great oath, (for which he was rebuked by the passengers) 'that he would rather ride in his shirt all his life, than suffer a fellow-creature to lie in so miserable a condition.'
>
> (I, xii, 70)

Not only is this passage ironic because it counterpoints the squeamishness of the respectable folk with the good-Samaritan-like behaviour of the postilion; it also problematizes this easy counterpointing by adding ironically that the good Samaritan will end up stealing to assuage his hunger and be transported for it. This hint by the omniscient narrator undercuts the moral status of the postilion, seemingly justifying the prudishness and scandalized disgust of the coach passengers; yet, at the same time, it releases another barb against social mores since the society which would have allowed Joseph to die at the roadside with no one to help him also allows a hungry man to starve, and if he should appropriate some bread, to be exiled from the country for having broken the law. Clearly both the law and understandings of decency are here exposed for their lack of Christian charity.

What are the advantages of authorial narration over the pseudo-autobiographical first-person mode? Following in the footsteps of the epic and historical writing, the authorial novel enjoys freedom from the limitations of a human perspective in the world. Where the first-person narrator can only relate what s/he has personally observed and participated in or what s/he has been told by others, the authorial narrator does not operate under any such restrictions. Novels that embrace a panoramic view of society, presenting us with many characters and a number of different plot strands, are therefore predominantly cast in the authorial mode, examples being Dickens's *Our Mutual Friend* (1864–65), George Eliot's *Middlemarch* (1871–72), Thomas Mann's *Buddenbrooks* (1901) and Tolstoy's *War and Peace* (1865–69). Since the authorial novel is a very flexible instrument, it allows for a variety of different modes: serious and facetious, flamboyant and ironic, realistic and metafictional. Its flexibility includes the easy combination of irony and sympathy, intrusive (if not obtrusive) narratorial meddling with the story as well as restrained covert telling, and it makes frequent forays into the minds of the protagonists on the sliding scale of the authorial-figural continuum:

> What is this by itself in a wood no longer green, no longer even russet; a wood, neutral tint – this dark blue moving object? Why, it is a schoolboy [. . .] now trudging home by the high road, and is seeking a certain tree [. . .].
>
> Professedly, Martin Yorke (it is a young Yorke, of course) tramples on the name of poetry: talk sentiment to him, and you would be answered by sarcasm. Here he

is, wandering alone, waiting duteously on Nature, while she unfolds a page of stern, of silent, and of solemn poetry, beneath his attentive gaze.

Being seated, he takes from his satchel a book – not the Latin grammar, but a contraband volume of Fairy tales [. . .].

He reads: he is led into a solitary mountain region; all round him is rude and desolate, shapeless, and almost colourless. He hears bells tinkle on the wind; forth-riding from the formless folds of the mist, dawns on him the brightest vision – a green-robed lady, on a snow-white palfrey; [. . .] he is spell-bound, and must follow her into Fairy-land.

(*Shirley* xxxii; Brontë 2006: 530–1)

Martin Yorke is introduced by a conspicuous narrative voice, but the text soon shifts to his perspective and takes us deep into what he is reading about. This shift is here aided by the narrative's use of the present tense. The internal focalization continues until Caroline appears and they start to exchange a few words, at which point the narrative shifts back into the past tense (532). From a distinct persona in communion with the narratee about a visual object they both seem to perceive within the fictional world, the narrator moves on to a knowledgeable rendering of young Martin's character and habits. Then, it seems, the narrator relinquishes control and draws the reader into Martin's fairy tale. The novel is such a fairy tale to the reader, and s/he, like Martin, forgets everything while reading it. But the fairy tale also, ironically, hints at Martin's jejune love for Caroline and at the role of magician that he will play in spiriting her into the presence of her beloved Robert Moore, who in his illness is guarded by a dragon of a nurse barring all visitors.

It is therefore the versatility of the authorial mode that has maintained the form's popularity. Criticism levelled against authorial narration focuses on its spurious authenticity – after all, the narrator figure is a mere substrate of the image of the author, and the truth to which fictional narrators lay claim is not very realistic at all. In the early twentieth century, the authority of the typical authorial narrator persona became increasingly questionable, and the confidential invasive garrulity of narratorial discourse started to be perceived as a liability. Under these circumstances, figural or reflector narrative developed, in which the narratorial voice dissolved to a covert scene-setting function of report, and the emphasis was shifted to the portrayal of characters' minds. To focus on consciousness is to focus on the 'myriad of impressions – trivial, fantastic, evanescent', the 'incessant shower of innumerable atoms' which, as Virginia Woolf claimed, portray 'life within' much more realistically than the external props of bourgeois life (Woolf 1957: 1989).

Reading people's minds

The new type of narrative which Stanzel calls figural or reflector-mode narrative and which is based on a predominance of internal focalization – seeing the fictional world through the perceptions of one or several characters – slowly developed in the nineteenth century and made its debut in the work of Henry James and Joseph Conrad. It has remained a popular mode of novel writing, especially in genre fiction (romance).

The allure of reflector-mode narrative lies in its ability to reproduce what life feels like in the living of it – in contrast to the retrospective first-person account (good, but not good enough) and the authoritative, quasi-divine view of the world in authorial narrative, which gives us unexpected insight but is again too neat (content-wise) and too confused and sprawling (formally) for some people's taste.

To illustrate the workings of reflector-mode narrative, I want to look at extracts from Sunetra Gupta's *Memories of Rain* (1992). The novel delves into the protagonist's mind from the very beginning, locating her (Moni) on a particular afternoon in London, and then moves into her memories.

> *She* saw, that afternoon, on Oxford Street, a woman crushing ice cream cones with her heels to feed the pigeons. She saw her fish out from a polythene bag a plastic tub that she filled with water for the pigeons, water that they would not be able to drink, for pigeons, her grandmother had told her many years ago, can only quench their thirst by opening their beaks to drops of rain. And she remembered a baby starling that, in the exhilaration of her first English spring, she had reached to hold, her hands sheathed in yellow kitchen gloves, for within her, as her husband had once observed, compassion had always been mingled with disgust.
>
> (1992: 3; my emphasis)

Notice the typical use of a referentless pronoun ('She') which has no antecedent, not even in the title of the novel; a shifted deictic *that* in 'that afternoon' which picks out a particular time of subjective existence and pinpoints the moment that triggers a series of memories: of her grandmother telling her about pigeons, of her tendency to mingle compassion and disgust, of 'her husband' and how she got to know him. With the move towards the husband, the text reaches further into the past and to Calcutta, where she fell in love with her brother's white student friend, Anthony. A page further on she remembers a visit by her brother to London ('Last year'). It must be a year ago from 'that afternoon'.

Although Gupta makes it easy for readers to retrieve the relevant information, the pattern is typical of figural narrative. There is no explicit exposition introducing the characters and the setting and time (compare, for example, an opening like 'On the afternoon of a warm summer's day in the early half of this century a tall, brawny man of middle age was strolling along a country lane in Sussex'). The scene (London) is implied by the reference to Oxford Street; in the memory of falling in love, her parents' house is first said to be located in Ballygunge, as part of a phrase ('for this was in the flood of '78, and he had just waded through knee-deep water, he and her brother, all the way from the Academy of Fine Arts to their house in Ballygunge', page 3). Here the definite articles for the academy and the flood presuppose knowledge clearly available to the protagonist, and it is only when Anthony's legs are said to drip with 'the sewage of Calcutta' (3) that the home of Moni (her name is yet to be divulged – on page 4) is located more explicitly for the Western reader. In particular, this opening reflects an entry into ongoing processes, thoughts, experiences – the reader finds him/herself confronted with a specific place and moment in the story and has to get his/her bearings. No orderly depiction of the basic information is given; one has to piece the chronology, the names of the characters, and so on, together. Yet despite these typically subjective features, Gupta's opening passage retains an orderly syntactic framework that does not entirely drop into Moni's consciousness. The repetition of 'She saw' rhetorically suggests an extradiegetic speaker. The elegant alignment of subsidiary clauses in the second sentence also hints at a rhetorical source of the discourse, at a speaker in control of words. The explicit 'She remembered' also smacks of psycho-narration, and it is odd that we get the husband's account of her ambivalence of compassion and disgust. The passage is not yet uncompromising in its internal focalization.

The strategy of placing the reader *in medias res* without sufficient preliminary orientation is typical of etic text beginnings and reflector-mode narrative. Most novels written in the figural mode cannot maintain the exclusively internal perspective throughout the entire text. After all, some information about the external world needs to be given, and protagonists' names need to be dropped at some point. Only very rare masters of the mode like James Joyce manage to invoke interiority even when depicting external action-oriented information. Thus, in the third chapter of *Ulysses* ('Proteus'), Stephen Dedalus strolls along Sandymount Beach, and the focus on his mind is so dominant that even reportative clauses such as 'He halted' (1993: 34.158) do not distract from the presentation of his consciousness since they are framed by snatches of interior monologue:

> He halted. I have passed the way to Aunt Sara's. Am I not going there? Seems not. No-one about. He turned northeast and crossed the firmer sand towards the Pigeonhouse.
> — *Qui vous a mis dans cette fichue position?*
> — *C'est le pigeon, Joseph.*
>
> (34.158–62)

By having Stephen remember this exchange about the Virgin Mary's pregnancy,[2] Stephen's change of direction towards the Pigeonhouse appears less externally focalized, as if he were observing himself turning towards that building. Later, this consciousness of his physical movements is emphasized even more subtly:

> His feet marched in sudden proud rhythm over the sand furrows, along by the boulders of the south wall. He stared at them proudly, piled stone mammoth skulls. Gold light on sea, on sand, on boulders. The sun is there, the slender trees, the lemon houses. (35.205–8)
> He had come nearer the edge of the sea and wet sand slapped his boots. The new air greeted him, harping in wild nerves, wind of wild air of seeds of brightness. Here, I am not walking out to the Kish lightship, am I? He stood suddenly, his feet beginning to sink slowly in the quaking soil. Turn back.
>
> (37.265–9)

Stephen sees his feet in movement, as if he were not acting deliberately. He perceives that he has arrived at the edge of the sea: the past perfect tense *had come* indicates his moment of perception. By such manipulations, Joyce is able to retain an internal perspective despite the sprinkling of reportative sentences in the narrative.

An especially good example of a resolutely figural text is Katherine Mansfield's short story 'The Little Governess' (1915). It starts with continuous free indirect discourse right in the middle of the little governess's thoughts:

> Oh, dear, how she wished that it wasn't night-time. She'd have much rather travelled by day, much much rather. But the lady at the Governess Bureau had said: "You had better take an evening boat [. . .]". [. . .]

It had been nice in the Ladies' Cabin. The stewardess was so kind and changed her money for her and tucked up her feet.

(Mansfield 1984: 166)

The story moves through the various stages of the little governess's horrible experiences, with the individual episodes always told from her perspective. It also ends with her final humiliation as she confronts the waiter (or, rather, hotel boy) maliciously enjoying her discomfiture. The succession of scenes which we witness from her frightened and naive point of view reflects on her lack of experience and prudishness. Since she has never been abroad she is frightened of being robbed. She therefore takes the porter to be a possible thief and refuses to pay him his franc. He takes his revenge by putting an old gentleman in her compartment (which is for Ladies only). She begins to trust the old gentleman and allows him to show her Munich. He invites her to lunch and ice cream and then takes her to his flat. When she becomes aware of his sexual intentions, she bolts and arrives back at the hotel too late to meet the lady who was to collect her for the agency. Having snubbed the hotel boy earlier (she was again unwilling to give him a tip), she now has to face his glee at her discomposure.

The presentation of everything from the governess's unenlightened perspective leads us as the readers to sympathize with her concern and alarm, yet quite soon we also have to recognize, from our more mature perspective, that she becomes a victim of her upbringing and the instructions she has been given. She believes the harmless waiter, the porter and the young men in the next compartment to be dangerous yet fails to notice that the old gentleman may have designs on her. She is overcautious and also stingy (because she is probably very poor), but then does not realize that she is accepting too much from the old man and that he will want something in return. She is as disgusted with sex as she is with money, both things presumably not talked about in her family and therefore subjects surrounded with horror and unease. The entire sequence of events is a nightmare for her as she is unable to control events and keep herself from harm. By showing everything through a series of misfortunes and hazardous episodes leading to what she sees as instances of near rape and of losing her reputation, the narrative leads us to participate in the constricted mental world of her penny-pinching and loveless existence.

Another strategy for avoiding narrative report, which is a reminder of telling, is the use of extended passages of dialogue. John McGahern's notorious novel *The Dark* (1965) was banned in Ireland on account of its sensitive material (most prominently, parental child abuse). It is a novel written entirely from the perspective of the protagonist Mahoney (whose first name we never learn). The opening is *in medias res* with a vengeance: The father, frustrated widower Mahoney, upbraids the son for having said 'fuck' and starts to chastise him with a leather strap. The scene is cast entirely in dialogue – the clash of the father's authoritative reprimands and the son's conciliatory and increasingly pathetic excuses ('I didn't mean it, Daddy. I didn't mean it, it just slipped out', 1983: 8) – interspersed with short reportative sentences that render the boy's horror, humiliation and self-loathing. The impact of the scene is terrifying. It is so even though the boy is never actually hit; the father only strikes the arm of the chair over which young Mahoney bends. The boy's fear and the immediacy of the presentation combine to stunning effect: we the readers immediately feel as if we were in young Mahoney's place.

Events in the novel are all related from this youth's perspective, but the boy is referred to variously as 'he', 'you' and 'I': the novel, in other words, alternates between third-person, second-person and first-person narration. The opening and the following three chapters come in the third person:

> The word [by his sister, who had to witness the scene] opened such a floodgate that he had to hurry out of the room with the last of his clothes in his hands, by the front door out to the old bolted refuge of the lavatory, with the breeze blowing in its one airhole. There they all rushed hours as these to sit in the comforting darkness and reek of Jeyes Fluid to weep and grope their way in hatred and self-pity back to some sort of calm. (10)

Chapter 5 moves into first-person narrative, but starts with what at first looks like interior monologue, and the fact that this is autodiegetic does not immediately register; we are still in the mind of young Mahoney, and only when we get to the first reportative clauses does it become clear that this is first-person present-tense narrative:

> One day she would come to me, a dream of flesh in woman, in frothing flimsiness of lace, cold silk against my hands.
>   An ad. Torn from the *Independent* by *my* face on the pillow, black and white of a woman rising. Her black lips open in a yawn. . . .
>   The pulsing dies away, a last gentle fluttering, and *I* can lie quiet.
>
> (30, 31)

Immediately his guilty thoughts take over again, and he worries about confessing his masturbatory excesses.

Chapter 6 moves on to second-person narrative, further underlining the focus on the young man's consciousness:

> Much of the worst in the house had shifted towards the others, you had your own room with the red shelves after long agitation, you had school and books, you were a growing man. (34)

Now he has to watch his father terrorizing and abusing his sister: 'You'd watched it come to this, hatred rising with every word and move he made, but you'd watched so many times it was little more than habit' (35).

As we continue to see the world through the eyes of young Mahoney – the change of pronoun matters very little – the cruelty, indifference and hypocrisy of Irish society are exposed. The protagonist's lack of orientation becomes palpable. The reader seems to be trapped in the protagonist's situation with no prospect of escaping from its horrors. No wonder the book aroused such outrage and led to McGahern being sacked from his teaching job.

With this device of providing a very close and intimate view of the fictional world, of drawing the reader into the consciousness and subjective stance of one fictional character, the technique of figural narrative caters to the reader's voyeuristic inclinations. Yet reflector-mode narrative also has its drawbacks since it fails to deliver a broader outline of the social and political context of events; it leaves it to the reader whether to credit and condone the protagonist's assertions, opinions and feelings. As critical debate about, for instance, Joyce's *Portrait of the Artist as a Young Man* or some of Henry James's short stories demonstrates, the lack of clear guidance on the part of a narrator can result in the reader's being at a loss. Are we to see Stephen Dedalus as a young and upcoming artist, or are we to take his aspirations ironically? Modernism, where reflector-mode narrative flourished extensively, is also the period during which irony (usually several layers of it) and ambiguity became key features of literary masterpieces. This effect was one aimed at not only in figural narrative but also in many first-person texts with a foregrounded narrating self. (Joseph Conrad's 'The Secret Sharer' and Henry James's 'The Figure in the Carpet' are prominent instances.)

The texts and extracts discussed in this chapter give some indication of the scope and   Envoy
range of techniques used in narrative. The interpretations offered are intended to show how narratological analysis can be a valuable tool when studying narrative texts. Obviously, it would be beyond the scope of this final chapter to exemplify all the aspects of narrative mentioned in Chapters 1 to 10. Nevertheless, it is my hope that it will help allay students' fear of a narratological approach to texts and may even encourage them to try out such an approach for themselves.

12 Guidelines for Budding Narratologists

This introduction to narratology is designed for an audience of first- to third-year students in BA programmes that incorporate extensive literary criticism and theory, for MA candidates starting on the theoretical study of narrative, and for a general audience of interested laypeople and researchers in other disciplines who would like to find out about literary approaches to narrative analysis. I have incorporated broader issues of fictional narrative and have tried to provide a more linguistic and a more historical survey than traditional introductions to narratology in English generally offer.

The book has also concentrated on introducing results from narratological research in German to a wider audience. Thus it lends itself as a complementary text to the many other excellent surveys of narratology available.

Other
introductions Among these one may note, for instance, Shlomith Rimmon-Kenan's *Narrative Fiction: Contemporary Poetics* (1983/ second edition, 2002), Mieke Bal's *Narratology: Introduction to the Theory of Narrative* (1985/ second edition, 1997), Steven Cohan and Linda M. Shires's *Telling Stories: A Theoretical Analysis of Narrative Fiction* (1988), Paul Cobley's *Narrative: The New Critical Idiom* (2001), Horace Porter Abbott's *The Cambridge Introduction to Narrative* (2002) and Suzanne Keen's *Narrative Form* (2003). Whereas Rimmon-Kenan and Bal are more structuralist in their approach, the other works mentioned include a number of topics that reflect how narrative study inevitably needs to pay attention to cultural and ideological issues. Thus, Paul Cobley includes a discussion of the history of narrative forms and discusses the relationship between narrative and identity. H. Porter Abbott, on the other hand, includes in his readable introduction a (considerable) number of ideologically significant aspects of narrative, treating such issues as normalization, master-plots, narrative negotiation and contestation as well as the constraints of the marketplace – to name only a few key concepts from the table of contents. Among these newer books Suzanne Keen's is the most narratological in its attention to form, appropriately reflected in its title *Narrative Form*. Unfortunately, one of the best pedagogical treatments is only available in an expensive facsimile edition: Seymour Chatman's *Reading Narrative Fiction* (1992).

Three works that can be used as complementary reading stand out by virtue of their special focus. Michael Toolan's *Narrative: A Critical Linguistic Introduction* (1988/ second edition, 2001) concentrates on the analysis of narrative texts for students of the English language, but also includes sections on children's storytelling and narrative's political relevance in the media and in law. Luc Herman's and Bart Vervaeck's *Handbook of Narrative Analysis* (2005) is a particularly good choice for students of comparative literature since it includes examples from many different languages; and

Jakob Lothe's *Narrative in Fiction and Film* (2000) is particularly good as a recent survey of narratological approaches to film.

Students of narratology will not only want to consult other introductions with a different focus on the topic but also to proceed to more complex prose by turning to the classic texts of narratology, perhaps those mentioned below. To start with, Gérard Genette's *Narrative Discourse: An Essay in Method* (1972/1980) and F. K. Stanzel's *A Theory of Narrative* (1979/1984) are the two classic texts to look at. These should be supplemented by a study of Gerald Prince's *Narratology: The Form and Functioning of Narrative* (1982), Mieke Bal's *Narratology: Introduction to the Theory of Narrative* (1985/second edition, 1997), mentioned above as an introduction but really a substantial work of criticism in its own right, as well as Seymour Chatman's *Story and Discourse* (1978). Chatman's follow-up *Coming to Terms* (1990) and Susan Lanser's *Fictions of Authority: Women Writers and Narrative Voice* (1992) may also be considered important classics of the discipline, as are Dorrit Cohn's *Transparent Minds: Narrative Modes for Presenting Consciousness in Fiction* (1978) and Meir Sternberg's *Expositional Modes and Temporal Ordering in Fiction* (1978/1993).

The classics of narratology

Among more recent books, there are also some weighty tomes that those who have decided on a career in narratology may want to turn to as particular challenges: Paul Ricoeur's *Time and Narrative* (1984–1988), Marie-Laure Ryan's *Possible Worlds, Artificial Intelligence, and Narrative Theory* (1991), Monika Fludernik's *Towards a 'Natural' Narratology* (1996) and David Herman's *Story Logic: Problems and Possibilities of Narrative* (2002). Of course, there are a huge number of worthwhile and inspiring books which deal with specific issues. It is impossible to name them all, but I will just select a few. On plot and causality, one could note Brian Richardson (*Unlikely Stories: Causality and the Nature of Modern Narrative*, 1997), Emma Kafalenos (*Narrative Causalities*, 2006) and Hilary P. Dannenberg (*Coincidence and Counterfactuality: Plotting Time and Space in Narrative Fiction*, 2008). On rhetoric and fictionality, see Richard Walsh (*The Rhetoric of Fictionality: Narrative Theory and the Idea of Fiction*, 2007) as well as James Phelan (*Experiencing Fiction: Judgments, Progressions, and the Rhetorical Theory of Narrative*, 2007). For the issue of narrative consciousness one should turn to Alan Palmer (*Fictional Minds*, 2004). Other key studies on frames, description, metalepsis and much more are noted in the body of the text and in the bibliography.

Recent studies

Four major reference works for students of narrative offer particularly useful information. The first and earliest is Gerald Prince's *Dictionary of Narratology* (1987/second edition, 2003), a glossary of narratological terms. David Herman, Manfred Jahn and Marie-Laure Ryan's *Encyclopedia of Narrative Theory* (2005), now available in paperback, updates and expands the dictionary format into a kind of handbook, providing entries from the key scholars in the field. James Phelan's and Peter J. Rabinowitz's 2005 Blackwell *Companion to Narrative Theory* and David Herman's *Cambridge Companion to Narrative* (2007) both provide an excellent survey of different approaches, issues and themes.

Reference works

When starting on a narratological research topic, one may of course search for material on specific issues in the *MLA Bibliography*, but looking through the issues of the journals *Poetics Today*, *Narrative*, *Style*, *The Journal of Narrative Theory*, *Poetica*, *The Journal of Literary Semantics* and *Language and Literature* may also prove instructive. In addition, consulting series specializing in narrative and narratology is another good way of finding out about new developments. Ohio State University Press has a series

Where to find narratological research

entitled Theory and Interpretation of Narrative, edited by James Phelan and Peter J. Rabinowitz, which publishes key studies in narrative. Likewise, the University of Nebraska Press has for a long time been one of the main publishers of narratological work, and David Herman is currently editing their Frontiers of Narrative series. De Gruyter needs to be mentioned as the home of the series Narratologia, edited by Wolf Schmid, Fotis Jannidis and John Pier. Most books published in this series are in English, though some are in German.

Research centres   If you are seriously planning to do research in narratology, studying with one of the key figures of the discipline may be a profitable and exciting experience. Recently several centres of narratological research have been created. There is, of course, the Porter Institute for Poetics and Semiotics in Tel Aviv (http://www.tau.ac.il/humanities/porter/). Ohio State University in Columbus, Ohio now boasts a centre called Project Narrative, with many lectures, seminars and conferences as well as scholarships for researchers (http://projectnarrative.osu.edu/). Paris has an important narratological research group at the École des Hautes Études en Sciences Sociales (EHESS) with the acronym CRAL (*Centre de recherches sur les arts et le langage*), see http://cral.ehess.fr/. In Germany, there is a narratology group in Hamburg under the directorship of Wolf Schmid, which organizes many conferences (see http://www.icn.uni-hamburg.de/index.php?lang=en). Finally, Wuppertal is currently creating a narratological research centre based on the cooperation between English studies (Roy Sommer, Astrid Erll) and the German department (Michael Scheffel, Matías Martínez); see http://www.fba.uni-wuppertal.de/zef/.

How to write about narratological issues

Writing about narrative using subject-specific terminology can become a hazard. Not only is it important to stick to *one* narratological model in one's terminology, but – more importantly, perhaps – the complexity of the models is such that it is extremely difficult for beginners to write an essay which does not include some narratological 'howlers'. My most basic advice is, therefore, to keep as closely as possible to the formulations you encounter in the books you have studied. Initially, do not experiment with turning phrases around, combining technical terms with different verbs, or using the active rather than the regular passive voice for formulas encountered in the classic texts. We will look at some of the problems that arise when talking or writing about the narrative aspects of a text below.

First-person narrative?   Even more fundamentally, beginners often find it difficult to apply narrratological categories to a text under discussion. For instance, many openings of modern short stories or novels make it initially quite difficult to tell whether the text is or is not a first-person narrative. Is the *I* in the text a character as well as the speaker? Who is the main protagonist? Let us look at the following passage which is the beginning of Nicolette Hardee's 'Wordperfect' (2003):

> 'This may be serious,' he said.
>   I have always put my faith in words, the reassembling of chaos into manageable phrases. Serious was a word that I would have used without hesitation. An OK word. Serious music, serious literature, serious money. I found that I did not like it applied to my state of health. I went off serious.
>   'If we operate there is a good chance of success.'

> Chance had always seemed an open sort of word. A sky-blue conjunction of possibility. Now chance became a chink of grey light seen through a closing door. Chance became dicey.
>   During the months which followed I found out other things.
>
>   ('Wordperfect'; Hardee 2003: 256)

Initially, one may suppose that the 'he' of the first line is the protagonist, the 'I' of the second line an opinionated narrative persona, an authorial narrator, a heterodiegetic narrator with no link to the story world. Only when we get to 'I found that I did not like it applied to *my* state of health' does it emerge that the 'I' is indeed a protagonist, the interlocutor of the 'he' (the doctor) on the level of the fictional world (the diegetic level): 'I' interacts with 'he'. The shift in tense from the present-tense system of the present perfect 'I *have* always *put* my faith' to the preterite of 'found', 'did not like', does not at first alert one to the time frame, but when the urgency of the doctor's utterances and the juxtaposition of 'now' with past-tense 'became' in 'Now chance became a chink of grey light' kicks in, in hindsight the past tense acquires the force of deictic distance between the 'I' of the narrator and the 'I' of the woman confronted with the cancer diagnosis. This is clearly a homodiegetic narrative: protagonist and narrator, experiencing and narrating self, are the same person, share a world. The 'now' in collocation with the past tense draws the reader into the moment of experience, erases the pastness of the preterite even in the act of narration. The narrator by these means dips into the moment of her confrontation with the bad news and thus foregrounds the experiencing self, underlining the protagonist's inability to distance herself from the impact, if only for the time being. The text then continues to move back to a more evaluative and critical perspective, holding on to the importance of words, of clichés – as if clichés will help her to keep her head clear and above water:

> For this was another thing that I learnt about words. A cliché is a wonderful artefact hacked from the mountain of the past, a sort of relay baton to keep you going to the finish line. It fits so neatly in your hand once you've grasped it, you'd be surprised. (256)

Most students have problems recognizing figural narrative. Is the text a report by the narrator, or is it a rendering of the situation that is focalized through the protagonist's mind? If there is no explicit narrator figure, the distinction between zero focalization and internal focalization – to use Genette's terms – can be difficult to trace. Let us look at another short story opening. Maria McCann's 'Minimal' starts with an exchange between Mark and Ellie about elderly people's inability to get rid of unneeded objects, their tendency to clutter their home with useless stuff:

Authorial or figural narrative?

> 'Total chaos,' Ellie says. 'Slippers under the sink, fuse wire in the bathroom cabinet. God knows how she found anything.'
>   'Old people don't mind,' says Mack. 'They're not in a hurry.'
>   'It was always like that, even when Nan was in her fifties.'
>
>   (McCann 2003: 296)

This opening does not provide any clear clues one way or the other. The passage continues:

> Mack knows all about Nan. He takes the big two-handled wok and pours soup into
> the bowls. They eat in silence, facing one another. Mack likes to concentrate on his
> food and Ellie, buffeted all week by office chatter, appreciates quiet intimacy. The
> soup is clear and spicy, studded with prawns. (296)

Once we get to 'Mack knows all about Nan', it becomes clear that this cannot be a first-
person narrative: not only is there no 'I' as a protagonist (or speaker); no first-person
narrator could see into Mack's mind. If read as a narrator's report on Mack's state of
knowledge, this sentence definitely rules out a homodiegetic reading of the text. Since
no later passages contradict this analysis, one can take this point as proven.

It is much more difficult to decide whether the text is written in the authorial mode
– with a covert extradiegetic narrator able to zoom in on the characters' minds – or in
the figural mode – written to convey the perspective of one of the two protagonists, with
internal focalization (Genette) or Mack or Ellie as focalizer (Bal). The story begins *in
medias res*, with a verbal exchange between Ellie and Mack, who are not introduced in
any way. Only in the course of the story do we learn that she works for an insurance
company as a telephonist and that he is unemployed and takes care of household
matters. There is also the underlying assumption that the reader knows who Nan is. No
explanations are provided about this grandmother or the fact that Mack and Ellie have
(possibly?) inherited her house. Or were they just cleaning it after her death? Note the
past tense in 'God knows how she *found* anything'; but this would have been *finds* if Nan
were still alive. And, indeed, later on there are several references to a 'landlord', who
owns the furniture which Mack, obsessed as he is with a minimalist lifestyle, gets rid of.
The fact that the opening takes it for granted that the people mentioned are known
would indicate an etic beginning and, therefore, a figural narrative situation. There is no
distinct narrator persona, no narrative voice ascribable to a narrator. So we have either
a very covert narrator, or (according to the no-narrator theory) no narrator at all.

This conclusion is belied, however, by the fact that neither Ellie nor Mack function
unmistakably as a reflector figure. Sentences like 'Mack likes to concentrate on his food
and Ellie, buffeted all week by office chatter, appreciates quiet intimacy' reflect the
habits and sentiments of both protagonists. In the succeeding paragraph we see things
through Ellie's consciousness, but, in the final paragraph of the passage quoted below,
it is Mack's perspective that seems to prevail:

> 'Delicious,' Ellie says, finishing up the last spoonful. How lucky to be chosen, to
> live with Mack, whose cookery is not, like some men's, an occasional self-indulgent
> performance. Mack devotes to their food his serious, inclusive attention. Now he
> nods, weighing the compliment, and glances at the rota taped to the fridge door:
> *Sunday — steamed chicken. Stock to fridge. Kedgeree*
> *Monday — cold chicken. Bean soup, chicken stock*
> *Tuesday*
> Mack frowns. He has evolved a system of radiant simplicity, each meal setting
> up the next with no junk food or waste, but so far he has not abolished midweek
> shopping. There are externals, as he calls them: bread, Cheddar. He has suggested
> to Ellie that they cut out dairy products. Lots of people do. (296)

The first section of the text does not, then, contain enough evidence to support the
claim that this is an instance of a figural narrative situation. Yet the passage is not

pronouncedly authorial either. There is no narrator (no 'I'); there is no emic text opening. Though the manner of presentation does afford us a glimpse of the thoughts and feelings of the two protagonists and shows very strong similarities to omniscient narration, there is an intimate feeling to the settings that seems to emerge from a perspective within the fictional world rather than from up and above the story world. The fact that the couple are on very good terms with one another, that they seem to exist on the same wavelength, so to speak, makes it possible to read the text from either of their perspectives, or even from a communal perspective. Many sentences allow themselves to be read as free indirect discourse of what the two say or think or reflect in their minds. Thus, 'Mack knows all about Nan' can be read as Mack *saying* that he knows all about Nan, agreeing with what Ellie says. Or this may be what she hears him say; or what she thinks: her awareness of Mack's awareness. The rest of the paragraph can be focalized through Mack's consciousness: he is aware of how he pours the soup that they eat in silence, how he likes to concentrate on his food while she enjoys the peace and quiet of home. But it may also be her impression of the scene, her vision of the soup 'studded with prawns'.

Only as the story unfolds does it become clear that Ellie is the reflector figure and that what we have, is actually a figural narrative in the present tense, with Ellie as the focalizer. With the wisdom of hindsight, we realize that the last paragraph of our extract is a reflection of what Ellie extrapolates about Mack's thoughts when she sees him frown. The phrase about being 'lucky [. . .] to live with Mack' first introduces Ellie's perspective; though, at a pinch, one could also have interpreted it as Mack's conceited awareness of Ellie's feelings. In either case, one needs to read the sentence as internally focalized. Since the entire paragraph after 'Mack frowns' seems to convey what he is thinking, ending in the free indirect discourse or interior monologue sentence[1] 'Lots of people do', taking Mack to be the focalizer is much more convincing at this point. (Alternatively, of course, one can go for alternating internal focalization.)

It soon emerges, though, that Ellie is to an ever-increasing extent falling victim to Mack's minimalism. He begins by eliminating the stove and the chairs and continues in this fashion until there is hardly any furniture or clothing left in the house and they have only uncooked spinach and raw onions to eat. The story ends with Ellie having him committed to a psychiatric hospital, the culmination of a sequence of actions which are depicted entirely from her point of view:

'Mack, where's the ottoman? Did you take our blankets out?'

'What blankets?'

Downstairs the dish of spinach and onion is on the table. Each place is set with a smaller bowl and a fork. There is no oil, salt or pepper. Ellie sits opposite Mack and watches him divide the salad between them.

'We could eat out of one bowl,' she says experimentally.

'And share a fork, take turns at using it.' He is excited. 'I never thought of that.'

Ellie forces down raw spinach and onion. She pictures the madness proliferating like yeast inside his skull: one fork, one spoon, one coat, one shoe.

After the meal Mack goes upstairs. Ellie checks the phone book and writes a number on the back of her hand. Soon, anorexic music threads its way down the stairwell: the computer. She steps outside, closing the front door behind her.

[. . .]

> Someone has to be there with Mack when the doctor arrives. Nevertheless she stays crouched against the car. It feels reliable. She thinks it may continue to support her weight, continue solid and real, until she can stand upright and begin the walk back to the house. (309–310)

Here Ellie is the focalizer of the story and, over long stretches of it, she functions as a reflector figure. Notwithstanding this, there are a good many narrative sentences – relatively speaking – describing the actions of both Mack and Ellie. Are these sentences written from an external or an internal perspective? An authorial narrator would be able to 'look down upon' both characters from outside. But the narrative discourse contains no indications of a narrator figure, a speaker who could be assumed to exist on the basis of the deictic signs in the text. This is why it is not advisable to use an expression such as 'The narrator describes Mack's skills as a cook', even though at the beginning the narrative seems to be authorial, in other words to have been written from an external (extradiegetic), higher-level perspective. In fact the apparent 'omniscience' of the narrative discourse soon dissolves into Ellie's point of view: she serves as the focalizer for the unfolding drama as Mack's obsession develops, assumes alarming proportions and finally threatens her very existence. Ellie is present when the two of them eat or converse; she can easily tell about both of them. She knows Mack's world view well enough to be able to extrapolate what he must be thinking.

Reading the story as Ellie's version of the events also opens the possibility of questioning her story. If Mack is as minimalist as she claims, or rather sees him to be (in fact, she does not speak, hence she doesn't claim anything), then why do they still have a computer, a phone, a telephone directory and a car? Is Mack's anorexia (see the 'anorexic music') a food and body thing (an obsession that extends from food preparation and sofas to kitchenware and bedrooms) that does not (yet?) touch on technology beyond that sphere? Is he trying to absorb a gradually starved Ellie into himself, with his body, mother-like, providing all the sustenance and comfort for her? Or is it Ellie who feels threatened, who is afraid of being reduced to nothing by his increasingly uncompromising minimania? Does Ellie overreact? And why does she not discuss the problem with him; why does she not say 'stop'? Instead of resisting his advance into suicidal minimalism, she helpfully proposes sharing one bowl and fork between them. Is she testing the extent of his insanity, or is this a sample of her inability to say 'No' openly, of her fear of confrontation? After all, she outmanoeuvres Mack as surreptitiously as he does her when he eliminates their furniture and physical comforts. Parading an apparent neutrality, the narrative in fact teases us with a linguistic minimalism of restrained style that only slowly discloses its deadly secrets.

Authorial narrative

Let us compare McCann's short story with the beginnings of two authorial narratives. Isaac Babel's story 'The End of the Almshouse' (1932) starts as follows:

> At the time of the famine there was no one in Odessa who could have lived better than the almsfolk at the Second Jewish Cemetery. The cloth merchant Kofman had once erected an almshouse beside the cemetery wall to the memory of his wife Izabella. Much fun was made of this location at the Café Franconi. But Kofman turned out to have done the right thing. After the revolution the old men and women who found refuge at the cemetery got jobs as gravediggers, cantors and washers of corpses. They got hold of an oak coffin and a pall with silver tassels, and hired it out to people who were poor.

Timber at that time had vanished from Odessa. The rented coffin did not lie idle. At home and during the funeral service the deceased person remained inside the oak box; but he was put into the grave wrapped only in a shroud. This is a forgotten Jewish law.

(Babel 1994: 289–90)

This opening is typical of authorial narration. It offers a wealth of information on the specific cultural background and also a historical survey, covering a longer period of time. The narrator is not referred to by the first-person pronoun, but he does put forward views of his own, as instanced in stylistic emphases such as the one in the last sentence of the passage cited. In Russian this sentence, through the lack of a verb, emphasizes the narrator's viewpoint: 'Takov zabyty evreiskii zakon' ('Konets bogadel'ik', Babel 1966: 232). Earlier, the reference to Kofman having been right also has a colloquial note that indicates the presence of a 'speaker', a narrator persona: 'Right he was' ('No prav okazalsya Kofmann', 232). Moreover, the phrase shows that the narrator can retrospectively evaluate the events; he knows that Kofman's almshouse turned out to be a good thing.[2] Yet, on the whole, the narrator of this story is a covert one. Many authorial narratives dispense with an intrusive narrator and are only identifiable as authorial because they present a bird's-eye view of the fictional world, offer an extensive introduction to the story world or are capable of depicting the thoughts of several protagonists. They are authorial by default, since the story is not focalized consistently from the perspective of one of the characters.

In contrast to the opening of Isaac Babel's story, a more bard-like approach by the narrator confronts us in the first paragraph of Washington Irving's 'The Broken Heart':

It is a common practice with those who have outlived the susceptibility of early feeling, or have been brought up in the gay heartlessness of dissipated life, to laugh at all love stories and to treat the tales of romantic passion as mere fictions of novelists and poets. My observations on human nature have induced me to think otherwise. They have convinced me that, however the surface of the character may be chilled and frozen by the cares of the world, or cultivated into mere smiles by the arts of society, still there are dormant fires lurking in the depths of the coldest bosom, which, when once enkindled, become impetuous and are sometimes desolating in their effects. Indeed, I am a true believer in the blind deity and go to the full extent of his doctrines. Shall I confess it? I believe in broken hearts and the possibility of dying of disappointed love. I do not, however, consider it a malady often fatal to my own sex; but I firmly believe that it withers down many a lovely woman into an early grave.

(Irving 1981: 72)

The narrator continues in this vein for several paragraphs, contrasting female pros-tration in unhappy love with male insouciance and men's sturdy ability to put the 'bitter pangs' (73) and 'blast[ed] . . . prospects of felicity' (73) behind them. Whereas for man, "[l]ove is but the embellishment of his early life' (72) and disappointments can be set aside through the 'dissipat[ion of] his thoughts in the whirl of varied occupation' (73), a woman has unhappy love gnaw at her health 'like some tender tree [. . .] with the worm preying at its heart' (74):

> We find it [the tree] suddenly withering when it should be most fresh and luxuriant. We see it drooping its branches to the earth and shedding leaf by leaf until, wasted and perished away, it falls even in the stillness of the forest; and as we muse over the beautiful ruin, we strive in vain to recollect the blast or thunderbolt that could have smitten it with decay. (74)

The narrator explicitly presents himself as a man ('my own sex') and lays out his opinions on the truth of love stories, claims superior knowledge on the strength of his long experience of life and even pleads guilty to believing in 'the blind deity' of love and the possibility of a broken heart ('Shall I confess it?'). Here the urbane and aloof stance of a covert narrator – as in Balzac's opening of *Le Père Goriot* – gives way to an involved, chatty and 'engaging' (Warhol 1989) narrator who assumes a distinct personality in his exchange with his audience. Such a text invokes the scenario of oral storytelling; it provides a mimesis of the act of narration (Nünning 2001).

Having gone over the most frequent problems in identifying narrative situations, I would now like to turn to expression-related problems.

Some do's and don't's: how to avoid narratologically infelicitous phrases

Most students find it difficult to write about narratological aspects of a text. Several types of error can be encountered.

The simplest type concerns the mixing up of narratological models. Ideally, one should abide by one model. In this book, I have needed to mix models all the time in order to make my remarks comprehensible to both Genettean and Stanzelian readers. Nevertheless, phrases like the *zero focalization of the authorial narrator* need to be avoided at all costs. Such a phrase not only combines Stanzel's and Genette's terminology; it is also illogical within either system. For Stanzel there is no such thing as focalization, and authorial narrative is constituted by *external perspective.* In Genette's model, on the other hand, the/a narrator does not have anything to do with focalization (in Bal's model, there is a narrator-focalizer); in fact, the narrator in Genette does not 'see', and does not belong to the category of mode (of which focalization is a subcategory).

A second type of recurring problem concerns remarks made about a narrator figure when the commentator is referring to a reflector mode text (Stanzel) or a narrative predominantly using internal focalization (Genette). I almost wanted to say 'written from an internal focalization', but that would have been a slip of type one; focalization does not have anything to do with the narrator and his narrational act in Genette's model. A similar slip occurs in the following sentence from an exam paper on Charles Maturin's *Melmoth the Wanderer* (1820), in which the narrative notes that the protagonist, Stanton, travelling in Spain, sees a 'cross erected as a memorial of a murder' (1992: iii, 28). The essay continues:

> The narrator anticipates future events [the death of the bride later in the scene] and the word *murder* foreshadows these and thereby creates an atmosphere of tension. To support this, **the narrator switches from external to internal focalization and back again.** (My emphasis)

Again, the narrator cannot be made responsible for handling focalization, which is usually held to apply between the story and the discourse levels of narrrative, not between the narrational level and the text. The essay extract shows further problematic features such as the linking of Stanton's plot-based vision of the cross with the narrator's actions, or with focalization. The fact that Stanton sees the cross can be said to foreshadow later developments only as the result of the author's design; hence it needs to be laid at the door of the implied author's responsibility (the implied author standing in for the role of the author as creator of the text). So the examination candidate also confuses the narrator and the (implied) author.

Generally, this problem arises when categories are mixed within one model. Thus, the following sentence about *Great Expectations* also falls into the trap of getting narrative person and perspective/focalization confused: 'The story is told from Pip's homodiegetic perspective (first-person narrator who is part of the story and knows only what he thinks and observes).' The collocation *homodiegetic perspective* does not work. First-person narrative and internal perspective are mixed up here: perspective cannot be homodiegetic (or heterodiegetic) since this term refers to the category person only. However, what the writer of the sentence *meant to say* is perfectly correct: what we get in *Great Expectations* is Pip's homodiegetic narrative, and this narrative is focalized (often internally) through the mind of Pip the child, Pip the character on the story level. To use Stanzel's terminology, the experiencing self predominates in this first-person narrative, and many scenes are presented from Pip's internal perspective. (Note that 'first-person perspective' is equally doubtful as a terminologically sound way of referring to a first-person narrative – the terms *first-person* and *homodiegetic* both relate to the category of *person*, and *perspective* to that of *voice*.) Better replace with: *from the perspective of Pip, the first-person narrator*. This formula uses 'perspective' in a loose sense but does not clash with *internal focalization*, or *experiencing self*, the more specific and appropriate terms.

The unacceptable conjunction of the narrator with focalization is also apparent in the phrase *a heterodiegetic narrator with shifting focalization* (from another exam paper), where the replacement of *narrator* by *narrative* converts the phrase into acceptable language: *heterodiegetic narrative with shifting focalization*. This third type of problem concerns terminology *tout court*. Just as it may not be appropriate to use *narrator* and *narrative* interchangeably, the term *perspective* needs to be handled carefully, especially if one uses Stanzel's model, where perspective is one of the three axes of the typology. Similarly, when using Stanzel's model, it is necessary to avoid the term *figural* in the sense of 'referring to a character' since this would seem to denote the figural narrative situation. Thus, when one encounters *an instance of a figural perspective*, one is justifiably puzzled; this phrase is extremely misleading. In Stanzel there is, of course, no *figural perspective* (only *external* and *internal perspective*), and the term *figural* should collocate with either *narrative* or *narrative situation* rather than *perspective*. Nevertheless, since the phrase *from a figural point of view* (i.e. 'a character's point of view') is fairly common, there is a great temptation to employ *figural perspective*. In some contexts, the mixing of terms does not mislead since it is obvious that a figural narrative situation is being discussed; yet in other contexts the imprecise collocation may be very confusing.

A final problem area for many beginners is that of the clear separation of spheres between the author and the narrator, the narratee and the reader. Obviously, a sentence like *Towards the end of the story, the author* [!] *comments on the action* mixes up the real-life author and the narrator. If a sentence 'comments on', i.e. discusses or evaluates, what the characters are doing, this indicates the existence of a foregrounded act of narration and hence the implicit (or explicit, if there is a first-person pronoun) presence of a narrator figure. On account of the act of narration, such comments need to be ascribed to the narrator persona and not the author, not even in his/her virtual persona as implied author. (Implied authors do not comment, speak or narrate; only narrators do.) So one rule to observe is to avoid phrases like *the author tells us, the author remarks, the author describes,* etc. All these acts are predicated on an act of speaking or narrating, and can therefore only be performed by the narrator. The real author has, of course, produced the text in its entirety, but what the text 'means' – here a very controversial issue raises its head – cannot easily be determined on the basis of authorial intention. Since we cannot ask the author (who is usually already dead), speculations about the author's intentions are to be avoided. It is much better to phrase such insights in a more cautious fashion, for instance by using phrases like *the text/story seems to suggest that . . . ; we next get a description of the mansion; the narrator comments on the actions of the hero or the actions of the hero receive some invidious criticism in the next paragraph.*

What is true of the author is true of the reader (figure). The real flesh-and-blood reader and the narratee have to be carefully kept apart. One should at all costs avoid saying something about the beliefs or feelings of the (real) reader – how could one tell? The following extract from an examination paper, again discussing *Melmoth the Wanderer,* Chapter iii, betrays a considerable lack of caution in this area:

> Stanton finds himself in an inhospitable country [Spain] where every door is shut against him as a heretic [he is an Anglican]. ***The narrator reminds the reader of Stanton's danger.*** While the protagonist "forgot [all this] in contemplating the glorious and awful scenery before him", ***the reader bears all this in mind*** as the storm begins to draw together in the distance. (My emphasis)

As we know, the narrator cannot communicate with the real reader, hence a direct address to the text-internal narratee would have to be clearly marked in the text for this sentence to be a correct rendering of the situation. The passage alluded to is the following:

> Stanton forgot his cowardly guide, his loneliness, his danger amid an approaching storm and an inhospitable country, where his name and country would shut every door against him, and every peal of thunder would be supposed justified by the daring intrusion of a heretic in the dwelling of an *old Christian,* as the Spanish Catholics absurdly term themselves, to mark the distinction between them and the baptised Moors. – All this was forgot in contemplating the glorious and awful scenery before him, – light struggling with darkness, – and darkness menacing a light still more terrible, and announcing its menace in the blue and livid mass of cloud that hovered like a destroying angel in the air, its arrows aimed, but their direction awfully indefinite.
>
> (1992: I, iii, 29–30)

As this extract shows, what the writer of this essay really wants to say is that the text hints at Stanton's impending danger. In consequence, we are actually (again!) talking about the implied author or, better, the text. A good way of rephrasing the sentence would be to say: *The way in which Stanton is represented implies that he may be in danger.* Second, the (real) reader cannot be said to *bear anything in mind* since we cannot look into his/her mind to check up on this! Much better to continue with, for instance:

> Stanton contemplates the sublime scenery before him, but this idyllic interlude should not let us forget about the previous hints at impending danger, which are also underlined by the references to the storm gathering in the distance.

Since the writer of the passage is part of the community of readers, s/he may give advice on how to read the text without lapsing into a communicational metaphor that conjoins narrators or authors in a mutual act of interlocution with the real reader.

Another tricky case is that of gnomic utterances on the part of the narrator, usually in an authorial role of omniscience. Such universal truths are often articulated by using the first-person plural (*we, our, us*). For instance, George Eliot frequently deploys gnomic utterances by the narrator such as in the opening sentence of Chapter 55 of *Middlemarch*: 'If youth is the season of hope, it is often so only in the sense that *our* elders are hopeful about *us*; for no age is so apt as youth to think its emotions, partings, and resolves are the last of their kind' (Eliot 1986: V, lv, 591). The *us* and *our* in this sentence include narrator and extradiegetic narratee in the awareness of their common humanity. 'We are all human', the narrator suggests, 'and so are you, dear reader', and so is Dorothea, to whose experience the dictum is meant to apply.

Such gnomic utterances, owing to their universality, reduce the distinction between the authorial narrator (clearly in charge of the text in *Middlemarch*) and the implied author 'George Eliot' while also obscuring the fact that *us* and *our* do not actually refer to *me* and *you*, the real readers, but to the reader persona, the implied reader, for whom the extradiegetic narratee is standing in. The extrafictional audience and the narratee are deliberately implicated by this kind of address: the real reader, Eliot presumably hoped, would assume the role of the narratee and agree with the sentiments expressed by the authorial narrator.

Owing to this deliberate fudging of the boundaries between reader role and actual reader, it is therefore not too surprising to see some novices at narratological research fall into Eliot's trap. Thus, still in reference to Melmoth, one candidate comments on Melmoth's sentence

> [...] he stood collected, and for a moment felt that defiance of danger which danger itself excites, and we love to encounter it as a physical enemy, to bid it 'do its worst,' and feel that its worst will perhaps be ultimately its best for us.
>
> (1992: I, iii, 30)

in the following manner: 'The authorial narrator closely depicts landscape and atmosphere. The presence of the narrator is striking in the comments he supplies in brackets. He even *refers to the reader*, or *addresses the reader indirectly*.' Naturally, the authorial narrator cannot 'address' the real reader; yet the strategy of involving the real reader through the reader role invoked by the narratee has been recognized by this writer, and it has proved successful. In fact, such passages get close to an implied or virtual transgression of narrative levels, a transgression perhaps effectuated in another aside by the authorial narrator of *Middlemarch*:

> Accordingly, he [Caleb] took the paper and lowered his spectacles, measured the space at his command, . . . lifted up his spectacles again . . . [*pardon these details for once – **you** would have learned to love them if **you** had known Caleb Garth*], and said in a comfortable tone . . .
>
> (Eliot 1986: III, xxiii, 265; my emphases)

The narrator addresses the extradiegetic narratee, but the passage, of course, plays with the effect of (implied) author directly addressing implied reader, hoping to get the real reader to agree with these sentiments. Such a transgression becomes even more obvious in the following extract, which one could even label an imagined or transferential metalepsis (punning on Bühler's *Deixis am Phantasma*, 'transferential deixis'):

> We are not afraid of telling over and over again how a man comes to fall in love with a woman and be wedded to her, or else be fatally parted from her. [. . .] For in the multitude of middle-aged men who go about their vocations in a daily course determined for them much in the same way as the tie of their cravats, there is always a good number who once meant to shape their own deeds and alter the world a little. The story of their coming to be shapen after the average and fit to be packed by the gross, is hardly ever told [. . .]. Nothing in the world more subtle than the process of their gradual change! In the beginning they inhaled it unknowingly; *you and I* may have sent some of our breath towards infecting them, when we uttered our conforming falsities or drew our silly conclusions: or perhaps it came with the vibrations from a woman's glance.
>
> (II, xv, 173–4)

Here *you* and *I*, narrator and narratee, appear to live in the world of everyman and everywoman, a world shared by real authors and readers just as by narrators/narratees and characters of the fictional world of Middlemarch. The world addressed here is a human universal; the man who does not realize his dreams is a type whom we all know and are supposed to recognize in Lydgate in the story world. Narrator and narratee suddenly seem to descend into Lydgate's world, where they behave as real readers allegedly do in their real world, which provides a model of interpretation for Middlemarch. Although the text here practises a benevolent deception of the reader, as critics we need to remain aloof from the sliding ground of categorial hollowing-out when venturing into the quicksands of the text's emotional appeals. Despite the *effect* – a very successful one – of Eliot's narrative strategy, therefore, as critics we are well advised to note that the speaker is still the authorial narrator assuming the role of the moralist and knowledgeable chronicler of human foibles, and that the addressee cannot but be a persona located on the same communicational level, a 'dear reader' figure, who cannot be identical with the flesh-and-blood reader (you!) and certainly cannot step into Lydgate's world and shake his hand, except in imaginative transference. At the same time, we can, of course, demonstrate that *in practice* the effect of Eliot's text undermines these neat categorial assumptions. The rhetoric of address manages to involve the reading audience didactically by its moral analysis and by its strategies of narratorial address. *Pragmatically*, to use a linguistic distinction, the reader feels involved; literally or semantically, s/he is not.

In the above, I have demonstrated a number of problems which may occur when narratological terminology is used as a tool for formulating arguments about narrative texts. Perhaps these don't's can now be supplemented with a number of do's, a list of suggestions as to how to set about writing narratological analyses.

- Reproduce locutions you find in the standard narratological reference literature. These are likely to reflect correct usage.
- Remember that the author – except at a reading – never talks to a real reader. If there is a distinct persona uttering opinions, comments and evaluations, this must be a narrator.
- It is best to stick to one narratological model and to note whose terminology you are using.
- Memorize categories and subcategories and do not combine subcategories from different supercategories.
- Remember that some texts present the fictional world through the mind of a character. In such texts there usually cannot be an overt narrator persona without ruining the overall simulation of unmediated access to the story world. Hence: Be careful in using the term *narrator* in connection with figural narrative (in accordance with Stanzel's model), respectively for texts with consistent internal focalization (*à la* Genette).

In the hope that this chapter has alerted narratological novices to some of the pitfalls which await the uninitiated, I would like to conclude by wishing readers much pleasure as they play the narratological game. As always, practice pays off in the long run. You gradually acquire the knack of analysing narratives, of juggling with terminology and interpreting complex narrative texts, and eventually you will be able to write about them with confidence or even panache.

Glossary of narratological terms

* Asterisked words cross-reference to other entries of this glossary.

Anachrony According to Genette, this is the temporal reordering of elements of the plot on the *discourse level in relation to their chronological order on the *story level. *Analepses (flashbacks) and *prolepses (flashforwards) are categorized as anachronies. See Chapter 4.

Analepsis According to Genette, the insertion of an account of previous events in the reporting of subsequent ones: in other words, a flashback to earlier stages of the story. Analepses are often found in connection with remembered events or with the introduction of new characters, whose history and experiences before this point have to be told. Modernist and postmodernist novels make use of analepsis in order to disrupt the chronological and teleological structure of the narrative.

Authorial narrative situation In Stanzel's model, one of his three prototypical narrative situations. Example: Henry Fielding's *Tom Jones*. In this narrative situation, there is an external perspective – a narrator reports on a fictional world which s/he is not part of. This narrator has an overview of the entire fictional world, tells the story from on high, as it were, in full knowledge of the outcome of the complications that exist on the plot level, and has access to the thoughts and minds of the characters whenever s/he wishes. This is why the authorial narrator is often referred to as 'omniscient' or godlike. In Genette's model, the equivalent term is that of an *extradiegetic *heterodiegetic narrator making use of zero *focalization.

Autodiegetic *Homodiegetic narrative in which the first-person narrator is the main protagonist. An autobiography is an autodiegetic narrative.

Consciousness, representation of The consciousness of characters may be rendered linguistically in a wide variety of ways. A formal distinction is made between *psycho-narration, *free indirect thought, *interior monologue and *stream of consciousness (which usually consists of a mixture of these forms). The standard work on the representation of consciousness is Dorrit Cohn's *Transparent Minds* (1978).

Consciousness, stream of The simulation of associative mental processes in the representation of consciousness using *interior monologue, *free indirect thought and *psycho-narration. Stream of consciousness is *not a *formal category but characterizes a type of consciousness and/or a manner of depicting the mind of a character. The focus is on the evocation of associative leaps and on providing the illusion that what is being represented is consciousness in flux. Outstanding examples are to be found in the works of Dorothy Richardson, Virginia Woolf and James Joyce (*Ulysses*).

Deictic centre According to Bühler (1934), the *origo* or reference point from which the speaker positions his discourse in time, space, social role or personal identity. Speaker A on the ground floor refers to himself as *I*, to the spot on the ceiling as *up* or *above*, to the book he holds as *this book* and to his telephone interlocutor (B) on the third floor as *you up there*. Speaker B in response will herself be *I* and address Speaker A as *you*, the spot on the ceiling will now be *down below*, and Speaker B will be holding *that book*. The deictic centre is the I-here-and-now of the speaker. In fiction it may be transferred to the I-here-and-now of a protagonist, a case of Bühler's *Deixis am Phantasma* or 'imaginary deixis'.

Deixis A linguistic category that consists of referring words, for example *now, this, that, here, up, there, behind* and many others. According to Bühler (1934), these words posit the existence of a centre of reference, an *origo*, that is located in the here and now of the speaker. *The house up there* is *up there* from the speaker's point of view. Verbs may also have deictic force, especially in English (*come, bring*) and in Japanese: in these languages a different word or prefix often has to be selected depending on the location of the speaker or on his/her social status. In narrative texts, deictics like *now* or *here* play an important role as markers of narrative perspective and voice. The deictic centre may be shifted from the speaker (narrator) to one of the characters. In *free indirect discourse and in *figural narrative, we read a character's thoughts and perceptions through his/her eyes, as it were, an effect which is achieved by the use of deictics relating to the character's deictic centre.

Diegesis vs. mimesis (1) Traditionally, this oppositional pair is used to characterize the difference between *telling and *showing, particularly in the discussion of the representation of speech and thought. Thus, for instance, speech report is more diegetic than *free indirect discourse (or the latter is more mimetic than speech report or indirect speech). *Interior monologue and direct speech are the most mimetic. The terms *mimesis* and *diegesis* are used in this way by Plato in Book III of the *Republic* (392D–394D) when he says the narrator of the Homeric epics speaks 'in his own voice' (diegesis), or lets the characters speak (mimesis). Narrative therefore mixes diegesis and mimesis. Lyric poetry has only the poet's voice and is exclusively diegetic; drama has the characters speak and is exclusively mimetic. Plato sees pure diegesis as the only legitimate mode and condemns dramatists and epic poets for their theatrical bent (the imitation of the speech of characters as mimesis). Aristotle, on the other hand, in his *Poetics*, sees all literature as mimesis or representation – his chosen example is actually drama. Poetic mimesis includes diegesis as a subcategory as in the diegesis (narrative discourse) of the poet in Homer's *Iliad*. (2) In Genette's terminology, *diégèse* ('diegesis') refers to the plot or story level of the narrative. This term is also used in film studies in reference to the story level (*histoire*).

Diegetic According to Genette, referring to the story level. The term can also, by analogy with the meaning of *diegesis (1), mean 'belonging to the narrator' as in the expression 'diegetic comment' (i.e. comment made by the narrator).

Discourse See narrative discourse.

Duration A subcategory of the category of *tense (Fr. *temps*) in Genette's model. It covers the relationship of *narrating time to *story time (G. Müller 1948). Genette,

Lämmert and others make a distinction between ellipsis (events are not related at all), summary (events are covered only briefly), simultaneous narration (isochrony, e.g. in dialogue), stretch (slow motion as in film) and pause (no events on the plot level, comment or discussion on the part of the narrator – the *narrative discourse continues but there is no corresponding action on the story level).

Embodied self A notion introduced by Stanzel in order to describe a *narrator on the level of communication (*extradiegetic level), who is described as more than a speaker: the narrator sits, writes, eats, speaks to his housekeeper, and so on. The term is used for authorial narrators who are personalized. A first-person narrator by implication is always an embodied self. As there is no narrator in *figural narrative, there cannot be a narrator's embodied self either.

Emic/etic openings After Harweg (1968), who borrows the terms from Kenneth Pike (*emic* vs. *etic* as in *phonemic* vs. *phonetic*), a distinction made between texts that start by introducing and explaining everything the reader needs to know (emic opening) and texts that do not provide such explanations but rather pretend that the reader is already familiar with what is referred to. Consequently, emic text beginnings make use of indefinite articles when they introduce people and places ('*a* tall man', '*a* small town'), whereas texts with etic beginnings feature definite articles ('*the* man', '*the* little town'). Stanzel identifies an etic opening as being typical of the *figural narrative situation.

Experiencing self In first-person narrative we distinguish between the function of the self as protagonist (experiencing self) and that of the (usually) retrospective narrator as the *narrating self. In many modern and postmodern texts, the experiencing self predominates. When the narrating self is suppressed or missing altogether, such first-person narratives are figural, according to Stanzel: the reflector mode predominates; the experiencing self is the *reflector figure.

Extradiegetic See narrative levels.

Fable, fabula See story.

Figural narrative situation According to Stanzel, a prototypical form of the novel in which the action is filtered through the consciousness of one (or more) characters. Figural narrative only came to the fore at the end of the nineteenth century and evolved into one of the main forms of the modernist novel (Dorothy Richardson, Virginia Woolf, James Joyce, Katherine Mansfield). Stanzel's term 'figural narrative situation' represents the fictional world as quasi im-mediate (see *mediacy), with the reader not being told things (*teller mode) but being shown them (*telling vs. showing), seeing them – as it were – unfold before his/her very eyes. The *reflector figure, through whose consciousness the fictional world is portrayed, offers a limited view on the fictional world (figural narrative is often discussed under the heading of *limited perspective*). Figural narrative corresponds to heterodiegetic narrative with internal focalization in Genette.

First-person narrative A form of narrative in which the hero/ine (or one of the protagonists) is the narrator. Equivalent to Genette's *homodiegesis. In cases where the narrator and the hero/heroine are identical, the first-person narrative is *autodiegetic, according to Genette: the main protagonist tells his/her own story. If the narrator is only a minor character, watching the hero's/heroine's deeds from afar and trying to interpret them, we are dealing with a *peripheral first-person narrator* (Stanzel 1979/84). We generally distinguish between the *I* as narrator (or narrating self) and the *I* as protagonist (or experiencing self). It can be assumed that first-person narrators are both inherently limited in their *perspective and potentially untrustworthy: they have an agenda when telling their stories, which could come into conflict with a true representation of what happened. For example, such a narrator will seek to justify his/her own behaviour or attitudes. In contrast, the *heterodiegetic narrator (third-person narrator) is trustworthy almost by definition – his/her account of the fictional world is a given, a seemingly objective depiction of the story world. Some first-person narrators are not only subjective, naive or at the mercy of their own feelings (fallible), they also expose themselves as *unreliable; their portrayal of events is obviously prejudiced, exaggerated or ideologically and morally suspect, biased or 'deviant'. Such *fallibility* (Chatman 1990) is located at one end of a scale ranging from the potential and unacknowledged bias of the first-person narrator to his/her extreme unreliability at the other end of this scale.

Focalization A central constitutive element of the *discourse level in narrative. Introduced by Genette in order to draw a more precise distinction between the terms *perspective* and *point of view*. In Genette's model, focalization is concerned with 'Who sees?' However, issues of visual representation (for example, the description of various scenarios) are often mixed up with the question of access to characters' minds. Genette's *external focalization* describes a view on the characters and the fictional world from the outside, whereas protagonists' inner lives remain a mystery to us. His *internal focalization* represents a view of the fictional world through the eyes of a character, in other words, a view from within. *Zero focalization* is equivalent to the perspective of an authorial narrator. For Genette, this is an unlimited (non-focalized) view, which combines external and internal perspectives, since an authorial narrator may also see things through the eyes of a protagonist. Mieke Bal (1985/1997) supplemented Genette's account by adding a second distinction between *focalizer* and *focalized*. In the case of Genette's external focalization, Bal contends, the focalizer is located on the extradiegetic level and focuses only on visible focalized objects. With internal focalization, on the other hand, the focalizer is on the diegetic level (in one of the protagonists) and can 'see' his/her own thoughts (i.e. perceive invisible focalized objects), but cannot perceive the mind content of other characters (i.e. perceives only visible focalized objects outside him/herself). Only in the case of authorial narrative do we find both visible and invisible (thoughts, feelings) focalized objects; here the focalizer is located on the extradiegetic level. Further important models are mentioned under *perspective below. More recently, Jahn (1999) and Nieragden (2002) have put forward significant new proposals for models of focalization. See also Herman/Vervaeck (2004).

Focalizer According to Mieke Bal, the person from whose perspective focalization is carried out. In the figural narrative situation, for example, the reflector focalizes his/her surroundings and him/herself. In authorial narrative, the narrator-focalizer focalizes visible and invisible focalized objects (persons and the consciousness of these people).

Frame (1) A term borrowed from the cognitive sciences and referring to a prototypical scenario (*frame, schema*). For example, the word *house* conjures up a frame and makes it possible to use the definite article to refer to further elements of this frame such as the window or the door. Within a particular frame, certain sequences of action can be activated as *scripts*: for instance, the restaurant script, with constituent parts such as the waiter or the menu, which are stored in the brain as standard components of 'eating out'. (2) Secondly, the term frame also refers more specifically to the framing of a narrative text. (For an account of framing in connection with works of art in general, see Wolf 1999, 2000, 2006.) In verbal literature the major representative examples are frame stories, that is to say narrative texts such as Joseph Conrad's *Heart of Darkness*, in which the main story (Kurtz in the jungle) is embedded in a frame narrative (Marlow tells his friends Kurtz's story while they are on a boat on the Thames). See Chapter 4 on different types of frame stories (introductory, terminal, interpolated).

Free indirect discourse (free indirect speech, free indirect thought) German: *erlebte Rede.* A form of speech and thought representation which is characterized by the freedom of its syntax and the presence of deictic and expressive elements reflecting the perspective of the original speaker or of the consciousness being portrayed. In contrast to regular indirect speech, free indirect discourse is syntactically 'free' in that it does not occupy the position of the complement of a verb of speaking or perceiving (*He said that . . ., She wondered whether . . .*) but as a main clause in its own right (*Had she observed him at all?* or *Tomorrow was Christmas*). Free indirect discourse also incorporates politeness markers (*Sir*), deictics (*now*), and evaluative or expressive phrases and sentences that are rarely found in indirect discourse but are typical of direct speech: *bother!*; *that sneak*; *mama*; *God rest his soul.* On the other hand, free indirect discourse is a non-direct, transposed or oblique form of speech representation since the tenses and pronouns shift to fit in with the surrounding narrative discourse. Thus, we find that, in the prototypical case of a third-person narrative in the past tense, the sequence of tenses is observed as prescribed for indirect speech: 'Henry strode along the road. *What, it was five o'clock already? He had to hurry. Sonja was due to arrive at seven.*'

Free indirect perception Description of the perceptions of a character in a novel, the dominant syntax being that of *free indirect discourse, detailing what the protagonist is seeing. Example: 'Henry looked out of the window. *The meadows stretched down to the river, where a few swans were undulating, their elegant necks held aloft in the breeze.*' The word 'elegant' expresses Henry's feelings; the whole sentence may be seen as a rendering of his visual impressions.

Frequency A subcategory introduced by Genette, of the utmost importance in connection with Proust's *À la recherche du temps perdu.* What happens once on the story level can be told once in the narrative discourse (*singulative narration*); what happens once can be told several times (*repetitive narration*); or what happens several times can be told once (*iterative narration*).

Heterodiegetic According to Genette, a narrative is heterodiegetic if the narrator is not a protagonist or, as Stanzel puts it, the spheres of existence of narrator and characters are non-identical. Traditionally, heterodiegesis is equated with third-person narrative, but this form is only the most common example of it. Some *you*-narratives as well as *they*-narratives and *one*-narratives are also heterodiegetic.

Homodiegetic Equivalent to first-person narrative. According to Genette, a narrative is homodiegetic if the narrator is the same person as (*homo*) a protagonist on the story level (*diegesis*). If the first-person narrator is the main protagonist, Genette calls this *autodiegesis. We*-narratives in which the self is a member of a group but features on his/her own as narrator are partially autodiegetic. In conversational narrative there can also be plural homo- or autodiegesis, for example when a couple tell of their joint adventures.

Implied author Introduced by Booth (1961) as that instance which guarantees the correct reading of a text when an *unreliable narrator proposes a world view different from the intended meaning of the text; hence the repository of the text's moral stance. The implied author is balanced in models of narrative communication by the figure of the *implied reader (Iser 1972, Chatman 1978). Nünning (1989) replaces the implied author by the 'meaning of the work as a whole' at the communicative level N3. Nünning (1997a) puts forward a heavy critique of Booth's term, but somewhat tones down this criticism in Nünning (2005).

Implied reader Term originally coined by Wolfgang Iser (*impliziter Leser*, 1972) to denote the (ideal) reader role projected by a text. Iser introduced the term in the context of his reader response criticism and focused on the 'social and historical norms' and the 'literary effects and responses' of fiction from Bunyan to Beckett (1974: xi). In narratology the implied reader remains a fairly shadowy counterpart to the *implied author. See also Rabinowitz (1977) on authorial audiences (*reader) and the distinction between real and implied readers and *narratees (Chapter 4).

Indirect discourse (indirect speech) Way of representing speech or utterances by using syntactically dependent clauses. The pronouns and tenses may have to be aligned with the referential and temporal frame of the narrative, depending on the introductory verb phrase: 'Frederick *told* us he *had* already *been* to see the exhibition.' In German there is a shift into the subjunctive. The use of the subjunctive also allows for indirect speech in German with no introductory verb phrase, where indirectness is already signalled by the subjunctive mode. Some languages do not have temporal shifts in indirect discourse, or only employ shifting irregularly. This is true of many medieval instances of indirect speech as well as of present-day Russian and Japanese. (See Fludernik 1993a.)

Interior monologue A form of representation of *consciousness: the representation of the mental processes of a character in direct speech (sentences with finite verbs in the present tense and referring to the person whose monologue it is in the first person. 'Frank reached the house. *For heaven's sake, where's my key?*') First used by Leo Tolstoy and Arthur Schnitzler and then by Dorothy Richardson, Virginia Woolf and James Joyce. Interior monologue can be found in single sentences (James Joyce's *Ulysses*, in the Bloom chapters) or as longer stretches of text (Penelope chapter in *Ulysses*). If the interior monologue makes extensive use of association, it is classified as *stream of consciousness. In such cases, it simulates the way the character's mind works.

Intradiegetic See narrative levels.

Isochrony See duration.

Mediacy (Ger. *Mittelbarkeit*) Central defining characteristic of narrative, proposed by Stanzel (1955, 1979/1984). In contrast to the representation of the fictional world in drama, in which the actions of the protagonists are shown in an unmediated fashion (in other words, the spectators see the actors before them, without any mediating instance), in narrative there is mediation by the narrator or the narrative discourse. This can be mimetic as the result of there being a teller or chronicler (*teller mode) or it can be focused through the consciousness of one of the characters in the novel (*reflector mode). The latter means that an impression of immediacy is created, but the representation is not really unmediated. Fludernik (1996) extends mediacy to the prototypical scenarios of consciousness-related cognitive perception – *telling* schema; *viewing* or *witness* schema; *experiencing* schema; *reflecting* schema (1996: 43–52).

Metafiction(al) A narrative strategy or a comment on the part of the narrator is metafictional if it explicitly or implicitly draws attention to the fictionality (fictitiousness or arbitrariness) of the story and the narrative discourse. *Frames and embedded stories (*mise-en-abyme*) are implicit metafictional strategies; comments by the narrator to the effect that s/he could have written the story differently are explicitly metafictional. The term 'metafiction' is sometimes used to refer to particularly metafictional postmodern texts, for example those known as *surfiction*, where the main protagonist is an author and reports on the difficulties he has with composing the story we are reading.

Metalepsis Genette's term for the transgression of boundaries between narrative levels. We can distinguish between ontological and discursive metalepsis (Ryan 2005). In the case of ontological metalepsis, the narrator is physically present on the story level (for example, the heterodiegetic narrator enters the fictional world and marries the heroine), or else a protagonist intrudes on the level of the narrator and performs actions there (for example, the characters visit their 'maker' and try to assassinate him). In the case of discursive or rhetorical metelepsis, the narrator imagines him/herself, or the reader, to be present in the world of the protagonists or, conversely, the narrator imagines the characters existing, as it were, in his/her world, without this having any impact on the plot. For instance, the narrator invites the reader to enter the house of the heroine, or says he wants to shake hands with the hero. This was a very common technique in the Victorian novel, in which the reader is frequently called upon to accompany the narrator into the drawing room and to observe the protagonists directly. See recent work in Fludernik (2003), Pier/Schaeffer (2005) and Wolf (2005).

Metanarrative Used to describe comments made by the narrator about the story, whether about making it up, formulating it in words or the ways of telling it. Metanarrative comments by the narrator can both foster and destroy the illusion of narrative mimesis. They are often metafictional. See Nünning (2001, 2004) and Fludernik (2003b).

Mimesis See diegesis.

Mise-en-abyme/mise en abîme A concept taken from art theory, referring to the inset–frame structure. A *frame and its inset can be called a mise-en-abyme structure if the framed element shows points of similarity to the frame. In narrative, one can speak of mise-en-abyme if an embedded story shares plot elements, structural features or themes with the main story and thus makes it possible to correlate plot and subplot. In Charles Maturin's *Melmoth the Wanderer* (1820), an evil monk tells the fugitive Alonzo de Monçada that he allowed two lovers, who sinned against his order, to starve to death in a dungeon. This embedded story leads the reader to suspect that the monk will also betray Monçada – a suspicion which proves to be justified. The standard work on mise-en-abyme is by Dällenbach (1977).

Mode (1) According to Genette, the way in which *focalization is treated, defined in the category of voice as 'Who sees?' (mode) vs. 'Who speaks?' (voice). (2) In

Stanzel's model, mode (Ger. *Modus*) refers to the distinction between *teller mode* and *reflector mode*, that is to say between the presentation of the story through the narrative act of a narrator and the presentation through the consciousness of a *reflector or Jamesian centre of consciousness.

Narratee (Fr. *narrataire*, Ger. *Leserfigur*) In contrast to the *reader (real or implied), a persona traceable in the narrative text through the use of address pronouns, imperatives and other markers of addresseehood. A diegetic or intradiegetic narratee is a character in the fictional world to whom another character tells a story; an extradiegetic narratee is a reader persona exhorted, harangued or hailed by the narrator as, for example, the 'madam' asked to shut the door in Sterne's *Tristram Shandy*.

Narrating time vs. story time (Germ. *Erzählzeit* vs. *erzählte Zeit*) A distinction introduced by Günther Müller (1948) between the time spent in the act of narrating (in minutes or pages) and the time represented on the story level (in days, months and years). Relates to the speed or *duration of narrative.

Narration, narrative act The telling of a story by a narrator, who may address a narratee. The narrative act, which corresponds to Genette's level of *narration*, forms the communicative framework of the narrative. According to Nünning (2001), this narrative act is often portrayed in such a lively manner that it constitutes a 'secondary mimesis' of the act of narration: the narrational process itself and the figure of the narrator seem to be part of a second fictional world, that of the narrator as s/he tells the story.

Narrative See narrativity.

Narrative discourse In contrast to the narrational level, the narrative discourse is to be found at the level of the printed text or the spoken words of a narrative. These are the end product or signified of the narrator's discourse, that is to say of the narrational process or act of narration. In the filmic or dramatic media, the corresponding narrative discourse refers to the sequence of sounds and images making up the film, or to the performance of a play. The narrative discourse has a double role as the *product* of the act of narration and as the *result* of temporal and focalizational rearrangements of the *story and *plot. In the first instance, the narrative discourse functions as the signified of the narrative act, the utterance; in the second, it operates as the surface level accommodating the transformations from the narrative deep structure. The story is in turn the signified of the narrative discourse (Genette).

Narrative levels Distinction between various levels of narrative which is of ontological relevance. A basic distinction is made between *story and *discourse. The story is what the narrative discourse refers to. Genette calls the story level *diegetic and the narrational level *extradiegetic*. The authorial narrator is located on the extradiegetic level whereas his/her protagonists live in the fictional world, on the diegetic level. If storytelling occurs within the narrative, as is the case when, for example, one character recounts something to another, this happens on what is called the *intradiegetic* level. The interpolated story is located one level below this, on the so-called *hypodiegetic* level. (See Chapter 4.)

Narrative report The discourse uttered by a narrator, or the narrative text, in so far as it refers to states or events in the story world.

Narrativity That which makes a text (in the widest sense) a narrative. Definitions of narrativity provide criteria for distinguishing between narrative and non-narrative texts (Fludernik 1996, Pier/Landa 2008). Gerald Prince (1982) and Hayden White (1978) use the term in different meanings. Prince distinguishes between *narrativehood* (i.e. criteria for defining what is, or is not, a narrative) and *narrativity* (degree of narrativity on a scale from the least to the most). White equates narrativity with the constructednesss of narrative, arguing that historical narratives share narrativity with fictional texts. Traditionally, narrativity is defined in terms of plot, the minimal definition being: the presence of at least two actions or events in chronological order which stand in some kind of relation to one another. Consistency of protagonists (the characters cannot change from one sentence to the next), the anthropomorphic quality of protagonists (speaking animals may be characters in a narrative but mute, immovable objects may not) and the foregrounding of the motives and intentions, goals and desires of the characters are other criteria that are often mentioned. Furthermore, protagonists must be locatable at a specific point on the space-time continuum (Prince 1982: 148–61). Fludernik (1996) includes plot in the schema of knowledge of the world that humans have. Plot is therefore treated as a subcategory of experientiality, which she posits to be the defining criterion of narrativity. The most recent contributions are in Pier/Landa (2008).

Narratology   Term coined by Todorov (1969). The academic study of narrative. Classic models of narratology adopt a structuralist approach and take up and develop further the ideas of Barthes, Bremond, Greimas or Genette. Since approximately 1980, the term narratology has also been used interchangeably with the more general terms narrative research, narrative theory and even narrative studies.

Narrator   In spoken narrative, the narrator is the person who utters the words of the story. In stories that are written down, in other words in written texts, we use the term narrator to refer to both *first-person (*homodiegetic) narrators and third-person (*heterodiegetic) narrators. Homodiegetic narrators are located on the extradiegetic level but are also characters in the story. Intradiegetic narrators are part of the fictional world: the text reproduces the situation of the conversational narrator at the story level. Heterodiegetic narrators that foreground their role as narrator function as the producer of the narrative text. They may even simulate the behaviour of a conversational narrator by using colloquial linguistic formulae. Signals for a heterodiegetic narrator are the use of the first-person singular pronoun (*I*), direct addresses to a narratee, the use of evaluative expressions (*the poor fisherman, the odious fellow*) and of expressive words and phrases such as *To be sure* or *By God!* as well as of metanarrative comments (*Now, let us see what has been happening to poor Henry*). Several narratologists assume that all narratives have a narrator; there is a covert narrator even in texts where no such person is explicitly mentioned, since they take it as given that a narrative text has a communicative framework. Narrators can be found in film and drama in the shape of frame narrators (voice-over, stage manager or a character or characters as in Thornton Wilder's *Our Town*); some theorists (Chatman) assume that film has a cinematic narrator.

Order   Genette's term. Concerned with the temporal ordering of the events depicted in the narrative discourse as compared with their chronology on the story level. A discrepancy between chronology and temporal order in the discourse is known as *anachrony. Genette posits *analepsis (flashback) and *prolepsis (flashforward) as subcategories.

Person Category traditionally distinguishing first and third-person narrative. This category of Stanzel's (1984) corresponds to Genette's category of *voice. The notion of 'person' derives from the fact that the main focus is on the person of the narrator in relation to the story, and this in turn determines the choice of personal pronouns used. In first-person narrative, the narrator uses the personal pronoun *I* to refer to the main protagonist in the story, who happens to be himself; in third-person narrative the hero or heroine is/are referred to using third-person pronouns i.e. *he, she* or *they* if there are multiple heroes. Stanzel (1979/1984) reformulates the category of person by making a distinction between the identity and non-identity of the realms of existence of narrator and protagonist (i.e. between the world of the narrator and the fictional world). Genette, by developing the terms *homodiegesis and *heterodiegesis, avoids the confusing reference to personal pronouns. Fludernik (1993b) suggests replacing Genette's homo/heterodiegesis (first- vs third-person narrative) with a distinction between *homo-communicative* and *hetero-communicative* narration, which would make it possible to incorporate *we*-narrative and *you*-narrative into the overall framework.

Perspective A synonym of the English term *point of view* (Lubbock). Originally used to describe the different kinds of access readers have to the consciousness of a novel's protagonists. (See *focalization.) In addition to the traditional visual (point of view) and psychological perspective (representation of consciousness), Uspensky (1973) and Lanser (1981) devised further subcategories, which take ideological and stylistic aspects into account. In Genette's model, these would be dealt with under the category of the narrator. In Stanzel's model, the oppositional pair *external* vs. *internal perspective* in fact characterizes a perspective continuum. Stanzel's external and internal perspective can be perceived of as locating point of view either on the intradiegetic level or on the extradiegetic level ('view from outside', 'view from within') as in Jean Pouillon's terms *vision sur* and *vision avec* (Pouillon 1946).

Perspective structure In connection with drama, Manfred Pfister (1977) suggested that, when all the ideological perspectives in a play are taken together, either a clear 'message' can be discerned (closed perspective structure) or else the various points of view are irreconcilable and simply exist alongside one another (open perspective structure). This idea has been appropriated for narratology by Nünning/Nünning (2000) and been developed into a model of narrative multi-perspectivism in which the narrator's and characters' perspectives (here ideological perspectives) are arbitrated and aligned with one another.

Plot See story. Cf. also Chapter 4.

Point of view Another term for *perspective, mainly used in the English-speaking world. See also *focalization.

Prolepsis Genette's term for an account of events that have not yet taken place. In this way the chronological order of the story is disrupted, the later event being recounted before the earlier. See *order and *anachrony.

Psycho-narration Dorrit Cohn's term for thought report. Extensively discussed in Cohn (1978) and Palmer (2004).

Reader/Narratee Alongside the real (empirical) reader, narratology also distinguishes external and internal readers and implied readers. The external *narratee* is located at the level of the extradiegetic narrator: s/he is the person explicitly addressed by the narrator. The internal narratee is a character who is addressed as reader by another character (e.g. in a letter). The *implied reader, correlating with the *implied author, is the ideal addressee invoked by a particular text: in the case of George Eliot or Goethe, for example, an educated person with a highly developed sense of moral values; or, with some feminist novels, a critical female; or with war stories, a cynical male; and so on. Rabinowitz (1977) calls implied readers the *authorial audience,* and the narrator's addressees narrative audience. Implied readers can also be specified, for example as regards gender (Lanser 1992).

Reflector (figure) A character in the fiction through whose consciousness *focalization takes place on the discourse level. Henry James calls such a protagonist a *centre of consciousness.* Stephen Dedalus in James Joyce's *Portrait of the Artist as a Young Man* is a reflector. In Stanzel's model, reflectors are found in texts in which the reflector mode predominates. See also *figural narrative situation.

Reflector mode In Stanzel's model the end of the mode axis which constitutes the *figural narrative situation. In reflector mode, mediacy is not generated by a narrator but through the consciousness of a reflector character, creating the illusion of immediacy.

Second-person narrative In second-person narrative, by analogy with third-person narrative, the character who is referred to as *you* is the protagonist or hero/heroine of the story. The reader focuses on the story of 'you' just as, in third-person narrative, for example *Tom Jones,* we are concerned with a person who is referred to by the third-person pronoun *he* or *she* (for instance Tom Jones or Mrs Dalloway). *You*-narratives utilize address forms and pronouns for protagonist reference. Texts from a variety of languages encompass all possible forms of address. The hero may, for instance, be referred to by polite forms like *vous* in French or *Lei* in Italian. A special feature of second-person narrative is that it may combine with first-person narrative: the story may include a narrator-protagonist as well as a narratee-protagonist; the speaker-narrator addressing the 'you' and hero is then also a character of the fiction like the narratee; *I* and *you* are located both on the intra- and the extradiegetic level of the story. In this case, both *I* and *you* have an existence determined by the continuity between their present narrating/listening selves and their past experiencing selves – *I* and *you* lived in the fictional world when the action took place (experiencing self, experiencing you), and at the same time, they either narrate or are addressed on the communicative level (narrating self, *you* as narratee). The narrator can also be an authorial narrator, located only on the level of communication. In this case the you-protagonist shares two spheres of existence (as narratee and protagonist), but the narrator is not part of the story world. An example of this is Joyce Carol Oates's 'You'. Finally, there are texts without any communicative level (figural narrative) in which the you-protagonist functions as a reflector character. Examples of these are Joyce Carol Oates's 'In a Public Place' and Edna O'Brien's *A Pagan Place.*

Speech report In fiction, the representation of the utterances of the protagonists in the narrative discourse, usually in a condensed and summary form, which may also be evaluative. In contrast to *free indirect discourse and indirect speech, which both preserve the propositional content (the message) of an utterance, speech report reduces a prior utterance to the fact of its articulation or gives the overall gist of the remarks. Example: *Mr March greeted the guests and bade them all welcome.* In Semino/Short (2004) called narrator's report of speech (NRS) or narrator's representation of speech acts (NRSA). In Genette: *discours narrativisé.*

Story Used with a number of different meanings. (1) Loosely, story is used in the sense of history: 'The real story behind this is . . .'. Story also refers to the events in the past. (2) In both narratology and in everyday usage, it can refer to what is told ('He told me a story'); in this sense it usually refers to the tale or the utterance. We have to distinguish between (3) story as motif and (4) story as plot, on the one hand, and between (1) story as what is told (motif and plot) and the narrative discourse as (2a) text or as (2b) narrative act, on the other. Genette calls the level of the story diegetic; the level of narration extradiegetic (see *narrative levels). The *plot is an elaborated version of the level of the motif (*fable, fabula*): it contains information concerning the reasons for and effects of the actions depicted (cf. E. M. Forster's example: 'The king died and then the queen died of *grief*'). When we move from the story level to the level of narrative discourse, we find temporal reordering is common (*anachrony), and decisions are also made with regard to focalization and selection of details. There is no consensus among narratologists as to whether decisions regarding chronology are already manifest on the plot level or only on the level of narrative discourse. Wolf Schmid (2005) additionally introduces the term *Geschehen* (unordered events as they happen, story material) in a four-part distinction between *Geschehen, Geschichte* ('plot'), *Erzählung* ('narrative discourse') and *Präsentation der Erzählung* (medial and evaluative presentation of the story by the narrator or in a medium). The term *plot* is frequently used simply to refer to the sequence of events in a narrative without providing more information about whether the reference is to the fable or includes causal links or temporal reordering. In Chatman (1978) the distinction story vs. discourse becomes the essential defining characteristic of *narrativity.

Stream of consciousness See consciousness, stream of.

Teller mode Narratives that have a prominent narrator persona belong to the teller mode. Opposed to *reflector mode in Stanzel's typology.

Telling vs. showing Distinction introduced by Percy Lubbock. Contrasts narrative texts in which everything is presented by the narrator (*telling*) and those in which the use of dialogue (as in drama) provides the reader with something akin to immediate access to the events represented (*showing*). Stanzel's *teller vs. *reflector mode relies on Lubbock's distinction and extends it.

Tense This is one of Genette's main categories, which is subdivided into three further areas: *duration, *frequency and *order.

Third-person narrative See heterodiegetic.

Thought report The most common way of reporting thought, in which feelings, hopes, motives and other mental states and processes (especially non-verbal aspects of consciousness) are represented in the narrative discourse. Example: 'Mary was choking with fear. She could hardly breathe.' In Semino/Short (2004) narrator's report of thought (NRT) or narrator's representation of thought acts (NRTA).

Unreliability A first-person (*homodiegetic) narrator who shows him/herself to be untrustworthy in his/her narration is referred to as unreliable. The reason for the narrator's untrustworthiness is not usually to be found in deliberate falsification on his/her part (the first-person narrator lies) but rather in a distorted view of things. It may be the case that the narrator is too naive to be able to describe what happens in a satisfactory way; s/he may also have a world view or moral attitudes which the reader cannot condone. The term was coined by Booth (1961) and has been significantly modified by Nünning (1998, 2005) and Cohn (2000). There is disagreement among researchers as to whether there is such a thing as an unreliable (or 'discordant' – Cohn) third-person (*heterodiegetic) narrator.

Voice (Fr. *voix*; Ger. *Stimme*) One of Genette's three basic categories, the others being *tense and *mode. Defined as 'Who speaks?' ('*Qui parle?*'). Covers largely the same ground as Stanzel's category of person, that is to say the distinction between first- and third-person narrators, which Genette calls *homodiegetic (*autodiegetic) and *heterodiegetic narrators. This categorization has been complicated by the discovery of second-person narratives (singular and plural), *we*-narratives, *one*-narratives, texts with invented pronouns, and texts with undefined narrators. In his category of voice, Genette also includes what he calls the *distance* between the narrative discourse and the story. Distance characterizes the degrees of narratorial mediation in speech and thought representation (minimal distance in interior monologue, maximal distance in speech report).

Notes

1 Narrative and narrating

1 Apart from many cartoons we might think here of Donald Barthelme's rewriting of the fairy tale in his novel *Snow White* (1967).
2 On gaps and their complementation by the reader during the reading process, see the very readable article by F. K. Stanzel 'The Complementary Story' (Stanzel 2004 [1977]).
3 In recent years there has a been debate as to what extent music, painting and poetry may be understood as narratives and approached through narratological analysis. See, for example, Nünning & Nünning (2002a), in particular the contribution of Wolf, and also Hühn (2004) and several of the papers in the Blackwell *Companion to Narrative Theory* (Phelan & Rabinowitz 2005).
4 For this reason in F. K. Stanzel's narrative theory (1984) the novel is opposed to drama.

2 The theory of narrative

1 On the subjects of German terminology, see Cornils/Schernus and others in Kindt/Müller (2003).
2 For more on the opposition narrator vs. narratee, see Chapter 4. For more on the opposition first person vs. third person narrative, see Chapters 4 and 9.
3 See, for example, Stanzel's three narrative situations (Chapter 9).
4 The concept of morphology is *not* based on modern linguistics, but rather on Goethe's *Formenlehre*, which presupposes an organic model within which narratives 'unfold'. The classic work of this type of narrative theory is Günther Müller's *Morphologische Poetik* (1948).
5 Even in non-fictional narratives, reality cannot be represented as it is. Rather, we reconstruct reality, though we do this assuming that this reconstruction equals reality.
6 The term *actant* refers to the protagonists in the plot and was established by Claude Bremond. It characterizes the plot functions which the protagonists fulfil. See Chapter 4.
7 See Nünning/Nünning (2002a).
8 See the somewhat contradictory views found in Kindt/Müller (2003).
9 V. N. Vološinov's 1929 monograph *Marxism and the Philosophy of Language* was supposedly written by Mikhail Bakhtin.
10 An overview may be found in the introductory chapter of Blackwell's *Companion* (Phelan and Rabinowitz 2005) and the introductory chapter by Fludernik and Margolin in the special edition of *Style* devoted to German narrative research (Fludernik and Margolin 2004).
11 For more information on homepages, etc., see Chapter 12.

3 Text and authorship

1 As Nathaniel Hawthorne complained to his publisher William D. Ticknor in a letter dated 19 January 1855: '[. . .] America is now wholly given over to a d——d mob of scribbling women [. . .]' – quoted in Davis 1998: 364.
2 See Siskin (1998) among others for the situation in England. On the author see also Bennett (2005).

3   The author was John Stubbs, and the proposed marriage was that between Elizabeth I and the French Catholic Duke of Anjou, brother of the French king.
4   For more on the serial publication of novels in the nineteenth century, see Brantlinger (2002), as well as Feltes (1986) and Hughes/Lund (1991).

4 The structure of narrative

1   On drama and narrative see Jahn (2001), Nünning/Sommer (2008) and Fludernik (2008).
2   But see Nünning (2001) for the discussion of a 'mimesis of narration' in texts that foreground the communicative scenario in fiction.
3   We shall look at perspective in film in a separate section in Chapter 10.

5 The surface of narrative

1   For German narrative, Konrad Ehlich has worked on conversational storytelling (1980, 1997). In the case of French, there is work by Elisabeth Gülich (1970). See also Chafe (1994).
2   Weydt (1983: 57) elaborates on this point with regard to German.

6 Realism, illusionism and metafiction

1   Anke Bauer and Cornelia Sander provide an excellent summary of Wolf's extremely complex book in Wenzel (2004: 201–21).

7 Language, speech and narrative

1   Cf. de Jong (1989), Fludernik (1993a: 26–32), and the entries on mimesis and diegesis in *The Routledge Encyclopedia of Narrative* (Herman *et al.* 2005).
2   On style in fiction see especially the classic by Leech and Short (1981).
3   See, among others, Goetsch (1994) and Winkgens (1997).
4   See also Fludernik (1993a: 266–75).
5   Genette's terms. The diegetic situation is one which occurs in the story-world, the non-diegetic one is brought in by the narrative discourse.

8 Thoughts, feelings and the unconscious

1   The French term *roman à courant de conscience* refers to the stream of consciousness novel, which is not precisely the same thing, since it is only a subcategory of the genre.
2   Free indirect discourse is frequently abbreviated as FID.
3   For relevant literature on mind style see Fowler (1977: 103–13), who coined the term, and Nischik (1993).
4   McHale sees the difference between modernism and postmodernism in the emphasis placed on knowledge-related questions in modernism – How do I see? – as opposed to the emphasis on ontological questions in postmodernism – What exists?

9 Narrative typologies

1   The following account of his work is based on the revised edition of his *Theorie des Erzählens* from 1982 (1st edn. 1979): *A Theory of Narrative* (1984).
2   Some examples are discussed in Chapter 12.
3   'In his works, the artist should be like God in His creation, invisible and omniscient; his presence should make itself felt everywhere but he should nowhere be seen' (trans. Patricia Häusler-Greenfield).
4   For more on the question of a neutral narrative situation, see Broich (1983).
5   See below, and also Chapter 4, the section on perspective.
6   Both translations by Patricia Häusler-Greenfield. Original: 'Ich weiß nicht, wie oft wir schon einander vorbeigegangen sind' – Zech 1925: 6. 'Erst beim Grauen des Morgens kamst du

nach Hause. [. . .] Du warst froh, als Du zu Hause warst, denn Du dachtest unwillkürlich: O, das ist die Gespensterstunde' – 67.
7 The same collection of essays also includes a piece on metalepsis in first- and third-person narrative by Dorrit Cohn. On metalepsis see also Fludernik (2003d) and Wolf (2005).
8 See also Banfield (1982) on impersonal narrative.
9 See Nünning (1995: I 259–91).

10 Diachronic approaches to narrative

1 For more on Russian *skaz*, see Eichenbaum (1971), Titunik (1977) or Vinogradov (1972).
2 To mention just four texts: Maria Edgeworth's *Castle Rackrent* (1800), Ford Madox Ford's *The Good Soldier* (1915), Ring Lardner's 'Haircut' (1925), and Faulkner's *The Sound and the Fury* (1929) (the Jason Compson section).
3 An excellent step in this direction has been made by Alan Palmer (forthcoming).

11 Practical applications

1 Sternberg (2007) makes much of the narrator's omnipotence.
2 The phrase comes from Léo Taxil's *La vie de Jésus* (Paris 1884). Taxil's real name was Gabriel Jogand-Pages (1854–1907). See the cartoon on Joseph asking Mary who made her pregnant on www.joyceimages.com/chapter/3/ (15/5/08).

12 Guidelines for budding narratologists

1 One cannot tell these apart because of the narrative present tense and the lack of a transposed personal pronoun.
2 Note that the café is spelled *Fankoni* in the Russian text, but *Franconi* in the English and German translation.

Bibliography

Texts

Aichinger, Ilse (1955) 'Story in a Mirror' [*Spiegelgeschichte*, 1949]. *The Bound Man and Other Stories*, trans. Eric Mosbacher. London: Secker & Warburg. 58–80.

Anderson, Sherwood (1983) *Winesburg, Ohio* [1919], Penguin Classics. Harmondsworth: Penguin.

Arnold, June (1973) *The cook and the carpenter; a Novel by the Carpenter*. Plainfield, VT: Daughters.

Austen, Jane (1971) *Emma* [1816]. London: Oxford University Press.

Austen, Jane (2001) *Pride and Prejudice* [1813], Norton Critical Editions. New York: Norton.

Babel, Isaac (1994) 'The End of the Almshouse' [1932]. *Isaac Babel: Collected Stories*, ed. Efraim Sicher, trans. David McDuff. London: Penguin. 289–99.

Babel, Isak (1966) 'Konets bogadel'ik' [1932]. *Izbrannoe*. Moscow: Isdatel'ctvo 'Chudozhestvennaya literatura', 232–9.

Balzac, Honoré de (2004) *Le Père Goriot* [1835]. Paris: Hatier. [*Old Goriot*, trans. Marion Ayton Crawford, Penguin Classics. London: Penguin, 1951.]

Barth, John (1981) *Lost in the Funhouse* [1963]. New York: Bantam Books.

Barthelme, Donald (1972) *Snow White* [1967]. New York: Atheneum.

Behn, Aphra (2004) *Oroonoko* [1688], Penguin Classics. London: Penguin.

Bond, Edward (1976) *Saved* [1965]. London: Methuen.

Brecht, Bertolt (2007) *Mother Courage and Her Children* [*Mutter Courage und ihre Kinder*, 1939], trans. John Willett, Penguin Classics. London: Penguin.

Brenton, Howard (1982) *The Romans in Britain* [1980]. London: Methuen.

Brink, André (2002) *The Other Side of Silence*. London: Secker & Warburg.

Brontë, Charlotte (2006) *Shirley* [1849], ed. Jessica Cox, Penguin Classics. Harmondsworth: Penguin.

Burgess, Anthony (1996) *A Clockwork Orange* [1962]. Stuttgart: Reclam.

Butor, Michel (1957) *La Modification*. Paris: Éditions de minuit. [*Second Thoughts, or a Change of Heart*, trans. Jean Stewart. London: Faber & Faber, 1958.]

Calvino, Italo (1982) *If on a Winter's Night a Traveller* [*Se una notte d'inverno un viaggiatore*, 1979], trans. William Weaver. London: Picador.

Champfleury (1973) *Le Réalisme* [1857], ed. Genevieve Lacambre. Paris: Hermann.

Chapman, George, Ben Jonson and John Marston (2001) *Eastward, Ho!* [1605]. *The Roaring Girl and Other City Comedies*, ed. James Knowles. Oxford: Oxford University Press.

Chaucer, Geoffrey (1989) *The Canterbury Tales*, ed. V.A. Kolve, Norton Critical Editions. New York: Norton.

Collins, Wilkie (1995) *Armadale* [1864–6], Penguin Classics. London: Penguin.

Conrad, Joseph (1949) *Four Tales: The Nigger of the Narcissus, Youth, The Secret Sharer, Freya of the Seven Isles*, intro. David Bone. London: Oxford University Press.

Conrad, Joseph (1995) *Heart of Darkness* [1899/1902], ed. D. C. R. A. Goonetilleke. Peterborough, Ont.: Broadview Press.

Davis, Rebbeca Harding (1998) *Life in the Iron-Mills* [1861], ed. Cecelia Tichi. Boston: Bedford.

Defoe, Daniel (1971) *The Fortunes and Misfortunes of the Famous Moll Flanders, &c.* [1722], ed. G.A. Starr. London: Oxford University Press.

Dick, Philip K. (1992) *The Man in the High Castle* [1962]. New York: Vintage.

Dickens, Charles (1962) *Bleak House* [1852–53], The New Oxford Illustrated Dickens. London: Oxford University Press.

Dickens, Charles (1981) *David Copperfield* [1849–50], ed. Nina Burgis. Oxford: Clarendon Press.

Dickens, Charles (2002) *Great Expectations* [1860–61]. Harmondsworth: Penguin.

Dickens, Charles (1996) *Hard Times* [1854]. Cambridge: Cambridge University Press.

Dickens, Charles (1953) *Little Dorrit* [1855–57]. London: Oxford University Press.

Dickens, Charles (1979) *Our Mutual Friend* [1864–65]. Penguin: Harmondsworth.

Diderot, Denis (1984) *Jack the Fatalist and His Master. A New Translation from the French of Denis Diderot* [*Jacques le fataliste*, 1778–80], trans. Wesley D. Camp and Agnes G. Raymond. New York: Peter Lang.

Döblin, Alfred (1980) *Berlin Alexanderplatz. Die Geschichte vom Franz Biberkopf* [1961]. Olten & Freiburg i. Brsg.: Walter. [*Berlin Alexanderplatz. The Story of Franz Biberkopf*, trans. Eugene Jolas. New York: Continuum, 2004.]

Dostoevsky, Fyodor Mikhailovich (1998) *The Karamazov Brothers* [1880], trans. Ignat Avsey, Oxford World's Classics. Oxford: Oxford University Press.

Dryden, John (1962) *The Indian Queen* [1664]. *The Works*, Vol. 8, ed. H. Swedenberg. Berkeley, CA: University of California Press. 181–231.

Edgeworth, Maria (1964) *Castle Rackrent* [1800], ed. George Watson. London: Oxford University Press.

Eliot, George (1986) *Middlemarch* [1871], ed. W.J. Harvey. Penguin Classics. Harmondsworth: Penguin.

Eliot, George (1980) *The Mill on the Floss* [1860], ed. Gordon S. Haight. Oxford: Clarendon.

Eliot, George (1985) 'Mr Gilfil's Love-Story', *Scenes of Clerical Life* [1858], ed. David Lodge, Penguin Classics. Harmondsworth: Penguin. 117–224.

Eliot, George (1996) *Silas Marner* [1861], Oxford World's Classics. Oxford: Oxford University Press.

Eugenides, Jeffrey (2002) *Middlesex.* London: Bloomsbury.

Faschinger, Lilian (1995) *Magdalena Sünderin.* Cologne: Kiepenheuer & Witsch. [*Magdelena the Sinner*, trans. Shaun Whiteside. London: Headline Review, 1996.]

Faulkner, William (1956) *The Sound and the Fury* [1929]. New York: The Modern Library.

Fielding, Henry (1983) *Amelia* [1751], ed. Martin Battestin. Oxford: Clarendon.

Fielding, Henry (1996) *The History of Tom Jones. A Foundling* [1749], ed. John Bender and Simon Stern, Oxford World's Classics. Oxford: Oxford University Press.

Fielding, Henry (1986) *Joseph Andrews* [1742]. Harmondsworth: Penguin.

Fielding, Henry (1999) *Shamela* [1741], *Joseph Andrews and Shamela*, ed. Judith Hawley. London: Penguin.

Fitzgerald, Francis Scott (1995) *The Great Gatsby* [1925]. Cambridge: Cambridge University Press.

Flaubert, Gustave (1927) *Correspondance.* Bd. IV. Paris: Louis Conard. [Letter to Mademoiselle Leroyer de Chantepie, 18 March 1857.]

Flaubert, Gustave (2005) 'A Simple Heart', *Three Tales* ['Un cœur simple', *Trois contes*, 1877], ed. Geoffrey Wall, trans. Roger Whitehouse. Harmondsworth: Penguin. 3–40.

Flaubert, Gustave (1972) *Madame Bovary* [1857]. Paris: Librairie Générale Française. [*Madame Bovary: Patterns of Provincial Life*, trans. Francis Steegmuller. New York: McGraw-Hill, 1982] see also http://www.online-literature.com/gustave-flaubert/madame-bovary/28/

Ford, Ford Madox (1999) *The Good Soldier: A Tale of Passion* [1915]. Oxford: Oxford University Press.

Fowles, John (1970) *The French Lieutenant's Woman.* London: Cape.

Fowles, John (1982) *Mantissa.* London: Cape.

Frayn, Michael (1981) *A Very Private Life* [1968]. Glasgow: Fontana.

Fugard, Athol (1993) *The Island* [1973]. Oxford: Oxford University Press.

Gaines, Ernest J. (1976) 'The Sky is Gray', *Bloodline.* New York: Norton. 83–117.

García Márquez, Gabriel (2000) *One Hundred Years of Solitude* [*Cien años de soledad*, 1967], trans. Gregory Rabassa. London: Penguin.

Gaskell, Elizabeth (1986) *North and South* [1855]. London: Penguin.

Gaskell, Elizabeth (1982) *Sylvia's Lovers*, ed. Andrew Sanders, World's Classics. Oxford: Oxford University Press.

The French Lieutenant's Woman (1980), dir. Karel Reisz, screenplay by Harold Pinter. United Artists.

Godden, Rumer (1968) 'You Need to Go Upstairs', *Gone: A Thread of Stories.* New York: Viking. 143–52.

Godwin, William (1949) *Political Justice* [1793]. London: Allen & Unwin.

Godwin, William (1991) *Caleb Williams* [1794], World's Classics. Oxford: Oxford University Press.

Goethe, Johann Wolfgang von (1994) *Elective Affinities* [*Die Wahlverwandschaften*, 1809], trans. David Constantine. London: Oxford University Press.

Golding, William (1974) *The Inheritors* [1955]. London: Faber & Faber.

Goldsmith, Oliver (1974) *The Vicar of Wakefield* [1766]. London: Oxford University Press.

Grass Günter (1993) *The Tin Drum* [*Die Blechtrommel*, 1959], trans. Ralph Manheim. New York: Everyman's Library.

Grass, Günter (1997) *Cat and Mouse* [*Katz und Maus: Eine Novelle*, 1961], trans. Ralph Manheim. London: Mandarin.

Gupta, Sunetra (1993) *Memories of Rain* [1992]. London: Orion.

Handke, Peter (1971) *Offending the Audience and Self-Accusation* [*Publikumsbeschimpfung und andere Sprechstücke*, 1966], trans. Michael Roloff. London: Methuen.

Hardee, Nicolette (2003) 'Wordperfect', *New Writing 12*, ed. Diran Adebayo, Blake Morrison and Jane Rogers. London: Picador. 256–63.

Hardy, Thomas (1986) *The Mayor of Casterbridge* [1886], ed. Martin Seymour-Smith, Penguin Classics. Harmondsworth: Penguin.

Hardy, Thomas (2005) *Tess of the D'Urbervilles* [1891], Oxford World's Classics. Oxford: Oxford University Press.

Hardy, Thomas (1998) *Under the Greenwood Tree*, ed. Tim Dolin, Penguin Classics. Harmondsworth: Penguin.

Hildesheimer, Wolfgang (1983) *Marbot: A Biography* [*Marbot: Eine Biographie*, 1981], trans. Patricia Crampton. London: Dent.

Hugo, Victor (1982) *Les Misérables* [*Les misérables*, 1862], trans. Norman Denny, Penguin Classics. London: Penguin.

Husson, Jules. *Le Réalisme* [1857]. See Champfleury.

Irving, Washington (1981) 'The Broken Heart', *The Sketch Book of Geoffrey Crayon, Gent.* [1820]. New York: Signet. 72–77.

Isherwood, Christopher (1964) *A Single Man.* London: Methuen.

James, Henry (1976) *The Ambassadors* [1903]. Harmondsworth: Penguin.

James, Henry (1964) 'The Figure in the Carpet' [1896]. *The Complete Tales of Henry James*, vol. 9, ed. Lion Edel. London: Hart-Davis. 273–315.

James, Henry (1999) *The Turn of the Screw* [1898], ed. Deborah Esch and Jonathan Warren, Norton Critical Editions. New York: Norton.

James, Henry (1999) *What Maisie Knew* [1897]. Thorndike/Bath: G. K. Hall.

Jandl, Ernst (1980) *Aus der Fremde.* Darmstadt: Luchterhand.

Jones, Lloyd (2008) *Mister Pip* [2006]. London: John Murray.

Joyce, James (1993) *A Portrait of the Artist as a Young Man* [1916]. Boston and New York: St. Martin's Press.

Joyce, James (1993) *Ulysses* [1922], ed. Hans Walter Gabler. New York: Vintage.

Kureishi, Hanif (1996) *The Black Album* [1995]. New York: Scribner.

Lardner, Ring (1984) *Haircut and Other Stories* [1925]. New York: Vintage.

McCann, Maria (2003) 'Minimal', *New Writing 12*, ed. Diran Adebayo, Blake Morrison and Jane Rogers. London: Picador. 296–310.

McGahern, John (1983) *The Dark* [1965]. London: Faber & Faber.

McLaren, Duncan (1997) 'Soap Circle', *New Writing 6*, ed. A. S. Byatt and Peter Porter. London: Vintage. 114–21.

Mann, Thomas (1991) *Die Buddenbrooks: Verfall einer Familie* [1901]. Frankfurt am Main: Fischer Verlag. [*Buddenbrooks*, trans. H.T. Lowe-Porter. New York: Vintage, 1984.]

Mann, Thomas (1991) *Doctor Faustus: The Life of the German Composer Adrian Leverkuhn as Told by a Friend* [*Doktor Faustus. Das Leben des deutschen Tonsetzers Adrian Leverkühn, erzählt von einem Freunde*, 1947], trans. John E. Woods. New York: Vintage, 1999.

Mansfield, Katherine (1984) 'The Little Governess' [1915]. *The Stories of Katherine Mansfield*, ed. Antony Alpers. Auckland: Oxford University Press. 166–76.

Maturin, Charles Robert (1992) *Melmoth the Wanderer* [1820], ed. Douglas Grant. London: Oxford University Press.

Maugham, William Somerset (1992) 'The Force of Circumstance' [1953], *Collected Short Stories: Volume 2*. Harmondsworth: Penguin. 42–64.

Maugham, William Somerset (2000) 'The Unconquered' [1944]. *Collected Short Stories: Volume 1*. London: Vintage. 343–74.

Meier, Gerhard (1977) *Der schnurgerade Kanal.* Bern: Zytglogge.

Meyer, E.Y. (1973) *In Trubschachen.* Frankfurt am Main: Suhrkamp.

Miller, Henry (1987) *Tropic of Cancer* [1934]. New York: Grove Press.

Modern Times (1936), dir. Charles Chaplin. United Artists.

O'Brien, Edna (1990) *A Pagan Place* [1970]. London: Weidenfeld & Nicolson.

O'Brien, Flann (1960) *At Swim-Two-Birds* [1939]. Harmondsworth: Penguin.

Oates, Joyce Carol (1975) 'In a Public Place', *The Poisoned Kiss and Other Stories from the Portugese*, Joyce Carol Oates and Fernandes. New York: Vanguard. 66–69.

Oates, Joyce Carol (1970) 'You', *The Wheel of Love and Other Stories.* New York: Vanguard. 362–87.

O'Neill, Eugene (1957) *A Touch of the Poet.* London: Jonathan Cape.

Ondaatje, Michael (1993) *The English Patient* [1992]. London: Macmillan.

Piercy, Marge (1987) *Woman on the Edge of Time* [1976]. London: The Women's Press.

Pirandello, Luigi (2003) *Six Characters in Search of an Author* [*Sei personaggi in cerca d'autore: Commedia da fare*, 1927], trans. Stephen Mulrine. London: Nick Hern.

Poe, Edgar Allan (1981) 'The Black Cat' [1843]. *The Annotated Tales of Edgar Allan Poe*, ed. Stephen Peithman. Garden City, NY: Doubleday. 140–8.

Poe, Edgar Allan (1981) 'The Tell-Tale Heart' [1843]. *The Annotated Tales of Edgar Allan Poe*, ed. Stephen Peithman. Garden City, NY: Doubleday. 134–9.

Proust, Marcel (2003) *In Search of Lost Time* [*A la recherche du temps perdu*, 1913–27], trans. C. K. Scott Moncrieff and Terence Kilmartin. New York: The Modern Library.

Pynchon, Thomas (1973) *Gravity's Rainbow.* New York: Viking.

Rabelais, François (1987) *Pantagruel* [1532–64]. Paris: Le club du meilleur livre.

Rabelais, François (1962) *Gargantua and Pantagruel* [1532–64], trans. J. M. Cohen, Penguin Classics. London: Penguin.

Radcliffe, Ann (1998) *The Mysteries of Udolpho* [1974], intro. Terry Castle. Oxford: Oxford University Press.

Robbe-Grillet, Alain (1959) *Jealousy* [*La jalousie*, 1957], trans. Richard Howard. London: Calder.

Robbe-Grillet, Alain (2000) *The Voyeur* [*Le voyeur*, 1955], trans. Richard Howard. New York: Grove.

Rushdie, Salman (1981) *Midnight's Children*. London: Cape.

Rushdie, Salman (1988) *The Satanic Verses*. London: Viking.

Sands, Donald B. (1986), ed., *Middle English Verse Romances*. Exeter: University of Exeter Press.

Schnitzler, Arthur (1998) *Fräulein Else* [1924], trans. F.H. Lyon. London: Pushkin.

Seymour-Ure, Kirsty (1998) 'The Russian', *New Writing 7*, ed. Carmen Callil and Craig Raine. London: Vintage. 96–109.

Shute, Nevil (1966) *On the Beach* [1957]. London: Pan Books.

Silko, Leslie (1988) *Ceremony* [1977]. New York: Penguin.

Simon, Claude (1960) *La Route des Flandres*. Paris: Éditions de Minuit. [*The Flanders Road*, trans. Richard Howard. London: Calder, 1985.]

Small, Judith (1991) 'Body of Work', *The New Yorker*, 8 July, 30–2.

Sterne, Laurence (1983) *The Life and Opinions of Tristram Shandy, Gentleman* [1759–67]. Oxford: Clarendon.

Stoker, Bram (1983) *Dracula* [1897], intro. A.N. Wilson. Oxford: Oxford University Press.

Storm, Theodor (1996) *The Dykemaster* [*Der Schimmelreiter*, 1888], trans. Denis Jackson, Angel Classics. London: Angel.

Stowe, Harriet Beecher (1981) *Uncle Tom's Cabin* [1851–52], Bantam Classic Editions. New York: Bantam.

Thackeray, William Makepeace (1963) *The History of Henry Esmond*. London: Dent.

Thackeray, William Makepeace (1994) *Vanity Fair* [1847/48], Norton Critical Editions. New York: Norton.

The Three Kings' Sons (1895), ed. F. J. Furnivall, EETS, E.S. 67. London: Kegan Paul.

Tolstoy, Leo (1985) *The Kreutzer Sonata and Other Stories* [1889], trans. David McDuff, Penguin Classics. London: Penguin.

Tolstoy, Leo (1985) *War and Peace* [1868–69], trans. Rosemary Edmunds, Penguin Classics. London: Penguin.

Trollope, Anthony (1990) *Doctor Thorne* [1867], Oxford World's Classics. Oxford: Oxford University Press.

Trollope, Anthony (1986) *Is He Popenjoy?* [1874–75], Oxford World's Classics. Oxford: Oxford University Press.

Vanbrugh, Sir John (2000) *The Relapse* [1696]. *Restoration Drama*, ed. David Womersley. Oxford: Blackwell. 595–645.

Waugh, Evelyn (1945) *Brideshead Revisited: The Sacred and Profane Memories of Captain Charles Ryder*. Boston: Little, Brown.

White, Edmund (1978) *Nocturnes for the King of Naples*. New York, NY: St. Martin's.

Wieland, Christoph Martin (2001) *Geschichte des Agathon* [1766/67], ed. Rolf Vollmann. Zurich: Manesse Verlag.

Wilder, Thornton (1964) *Our Town: A Play in Three Acts* [1938]. Harper Colophon Books. New York: Harper & Row.

Wittig, Monique (1996) *The Opoponax* [*L'Opoponax*, 1964], trans. Helen Weaver. London: Peter Owen.

Wolf, Christa (1980) *A Model Childhood* [*Kindheitsmuster*, 1976], trans. Ursula Molinaro and Hedwig Rappolt. New York: Farrar, Straus, Giroux.

Woolf, Virginia (1957) 'Modern Fiction' [1919], *The Common Reader: First Series*. London: Hogarth.

Woolf, Virginia (2008) *Mrs Dalloway* [1925], World's Classics. Oxford: Oxford University Press.

Zech, Paul (1925) *Die Geschichte einer armen Johanna*. Berlin: Dietz.

Criticism

Abbott, Horace Porter (2002) *The Cambridge Introduction to Narrative*. Cambridge: Cambridge University Press.

Alber, Jan (2007) *Narrating the Prison: Role and Representation in Charles Dickens' Novels, Twentieth-Century Fiction, and Film*. Youngstown, NY: Cambria Press.

Aristoteles (1982) *Aristotelus peri poiètikès/The Poetics*, with an English translation by W. Hamilton Fyfe, Loeb Classical Library, 199. London: Heinemann.

Armstrong, Nancy, and Leonard Tennenhouse (1993) 'History, Poststructuralism, and the Question of Narrative', *Narrative* 1: 45–58.

Backus, Joseph M. (1965) '"He Came into her Line of Vision Walking Backward": Nonsequential Sequence Signals in Short Story Openings'. *Language Learning* 15: 67–83.

Bakhtin, Mikhail (1981) *The Dialogic Imagination*, ed. Michael Holquist. Austin, TX: University of Texas Press.

Bakhtin, Mikhail (1984) *Problems of Dostoevsky's Poetics* [1963], trans. and ed. Caryl Emerson, intro. Wayne C. Booth. Minneapolis, MN: University of Minnesota Press.

Bal, Mieke (1982) 'On Meanings and Descriptions', *Studies in Twentieth Century Literature* 6.1–2: 100–48.

Bal Mieke (1997) *Narratology: Introduction to the Theory of Narrative* [1985]. Toronto, Ont.: University of Toronto Press.

Bally, Charles (1912a) 'Le style indirect libre en français moderne I'. *Germanisch-Romanische Monatsschrift* 4: 549–56.

Bally, Charles (1912b) 'Le style indirect libre en français moderne II'. *Germanisch-Romanische Monatsschrift* 4: 597–606.

Banfield, Ann (1982) *Unspeakable Sentences: Narration and Representation in the Language of Fiction*. Boston, MA: Routledge & Kegan Paul.

Barcelona, Antonio (2000), ed., *Metaphor and Metonymy at the Crossroads: A Cognitive Perspective*, Topics in English Linguistics, 30. Berlin: Mouton de Gruyter.

Barchas, Janine (2003) *Graphic Design, Print Culture, and the Eighteenth-Century Novel*. Cambridge: Cambridge University Press.

Barthes, Roland (1968) 'L'effet de réel', *Communications* 11: 84–89.

Barthes, Roland (2002) 'The Death of the Author' [1968], *The Book History Reader*, ed. David Finkelstein and Alistair McCleery. London: Routledge. 221–24.

Bauer, Anke, and Cornelia Sander (2004) 'Zur Analyse der Illusionsbildung und der Illusionsdurchbrechung', *Einführung in die Erzähltextanalyse: Kategorien, Modelle, Probleme*. Ed. Peter Wenzel. Trier: Wissenschaftlicher Verlag Trier, 2004. 197–222.

Bennett, Andrew (2005) *The Author*. London: Routledge.

Benveniste, Émile (1971) *Problems in General Linguistics* [1966], Miami Linguistics Series, 8. Coral Gables, FL: University of Miami Press.

Booth, Wayne C. (1983) *The Rhetoric of Fiction* [1961]. Chicago/London: Chicago University Press.

Bordwell, David (1985) *Narration in the Fiction Film*. Madison, WI: University of Wisconsin Press.

Bortolussi, Marisa, and Peter Dixon (2003) *Psychonarratology: Foundations for the Empirical Study of Literary Response*. Cambridge: Cambridge University Press.

Branigan, Edward R. (1984) *Point of View in the Cinema: A Theory of Narration and Subjectivity in Classical Film*. Berlin: Mouton.

Branigan, Edward (1992) *Narrative Comprehension and Film*. London and New York: Routledge.

Brantlinger, Patrick (2002) *A Companion to the Victorian Novel*. Malden, MA: Blackwell.

Bremond, Claude (1973) *Logique du récit*. Paris: Seuil.

Broeder, Peter (1995) 'Adult Language Acquisition: The Establishment, Shift, and Narrative Maintenance of Reference in Narratives', *Reference in Multidisciplinary Perspective*, ed. Richard A. Geiger. Hildesheim: Olms. 584–610.

Broich, Ulrich (1983) 'Gibt es eine "neutrale Erzählsituation"?' *Germanisch-Romanische Monatsschrift* 33: 129–45.

Bronzwaer, W. J. M. (1970) *Tense in the Novel: An Investigation of Some Potentialities of Linguistic Criticism.* Groningen: Wolters–Noordhoff.

Brooks, Peter (1985) *Reading for the Plot. Design and Intention in Narrative.* New York: Vintage.

Bühler, Karl (1934) *Sprachtheorie: Die Darstellungsfunktion der Sprache.* Jena: Gustav Fischer.

Butter, Michael (2007) 'The Epitome of Evil: Hitler in American Fiction, 1939–2002'. Dissertation, University of Freiburg. (Forthcoming, with Palgrave.)

Chafe, Wallace (1980), ed., *The Pear Stories: Cognitive, Cultural, and Linguistic Aspects of Narrative Production.* Advances in Discourse Processes, 3. Norwood, NJ: Ablex.

Chafe, Wallace (1994) *Discourse, Consciousness and Time: The Flow and Displacement of Conscious Experience in Speaking and Writing.* Chicago: University of Chicago Press.

Chambers, Ross (1984) *Story and Situation: Narrative Seduction and the Power of Fiction,* Theory and History of Literature, 12. Minneapolis, MN: University of Minnesota Press.

Champfleury, Husson, Jules (1973) *Le réalisme* [1857], ed. Geneviève Lacambre. Paris: Hermann.

Chatman, Seymour (1978) *Story and Discourse: Narrative Structure in Fiction and Film.* Ithaca, NY: Cornell University Press.

Chatman, Seymour (1990) *Coming to Terms: The Rhetoric of Narrative in Fiction and Films.* Ithaca, NY: Cornell University Press.

Chatman, Seymour (1992) *Reading Narrative Fiction.* Upper Saddle River, NJ: Prentice Hall. [Currently available in a facsimile edition from Prentice Hall, 1993.]

Clare, Janet (1990) *Art Made Tongue-Tied by Authority: Elizabethan and Jacobean Dramatic Censorship.* Manchester: Manchester University Press.

Cobley, Paul (2001) *Narrative: The New Critical Idiom.* London: Routledge.

Cohan, Steven, and Linda M. Shires (1988) *Telling Stories: A Theoretical Analysis of Narrative Fiction.* New York: Routledge.

Cohn, Dorrit (1978) *Transparent Minds: Narrative Modes for Presenting Consciousness in Fiction.* Princeton, NJ: Princeton University Press.

Cohn, Dorrit (1981) 'The Encirclement of Narrative', *Poetics Today* 2.2: 157–82.

Cohn, Dorrit (1999) *The Distinction of Fiction.* Baltimore, MD: Johns Hopkins University Press.

Cohn, Dorrit (2000) 'Discordant Narration', *Style* 34.2: 307–16.

Cornils, Anja, and Wilhelm Schernus (2003) 'On the Relationship between Theory of the Novel, Narrative Theory, and Narratology', in Kindt/Müller (2003): 137–74.

Coste, Didier (1989) *Narrative as Communication.* Theory and History of Literature, 64. Minneapolis, MN: University of Minnesota Press.

Culler, Jonathan D. (2004) 'Omniscience', *Narrative* 12.1: 22–34.

Currie, Gregory (1990) *The Nature of Fiction.* Cambridge: Cambridge University Press.

Dällenbach, Lucien (1989) *The Mirror in the Text,* trans. Jeremy Whitely. Cambridge: Polity Press. [*Le récit spéculaire: Essai sur la mise en abyme.* Paris: Seuil, 1977.]

Dannenberg, Hilary P. (2004a) 'A Poetics of Coincidence in Narrative Fiction', *Poetics Today* 25.3: 399–436.

Dannenberg, Hilary (2004b) 'Ontological Plotting: Narrative as a Multiplicity of Temporal Dimensions', *The Dynamics of Narrative Form.* Papers in Narratology at ESSE 6 (Strasbourg, September 2002) and Other Contributions, ed. John Pier. Narratologia, 4. Berlin: de Gruyter. 159–90.

Dannenberg, Hilary P. (2008) *Coincidence and Counterfactuality: Plotting Time and Space in Narrative Fiction.* Lincoln, NE: University of Nebraska Press.

Darby, David (2001) 'Form and Context: An Essay in the History of Narratology'. *Poetics Today* 22.4: 829–52.

Diengott, Nilli (1988) 'Narratology and Feminism', *Style* 22.1: 42–51.

Dijk, Teun A. van (1972) *Some Aspects of Text Grammars: A Study in Theoretical Poetics and Linguistics.* The Hague: Mouton.

Dutton, Richard (1997) 'Censorship', *A New History of Early English Drama*, eds. John D. Cox and David Scott Kastan. New York: Columbia University Press. 287–304.

Ehlich, Konrad (1980), ed. *Erzählen im Alltag.* Frankfurt am Main: Suhrkamp.

Ehlich, Konrad (1997) 'Alltagserzählung', *Reallexikon der deutschen Literaturwissenschaft*, ed. Klaus Weimar in collaboration with Harald Fricke, Klaus Grubmüller and Jan-Dirk Müller, Vol. I (A-G). Berlin/New York: de Gruyter. 49–53.

Eichenbaum, Boris (1971) 'Wie Gogols 'Mantel' gemacht ist' [1919]. *Russischer Formalismus. Texte zur allgemeinen Literaturtheorie und zur Theorie der Prosa*, ed. Jurij Striedter, UTB, 40. Munich: Fink. 125–59.

Emmott, Catherine (1997) *Narrative Comprehension: A Discourse Perspective.* Oxford: Clarendon.

Engler, Bernd (2004) 'Metafiction', <http://www.litencyc.com> 4 Sept 2005.

Erne, Lukas (2003) *Shakespeare as Literary Dramatist.* Cambridge: Cambridge University Press.

Faulstich, Werner, and Hans-Werner Ludwig (1985) *Erzählperspektive empirisch. Untersuchungen zur Rezeptionsrelevanz narrativer Strukturen.* Tübingen: Narr.

Feltes, Norman (1986) *Modes of Production of Victorian Novels.* Chicago: University of Chicago Press.

Fill, Alwin (2003) *Das Prinzip Spannung: Sprachwissenschaftliche Betrachtungen zu einem universalen Phänomen.* Tübingen: Narr.

Fischer-Lichte, Erika (1991) *Heinrich von Kleist: Michael Kohlhaas.* Grundlagen und Gedanken zum Verständnis erzählender Literatur. Frankfurt am Main: Diesterweg.

Fleischman, Suzanne (1990) *Tense and Narrativity: From Medieval Performance to Modern Fiction.* London: Routledge.

Fludernik, Monika (1988) '"The Divine Accident of Life": Metaphoric Structuring and Meaning in *Winesburg, Ohio*'. *Style* 22.1: 116–35.

Fludernik, Monika (1990) 'Byron, Napoleon, and Thorough-Bred Mares: Symbolism and Semiosis in Eugene O'Neill's *A Touch of the Poet*', *Sprachkunst* 21.1: 335–52.

Fludernik, Monika (1993a) *The Fictions of Language and the Languages of Fiction: The Linguistic Representation of Speech and Consciousness.* London: Routledge.

Fludernik, Monika (1993b) 'Second-Person Fiction: Narrative YOU as Addressee and/or Protagonist', *Arbeiten aus Anglistik und Amerikanistik (AAA)* 18.2: 217–47.

Fludernik, Monika (1994a) 'Introduction: Second-Person Narrative and Related Issues', *Style* 28.3: 281–311.

Fludernik, Monika (1994b) 'Second-Person Narrative as a Test Case for Narratology: The Limits of Realism', *Style* 28.3: 445–79.

Fludernik, Monika (1994c), ed., *Second-Person Narrative*, Special issue *Style*, 28.3.

Fludernik, Monika (1994d) 'Second-Person Narrative: A Bibliography', *Style* 28.4: 525–48.

Fludernik, Monika (1996) *Towards a 'Natural' Narratology.* London/New York: Routledge.

Fludernik, Monika (1999) 'The Genderization of Narrative', in Pier (1999): 153–75.

Fludernik, Monika (2000) 'Genres, Text Types, or Discourse Modes – Narrative Modalities and Generic Categorization', *Style* 34.2: 274–92.

Fludernik, Monika (2001) 'William Godwin's *Caleb Williams*: The Tarnishing of the Sublime', *English Literary History* 68.4: 857–96. [Reprinted in *Nineteenth-Century Literature*, 130. Gale Publishers, 2003. 169–89.]

Fludernik, Monika (2003a) 'The Diachronization of Narratology', *Narrative* 11.3: 331–48.

Fludernik, Monika (2003b) 'Metanarrative and Metafictional Commentary', *Poetica* 35: 1–39.

Fludernik, Monika (2003c) 'Natural Narratology and Cognitive Parameters', *Narrative Theory and the Cognitive Sciences*, ed. David Herman. Stanford, CA: CSLI Publications. 243–67.

Fludernik, Monika (2003d) 'Scene Shift, Metalepsis, and the Metaleptic Mode', *Style* 37.4: 382–400.

Fludernik, Monika (2005) 'Middle English from a Narratological Perspective', Paper read at the SSNL Conference, Louisville, KY, April 2005.

Fludernik, Monika (2008) 'Narrative and Drama', in Pier/Landa (2008): 355–83.

Fludernik, Monika, and Uri Margolin (2004), eds. *German Narratology*. Special issue *Style* 38.2–3.

Forceville, Charles (1996) *Pictorial Metaphor in Advertising*. London: Routledge.

Forster, E. M. (1949) *Aspects of the Novel* [1927]. London: Arnold.

Fowler, Roger (1977) *Linguistics and the Novel*. London: Methuen.

Friedemann, Käte (1965) *Die Rolle des Erzählers in der Epik* [1910]. Darmstadt: Wissenschaftliche Buchgesellschaft.

Friedman, Norman (1955) 'Point of View in Fiction. The Development of a Critical Concept', *PMLA* 70: 1160–84.

Füger, Wilhelm (2004) 'Limits of the Narrator's Knowledge in Fielding's *Joseph Andrews*: A Contribution to a Theory of Negated Knowledge in Fiction,' *Style* 38.3: 278–89. ['Das Nichtwissen des Erzählers in Fieldings *Joseph Andrews*: Baustein zu einer Theorie negierten Wissens in der Fiktion, *Poetica* 10.2–3 (1978): 188–216.]

Genette, Gérard (1980) *Narrative Discourse: An Essay in Method*. ['Discours du récit', *Figures III*, 1972], trans. Jane E. Lewin. Ithaca, NY: Cornell University Press.

Genette, Gérard (1988) *Narrative Discourse Revisited* [*Nouveau discours du récit*, 1983], trans. Jane E. Lewin. Ithaca, NY: Cornell University Press.

Genette, Gérard (1997) *Paratexts: Thresholds of Interpretation*. [*Seuil*, 1987.], trans. Jane E. Lewin. Cambridge: Cambridge University Press.

Goetsch, Paul (1985) 'Fingierte Mündlichkeit in der Erzählkunst entwickelter Schriftkulturen', *Poetica* 17.3–4: 202–18.

Goetsch, Paul (1994) *Hardys Wessex-Romane: Mündlichkeit, Schriftlichkeit, kultureller Wandel*. Tübingen: Narr.

Grabes, Herbert (1978) 'Wie aus Sätzen Personen werden . . . Über die Erforschung literarischer Figuren', *Poetica* 10: 405–28.

Grice, H.P. (1996) 'Logik und Konversation [1975]', *Sprachwissenschaft: Ein Reader*, ed. Ludger Hoffmann. Berlin: de Gruyter. 163–182.

Grice, H. Paul (1975) 'Logic and Conversation', *Speech Acts*. Syntax and Semantics, 3. Ed. Peter Cole and Jerry L. Morgan. New York: Academic Press. 41–58.

Gülich, Elisabeth (1990) *Makrosyntax der Gliederungssignale im gesprochenen Französisch* [1970]. Munich: Fink.

Hamburger, Käte (1993) *The Logic of Literature* [*Die Logik der Dichtung*, 1957], trans. Marilynn J. Rose. Bloomington, IN: Indiana University Press.

Hamon, Philippe (1972) 'Qu'est-ce qu'une description?' *Poetique: Revue de Théorie et d'Analyse Litteraires* 12: 465–85.

Harvey, Sir Paul (1932) *The Oxford Companion to English Literature*. Oxford: Clarendon.

Harweg, Roland (1968) *Pronomina und Textkonstitution*. Munich: Fink.

Heinen, Sandra (2002) 'Das Bild des Autors. Überlegungen zum Begriff des "impliziten Autors" und seines Potentials zur kulturwissenschaftlichen Beschreibung von inszenierter Autorschaft', *Sprachkunst* 33: 329–345.

Heinze, Rüdiger (2008) 'Violations of Mimetic Epistemology in First-Person Narrative Fiction', *Narrative* 16.3: 279–97.

Helbig, Jörg (1988) *Der parahistorische Roman: Ein literarhistorischer und gattungstypologischer Beitrag zur Allotopieforschung*. Frankfurt am Main: Lang.

Herman, David (1999) 'Toward a Socionarratology: New Ways of Analyzing Natural-Language Narratives'. *Narratologies*, ed. David Herman. Columbus, OH: Ohio State University Press. 218–46.

Herman, David (2001) 'Story Logic in Conversational and Literary Narratives', *Narrative* 9.2: 130–37.

Herman, David (2002) *Story Logic: Problems and Possibilities of Narrative*. Lincoln, NE: University of Nebraska Press.

Herman, David (2005) 'Histories of Narrative Theory (I): A Genealogy of Early Developments'. *The Blackwell Companion to Narrative Theory*, ed. James Phelan and Peter J. Rabinowitz. Malden, MA: Blackwell. 1–35.

Herman, David (2007), ed., *The Cambridge Companion to Narrative*. Cambridge: Cambridge University Press.

Herman, David (forthcoming), ed., *The Emergence of Mind: Representations of Consciousness in Narrative Discourse in English, 700 – the Present*. Lincoln, NE: University of Nebraska Press.

Herman, David, Manfred Jahn and Marie-Laure Ryan (2005), eds., *Encyclopedia of Narrative Theory*. London: Routledge.

Herman, Luc, and Bart Vervaeck (2004) 'Focalization Between Classical and Postclassical Narratology', in Pier (2004): 115–38.

Herman, Luc, and Bart Vervaeck (2005) *Handbook of Narrative Analysis*. Lincoln/London: University of Nebraska Press. [*Vertelduivels: handboek verhaalanalyse*. Tekst en tijd 7. Nijmegen: Vantilt, 2001.]

Hrushovski, Benjamin (1982) 'Integrational Semantics. An Understander's Theory of Meaning in Context', *Contemporary Perceptions of Language: Interdisciplinary Dimensions. Georgetown University Round Table on Languages and Linguistics 1982*, ed. Heidi Byrnes. Washington, DC: Georgetown University Press. 156–190.

Hühn, Peter (2004) 'Transgeneric Narratology: Applications to Lyric Poetry', in Pier (2004): 139–58.

Hughes, Linda, and Michael Lund (1991) *The Victorian Serial*. Charlottesville, VA: University Press of Virginia.

Hume, Kathryn (2005) 'Narrative Speed', *Narrative* 13: 105–24.

Hume, Kathryn, and Jan Baetens (2006) 'Narrative Speed, Rhythm, Movement: A Dialogue on K. Hume's Article "Narrative Speed"'. *Narrative* 14: 349–55.

Hyvärinen, Matti (2006) 'Towards a Conceptual History of Narrative', *The Travelling Concept of Narrative*, ed. Matti Hyvärinen, Anu Korhonen and Juri Mykkänen. Studies Across Disciplines in the Humanities and Social Sciences, 1. Helsinki: Helsinki Collegium for Advanced Studies. 20–41.

Iser, Wolfgang (1974) *The Implied Reader: Patterns of Communication in Prose Fiction from Bunyan to Beckett* [*Der implizite Leser: Kommunikationsformen des Romans von Bunyan bis Beckett*, 1972.]. Baltimore, MD: John Hopkins University Press.

Jahn, Manfred (1996) 'Windows of Focalization: Deconstructing and Reconstructing a Narratological Concept', *Style* 30.2: 241–67.

Jahn, Manfred (1999) 'More Aspects of Focalization: Refinements and Applications', in Pier (1999): 85–110.

Jahn, Manfred (2001) 'Narrative Voice and Agency in Drama: Aspects of a Narratology of Drama', *New Literary History* 32.3: 659–79.

Jahn, Manfred (2003) *A Guide to Narratological Film Analysis. Poems, Plays, and Prose: A Guide to the Theory of Literary Genres*. English Department, University of Cologne. Version: 1.7. 2 August 2003. <http://www.uni-koeln.de/~ame02/pppf.htm>. 28 Feb. 2005

Jakobson, Roman (1956) 'Two Aspects of Language and Two Types of Aphasic Disturbances', *Fundamentals of Language*, ed. Roman Jakobson and Morris Halle. S'Gravenhage: Mouton, 53–82.

Jakobson, Roman (1987) 'Closing Statement: Linguistics and Poetics [1958]', *Roman Jakobson: Language and Literature*, ed. Krystyna Pomorska and Stephen Rudy. Cambridge, MA: Belknap Press of Harvard University Press. 62–94.

James, Henry (1953) *The Art of the Novel* [1934], intro. R.P. Blackmur. New York: Scribner.

Jannidis, Fotis *et al.* (1999), eds., *Rückkehr des Autors*. Tübingen: Niemeyer.

Jauss, Hans-Robert (1982) *Toward an Aesthetic of Reception* [1989], trans. Timothy Bahti. Minneapolis, MN: University of Minnesota Press. 46–75.

Jong, Irene J.F. de (1989) *Narrators and Focalizers: The Presentation of the Story in the Iliad* [1987], 2nd edn, Amsterdam: Grüner.

Kafalenos, Emma (2006) *Narrative Causalities.* Columbus, OH: Ohio State University Press.

Karpf, Fritz (1933) 'Die erlebte Rede im Englischen', *Anglia* 57: 227–76.

Keen, Suzanne (2003) *Narrative Form.* Basingstoke: Palgrave Macmillan.

Kindt, Tom, and Hans-Harald Müller (2003), eds. *What is Narratology? Questions and Answers Regarding the Status of a Theory.* Narratologia, 1. Berlin: de Gruyter.

Kittay, Jeffrey, and Wlad Godzich (1987) *The Emergence of Prose: An Essay in Prosaics.* Minneapolis, MN: University of Minnesota Press.

Kövecses, Zoltán, and Günter Radden (1998) 'Metonymy: Developing a Cognitive Linguistic View', *Cognitive Linguistics* 9.1: 37–77.

Korte, Barbara (1993) *Körpersprache in der Literatur: Theorie und Geschichte am Beispiel des englischsprachigen Romans.* Tübingen: Francke. Trans: *Body Language in Literature.* Toronto: University of Toronto Press, 1997.

Kuno, Susumu (1987) *Functional Syntax. Anaphora, Discourse and Empathy.* Chicago: University of Chicago Press.

Labov, William, and Joshua Waletzky (1967) 'Narrative Analysis: Oral Versions of Personal Experience', *Essays on the Verbal and Visual Arts,* ed. J. Helms. Seattle, WA: University of Washington Press. 12–44.

Lacan, Jacques (1977) *Écrits: A Selection* [1966], trans. Alan Sheridan. New York: Norton.

LaCapra Dominick (1982) *Madame Bovary on Trial.* Ithaca, NY: Cornell University Press.

Lamarque, Peter, and Stein Haugom Olsen (1994) *Truth, Fiction, and Literature: A Philosophical Perspective.* Oxford: Clarendon Press.

Lämmert, Eberhard (1993) *Bauformen des Erzählens* [1955]. Stuttgart: Metzler.

Lanser, Susan S. (1981) *The Narrative Act: Point of View in Prose Fiction.* Princeton, NJ: Princeton University Press.

Lanser, Susan S. (1986) 'Toward a Feminist Narratology', *Style* 20.3: 341–63.

Lanser, Susan S. (1988) 'Shifting the Paradigm: Feminism and Narratology', *Style* 22.1: 52–60.

Lanser, Susan S. (1992) *Fictions of Authority: Women Writers and Narrative Voice.* Ithaca, NY: Cornell University Press.

Leech, Geoffrey N., and Michael Short (2007) *Style in Fiction: A Linguistic Introduction to English Fictional Prose* [1981]. London: Longman.

Linde, Charlotte (1993) *Life Stories: The Creation of Coherence.* New York: Oxford University Press.

Lodge, David (1977) *The Modes of Modern Writing: Metaphor, Metonymy and the Typology of Modern Literature.* London: Edward Arnold.

Löschnigg, Martin (1999) 'Narratological Categories and the (Non-)Distinction Between Factual and Fictional Narratives', in Pier (1999): 31–48.

Lothe, Jakob (2000) *Narrative in Fiction and Film: An Introduction.* Oxford: Oxford University Press.

Love, Harold (2002) *Attributing Authorship.* Cambridge: Cambridge University Press.

Lubbock, Percy (1966) *The Craft of Fiction* [1921]. London: Jonathan Cape.

Ludwig, Otto (1891) 'Formen der Erzählung', *Studien 1. Gesammelte Schriften,* Vol. 5, ed. Adolf Stern. Leipzig: Grunow.

McHale, Brian (1987) *Postmodernist Fiction.* New York/London: Methuen.

McHale, Brian (1992) *Constructing Postmodernism.* London: Routledge.

Margolin, Uri (1990) 'Individuals in Narrative Worlds: An Ontological Perspective', *Poetics Today* 11.4: 843–71.

Margolin, Uri (1995) 'Characters in Literary Narrative: Representation and Signification', *Semiotica* 106.3–4: 373–92.

Margolin, Uri (1996) 'Characters and Their Versions', *Fiction Updated: Theories of Fictionality,*

Narratology, and Poetics, eds. Calin-Andrei Mihailescu and Walid Hamarneh. Toronto, Ont.: University of Toronto Press. 113–32.

Margolin, Uri (2000) 'Telling in the Plural: From Grammar to Ideology', *Poetics Today* 21.3: 591–618.

Marnette, Sophie (1996) 'Réflexions sur le discours indirect libre en français médiéval', *Romania* 114: 1–149.

Martínez, Matías, and Michael Scheffel (1999) *Einführung in die Erzähltheorie*. Munich: Beck.

Meister, Jan Christoph (2005), ed., *Narratology Beyond Literary Criticism: Mediality, Disciplinarity*. Berlin: Mouton de Gruyter.

Mosher, Harald F. (1991) 'Toward a Poetics of "Descriptized" Narration', *Poetics Today* 12 : 425–45.

Müller, Günther (1968) 'Erzählzeit und erzählte Zeit' [1948]. *Morphologische Poetik*. Günther Müller. Darmstadt: Wissenschaftliche Buchgesellschaft.

Nelles, William (1997) *Frameworks: Narrative Levels and Embedded Narrative*. American University Studies, Ser. 19, General literature, 33. New York: Lang.

Nielsen, Henrik Skov (2004) 'The Impersonal Voice in First-Person Fiction', *Narrative* 12: 133–50.

Nieragden, Göran (2002) 'Focalization and Narration: Theoretical and Terminological Refinements', *Poetics Today* 23: 685–97.

Nischik, Reingard M. (1981) *Einsträngigkeit und Mehrsträngigkeit der Handlungsführung in literarischen Texten: Dargestellt insbesondere an englischen, amerikanischen und kanadischen Romanen des 20. Jahrhunderts*. Tübinger Beiträge zur Anglistik, 1. Tübingen: Narr.

Nischik, Reingard M. (1993) 'Mind Style Analysis and the Narrative Modes for the Presentation of Consciousness', *Tales and 'Their Telling Difference': Zur Theorie und Geschichte der Narrativik*, ed. Herbert Foltinek, Wolfgang Riehle and Waldemar Zacharasiewicz. Heidelberg: Winter. 93–107.

Nischik, Reingard M. (1994) 'Sukzessive und simultane Aufspaltung der Erzählinstanz im Erzählwerk Margaret Atwoods', *Orbis Litterarum* 49: 233–51.

Nünning, Ansgar (1989) *Grundzüge eines kommunikationstheoretischen Modells der erzählerischen Vermittlung: Die Funktion der Erzählinstanz in den Romanen George Eliots*, Horizonte, 2. Trier: Wissenschaftlicher Verlag Trier.

Nünning, Ansgar (1995) *Von historischer Fiktion zu historiographischer Metafiktion*. 2 vols. Trier: Wissenschaftlicher Verlag Trier.

Nünning, Ansgar (1997a) '"But why *will* you say that I am mad?" On the Theory, History, and Signals of Unreliable Narration in British Fiction', *Arbeiten aus Anglistik und Amerikanistik* (*AAA*) 22: 83–105.

Nünning, Ansgar (1997b) 'Die Funktion von Erzählinstanzen: Analysekategorien und Modelle zur Beschreibung des Erzählverhaltens', *Literatur in Wissenschaft und Unterricht* 30: 323–49.

Nünning, Ansgar (1998), ed., *Unreliable Narration. Studien zur Theorie und Praxis unglaubwürdigen Erzählens in der englischsprachigen Erzählliteratur*. Trier: Wissenschaftlicher Verlag Trier.

Nünning, Ansgar (2001) 'Mimesis des Erzählens: Prolegomena zu einer Wirkungsästhetik, Typologie und Funktionsgeschichte des Akts des Erzählens und der Metanarration', *Erzählen und Erzähltheorie im 20. Jahrhundert: Festschrift für Wilhelm Füger*, ed. Joerg Helbig. Heidelberg: Winter, 2001. 13–47.

Nünning, Ansgar (2004) 'On Metanarrative: Towards a Definition, a Typology and an Outline of the Functions of Metanarrative Commentary', in Pier (2004): 11–58.

Nünning, Ansgar (2005) 'Reconceptualizing Unreliable Narration: Synthesizing Cognitive and Rhetorical Approaches', in Phelan/Rabinowitz (2005): 89–107.

Nünning, Ansgar (2007) 'Towards a Typology, Poetics and History of Description in Fiction', Description in Literature and Other Media, in Wolf/Bernhart (2007): 91–128.

Nünning, Ansgar, and Vera Nünning (2002a), eds., *Erzähltheorie transgenerisch, intermedial, interdisziplinär.* WVT-Handbücher zum literaturwissenschaftlichen Studium 5. Trier: Wissenschaftlicher Verlag Trier.

Nünning, Ansgar, and Vera Nünning (2002b) *Neue Ansätze in der Erzähltheorie.* WVT–Handbücher zum literaturwissenschaftlichen Studium, 4. Trier: Wissenschaftlicher Verlag Trier.

Nünning, Ansgar, and Vera Nünning (2002c) 'Produktive Grenzüberschreitungen: Transgenerische, intermediale und interdisziplinäre Ansätze in der Erzähltheorie', in Nünning/Nünning (2002a): 1–22.

Nünning, Ansgar, and Roy Sommer (2008) 'Diegetic and Mimetic Narrativity: Some Further Steps Towards a Transgeneric Narratology of Drama', in Pier/Landa (2008): 331–54.

Nünning, Vera (1998) '*Unreliable Narration* und die historische Variabilität von Werten und Normen. *The Vicar of Wakefield* als Testfall für eine kulturgeschichtliche Erzählforschung'. In A. Nünning (1998): 257–285.

Nünning, Vera, and Ansgar Nünning (2000), ed., *Multiperspektivisches Erzählen: Zur Theorie und Geschichte der Perspektivenstruktur im englischen Roman des 18. bis 20. Jahrhunderts.* Trier: Wissenschaftlicher Verlag Trier.

Palmer, Alan (2004) *Fictional Minds.* Lincoln, NE: University of Nebraska Press.

Palmer, Alan (2005a) 'Intermental Thought in the Novel: The Middlemarch Mind', *Style* 39: 427–39.

Palmer, Alan (2005b) 'The Lydgate Storyworld', *Narratology Beyond Literary Criticism*, ed. Jan Christoph Meister. Berlin: de Gruyter. 151–72.

Palmer, Alan (forthcoming) 'Large Intermental Units in *Middlemarch*', *Postclassical Narratology: New Essays*, ed. Jan Alber and Monika Fludernik.

Pascal, Roy (1977) *The Dual Voice.* Manchester: Manchester University Press.

Petersen, Jürgen H. (1992) 'Erzählen im Präsens. Die Korrektur herrschender Tempus-Theorien durch die poetische Praxis in der Moderne', *Euphorion* 86: 65–89.

Pfister, Manfred (2000) *Das Drama: Theorie und Analyse* [1977]. UTB 580; Literaturwissenschaft; Information und Synthese, 3. Munich: Fink. [*The Theory and Analysis of Drama*, trans. John Halliday. Cambridge: Cambridge University Press, 1988.]

Phelan, James (2007) *Experiencing Fiction: Judgments, Progressions, and the Rhetorical Theory of Narrative.* Columbus, OH: Ohio State University Press.

Phelan, James, and Peter J. Rabinowitz (2005), eds., *A Companion to Narrative Theory.* Malden, MA: Blackwell.

Pier, John (1999), ed. *GRAAT: Revue des Groupes de Recherches Anglo-Américaines de L'Université François Rabelais de Tours* 21. (Recent Trends in Narratological Research: Papers from the Narratology Round Table, ESSE 4, September 1997, Debrecen, Hungary.) Tours: University of Tours.

Pier, John (2004), ed. *The Dynamics of Narrative Form: Studies in Anglo-American Narratology.* Narratologia, 4. Berlin: de Gruyter.

Pier, John, and José Ángel García Landa (2008), eds., *Theorizing Narrativity.* Narratologia, 12. Berlin: de Gruyter.

Pier, John, and Jean-Marie Schaeffer (2005), eds., *Métalepses. Entorses au pacte de la représentation.* Paris: Éditions de l'Ecole des Hautes Etudes en Sciences Sociales.

Plato (1993) *The Republic,* trans. Robin Waterfield. Oxford World's Classics. Oxford: Oxford University Press.

Polanyi, Livia (1978) 'False Starts Can Be True', *Berkeley Linguistics Society* 4: 628–39.

Polkinghorne, Donald E. (1988) *Narrative Knowing and the Human Sciences.* Albany: State University of New York Press.

Pouillon, Jean (1946) *Temps et roman.* Paris: Gallimard.

Prince, Gerald (1982) *Narratology: The Form and Functioning of Narrative.* Berlin: Mouton de Gruyter.

Prince, Gerald (2003) *A Dictionary of Narratology* [1987]. Lincoln, NE: University of Nebraska Press.

Propp, Vladimir (1968) *Morphology of the Folktale* [1928], 2nd edn, trans. Laurence Scott. Austin, TX: University of Texas Press.

Quasthoff, Uta M. (1980) *Erzählen in Gesprächen. Linguistische Untersuchungen zu Strukturen und Funktionen am Beispiel einer Kommunikationsform des Alltags.* Kommunikation und Institution, 1. Tübingen: Narr.

Rabinowitz, Peter J. (1977) 'Truth in Fiction: A Reexamination of Audiences,' *Critical Inquiry* 4: 121–41.

Randall, William Lowell (1995) *The Stories We Are: An Essay on Self-Creation.* Toronto: University of Toronto Press.

Richardson, Brian (1997) *Unlikely Stories: Causality and the Nature of Modern Narrative.* Newark, NJ: University of Delaware Press.

Richardson, Brian (2006) *Unnatural Voices. Extreme Narration in Modern and Contemporary Fiction.* Columbus, OH: Ohio State University Press.

Ricoeur, Paul (1988) *Time and Narrative* [1984–1988]. Vol. I–III. Trans. Kathleen McLaughlin and David Pellauer. Chicago: Chicago University Press.

Riffaterre, Michael (1959) 'Criteria of Style Analysis', *Word* 15: 154–74.

Riffaterre, Michael (1961) 'Vers la définition linguistique du style', *Word* 17: 318–44.

Riffaterre, Michael (1982) 'Trollope's Metonymies', *Nineteenth-Century Fiction* 37: 272–92.

Rimmon-Kenan, Shlomith (2002) *Narrative Fiction: Contemporary Poetics* [1983]. 2nd edn. London: Routledge.

Rodiek, Christoph (1997) *Erfundene Vergangenheit: Kontrafaktische Geschichtsdarstellung (Uchronie) in der Literatur.* Frankfurt am Main: Klostermann.

Ryan, Marie-Laure (1986) 'Embedded Narratives and Tellability', *Style* 20.3: 319–40.

Ryan, Marie-Laure (1987) 'On the Window Structure of Narrative Discourse', *Semiotica* 64: 59–81.

Ryan, Marie-Laure (1990) 'Stacks, Frames and Boundaries, or Narrative as Computer Language', *Poetics Today* 11.4: 873–900.

Ryan, Marie-Laure (1991) *Possible Worlds, Artificial Intelligence, and Narrative Theory.* Bloomington, IN: Indiana University Press.

Ryan, Marie-Laure (1992) 'The Modes of Narrativity and their Visual Metaphors', *Style* 26.3: 368–87.

Ryan, Marie-Laure (1993) 'Narrative in Real Time: Chronicle, Mimesis and Plot in the Baseball Broadcast', *Narrative* 1.2: 138–55.

Ryan, Marie-Laure (1999), ed., *Cyberspace Textuality: Computer Technology and Literary Theory.* Indianapolis, IN: Indiana University Press.

Ryan, Marie-Laure (2001a) *Narrative as Virtual Reality: Immersion and Interactivity in Literature and the Electronic Media.* Baltimore, MD: Johns Hopkins University Press.

Ryan, Marie-Laure (2001b) 'The Narratorial Functions: Breaking Down a Theoretical Primitive', *Narrative* 9.2: 146–52.

Ryan, Marie-Laure (2004), ed., *Narrative Across Media: The Languages of Storytelling.* Lincoln, NE: University of Nebraska Press.

Ryan, Marie-Laure (2005) 'Logique culturelle de la métalepse, ou: La métalepse dans tous ses états', in Pier/Schaeffer (2005): 201–24.

Schiffrin, Deborah (1987) *Discourse Markers.* Studies in Interactional Sociolinguistics, 5. Cambridge: Cambridge University Press.

Schmid, Wolf (2005) *Elemente der Narratologie*, Narratologia, 8. Berlin: de Gruyter.

Schnitzler, Marion (1983) *Die Kapitelüberschrift im französischen Roman des 19. Jahrhunderts: Formen und Funktionen.* Heidelberg: Winter.

Sell, Roger D. (2000) *Literature as Communication: The Foundations of Mediating Criticism.* Amsterdam/Philadelphia: John Benjamins.

Semino, Elena, and Michael M. Short (2004) *Corpus Stylistics: Speech, Writing and Thought Presentation in a Corpus of English Writing*. London and New York: Routledge.

Siskin, Clifford (1998) *The Work of Writing: Literature and Social Change in Britain, 1700 –1830*. Baltimore, MD: Johns Hopkins University Press.

Shklovsky, Viktor (1991) *Theory of Prose* [1925], trans. B. Sher, Intr. G.L. Burns. Elmwood Park, IL: Dalkey Archive Press.

Smith, Nigel (1993) *Literature and Censorship*. Cambridge: Brewer.

Spielhagen, Friedrich (1967) *Beiträge zur Theorie und Technik des Romans* [1883]. Göttingen: Vandenhoeck & Ruprecht.

Stanzel, Franz K. (1955) *Die typischen Erzählsituationen im Roman: Dargestellt an Tom Jones, Moby-Dick, the Ambassadors, Ulysses u.a.* Wiener Beiträge zur englischen Philologie Bd. 63. Vienna/Stuttgart: Braumüller. [Translation: Stanzel (1971)]

Stanzel, Franz K. (1971) *Narrative Situations in the Novel: Tom Jones, Moby-Dick, the Ambassadors, Ulysses* [1955], trans. J.P. Pusack. Bloomington, IN: Indiana University Press.

Stanzel, Franz K. (1977) 'Die Komplementärgeschichte: Entwurf einer leserorientierten Romantheorie', *Erzählforschung* 2, ed. W. Haubrichs. *Zeitschrift für Literaturwissenschaft und Linguistik*, Beiheft 6. 240–59. [Wiederabdruck in: Franz K. Stanzel (2002) *Unterwegs – Erzähltheorie für Leser*. Göttingen: Vandenhoeck & Ruprecht.]

Stanzel, Frank K. (1981) 'Wandlungen des narrativen Diskurses in der Moderne', *Erzählung und Erzählforschung im 20. Jahrhundert. Tagungsbeiträge eines Symposiums der Alexander von Humboldt-Stiftung Bonn-Bad Godesberg vom 9.–14. September 1980 in Ludwigsburg*, ed. Rolf Kloepfer and Gisela Janetzke-Diller. Stuttgart: Kohlhammer. 371–83.

Stanzel, Franz K. (1982) *Theorie des Erzählens* [1979]. 2nd edition. Göttingen: Vandenhoeck & Ruprecht.

Stanzel, Franz K. (1984) *A Theory of Narrative* [1979/1982], trans. Charlotte Goedsche. Preface by Paul Hernadi. Cambridge: Cambridge University Press.

Stanzel, Franz K. (1990) 'A Low-Structuralist at Bay? Further Thoughts on a Theory of Narrative', *Poetics Today* 11.4: 805–16.

Stanzel, Franz K. (2001) *Theorie des Erzählens* [1982]. 7th edition; third, expanded and revised version. Göttingen: Vandenhoeck & Ruprecht

Stanzel, Franz K. (2004) 'The 'Complementary Story': Outline of a Reader-Oriented Theory of the Novel' [1977], special issue German Narratology 1, *Style* 38.2: 203–20.

Steinberg, Erwin R. (1969) *The Stream of Consciousness and Beyond in 'Ulysses'* [1958]. Pittsburgh, PA: Pittsburgh University Press.

Steinberg, Günther (1971) *Erlebte Rede. Ihre Eigenarten und ihre Formen in neuerer deutscher, französischer und englischer Erzählliteratur*. Göppingen: Alfred Kümmerle.

Stempel, Wolf-Dieter (1987) 'Die Alltagserzählung als Kunst-Stück. Wolfgang Iser zum 60. Geburtstag'. *Mündliches Erzählen im Alltag*, eds. Willi Erzgräber and Paul Goetsch. Tübingen: Narr. 105–135.

Sternberg, Meir (1974) 'What is Exposition? An Essay in Temporal Delimitation', *The Theory of the Novel: New Essays*, ed. John Halperin. New York: Oxford University Press. 25–70.

Sternberg, Meir (1993) *Expositional Modes and Temporal Ordering in Fiction* [1978]. Bloomington, IN: Indiana University Press.

Sternberg, Meir (2005) 'The World from the Addressee's Viewpoint: Hearing Revisited', Paper read at the SSNL Conference, Louisville, KY, April 2005.

Sternberg, Meir (2007) 'Omniscience in Narrative Construction: Old Challenges and New', *Poetics Today* 28.4: 683–794.

Stockwell, Peter (2002) *Cognitive Poetics: An Introduction*. London: Routledge.

Tannen, Deborah (1984) *Talking Voices: Repetition, Dialogue, and Imagery in Conversational Discourse*. Cambridge: Cambridge University Press.

Titunik, Irwin R. (1977) 'Das Problem des *skaz*. Kritik und Theorie', *Erzählforschung 2*. Zeitschrift für Literaturwissenschaft und Linguistik, Beiheft 6, ed. Wolfgang Haubrichs. Göttingen: Vandenhoeck & Ruprect. 114–40.

Todorov, Tzvetan (1969) *Grammaire du Décaméron*. The Hague: Mouton.

Todorov, Tzvetan (1977) *The Poetics of Prose* [1971], trans. Richard Howard, foreword Jonathan Culler. Oxford: Blackwell.

Todorov, Tzvetan (1993) *The Fantastic: A Structural Approach to a Literary Genre* [1970], trans. Richard Howard, preface Robert Scholes. Ithaca, NY: Cornell University Press.

Toolan, Michael (2001) *Narrative: A Critical Linguistic Introduction* [1988], 2nd edition. London: Routledge.

Tynjanov, Jurij N. (1982) *Poetik. Ausgewählte Essays*. Leipzig/Weimar: G. Kiepenheuer.

Uspensky, Boris (1973) *A Poetics of Composition*, trans. Valentina Zavarin and Susan Wittig. Berkeley, CA: University of California Press.

Vinogradov, Viktor (1972) 'Das Problem des *skaz* in der Stilistik [1925]', *Texte der russischen Formalisten. Band I: Zur allgemeinen Literaturtheorie und zur Theorie der Prosa*, Theorie und Geschichte der Literatur und der schönen Künste, 6.1. Munich: Fink. 169–207.

Vološinov, V. N. (1993) *Marxism and the Philosophy of Language* [1929], trans. Ladislav Matejka and I. R. Titunik. Cambridge, MA: Harvard University Press.

Walsh, Richard (2007) *The Rhetoric of Fictionality: Narrative Theory and the Idea of Fiction*. Columbus, OH: Ohio State University Press.

Warhol, Robyn (1986) 'Toward a Theory of the Engaging Narrator: Earnest Interventions in Gaskell, Stowe, and Eliot', *PMLA* 101: 811–18.

Warhol, Robyn (1989) *Gendered Interventions: Narrative Discourse in the Victorian Novel*. New Brunswick, NJ: Rutgers University Press.

Warhol, Robyn (2003) *Having a Good Cry: Effeminate Feelings and Pop-Culture Forms*. Columbus, OH: Ohio State University Press.

Watt, Ian (1957) *The Rise of the Novel: Studies in Defoe, Richardson and Fielding*. London: Chatto & Windus.

Wellek, René, and Austin Warren (1949) *Theory of Literature*. New York: Harcourt.

Wenzel, Peter (2004), ed., *Einführung in die Erzähltextanalyse: Kategorien, Modelle, Probleme*. WVT–Handbücher zum literaturwissenschaftlichen Studium, 6. Trier: Wissenschaftlicher Verlag Trier.

Weydt, Harald (1983) *Partikeln und Interaktion*. Tübingen: Niemeyer.

White, Hayden (1978) *Tropics of Discourse: Essays in Cultural Criticism*. Baltimore, MD: Johns Hopkins University Press.

Wieckenberg, Ernst-Peter (1969) *Zur Geschichte der Kapitelüberschrift im deutschen Roman vom 15. Jahrhundert bis zum Ausgang des Barock*. Göttingen: Vandenhoeck & Ruprecht.

Winkgens, Meinhard (1997) *Die kulturelle Symbolik von Rede und Schrift in den Romanen von George Eliot. Untersuchungen zu ihrer Entwicklung, Funktionalisierung und Bewertung*. ScriptOralia, 93.Tübingen: Narr.

Winnett, Susan (1990) 'Coming Unstrung: Women, Men, Narrative, and Principles of Pleasure', *PMLA* 105: 505–18.

Wolf, Werner (1993) *Ästhetische Illusion und Illusionsdurchbrechung in der Erzählkunst: Theorie und Geschichte mit Schwerpunkt auf englischem illusionsstörenden Erzählen*. Tübingen: Niemeyer.

Wolf, Werner (1999) 'Framing Fiction. Reflections on a Narratological Concept and an Example: Bradbury, *Mensonge*', *Grenzüberschreitungen: Narratologie im Kontext/Transcending Boundaries: Narratology in Context*, ed. Walter Grünzweig and Andreas Solbach. Tübingen: Narr. 97–124.

Wolf, Werner (2000) 'Multiperspektivität: Das Konzept und seine Applikationsmöglichkeit auf Rahmungen in Erzählwerken', in Nünning/Nünning (2000): 79–109.

Wolf, Werner (2002) 'Das Problem der Narrativität in Literatur, bildender Kunst und Musik: ein Beitrag zu einer intermedialen Erzähltheorie', in Nünning/Nünning (2002a): 23–104.

Wolf, Werner (2005) 'Metalepsis as a Transgeneric and Transmedial Phenomenon', in Meister (2005): 83–108.

Wolf, Werner (2006) 'Framing Borders in Frame Stories', *Framing Borders in Literature and Other Media*, ed. Werner Wolf and Walter Bernhart. Amsterdam: Rodopi. 179–206.

Wolf, Werner, and Walter Bernhart (2007), eds., *Description in Literature and Other Media*. Amsterdam: Rodopi.

Zerweck, Bruno (2001) 'Historicizing Unreliable Narration: Unreliability and Cultural Discourse in Narrative Fiction', *Style* 35.1: 151–78.

Subject Index

Alphabetical entries in the glossary of narratological terms are not indexed.

Author Index